Religion, Morality and Socio-Political Philosophy

Religion, Morality and Socio-Political Philosophy

A Comparative Study of John Dewey and Ambedkar's

Seshagiri Rao Regulagadda

KALPAZ

ISBN: 978-93-5128-130-6

Price: ₹ 720

First Published, 2015

Published by

Kalpaz Publications
C-30, Satyawati Nagar,
Delhi-110052
Ph. : 9212142040
E-mail: kalpaz@hotmail.com

Printed at : G. Print Process, Delhi

Cataloging in Publication Data—DK
Courtesy: D.K. Agencies (P) Ltd. <docinfo@dkagencies.com>

Regulagadda, Seshagiri Rao, author.
Religion, morality and socio-political philosophy : a comparative study of John Dewey and Ambedkar's / by Seshagiri Rao Regulagadda.
pages cm
Includes bibliographical references (pages).
ISBN 9789351281306

1. Dewey, John, 1859-1952. 2. Ambedkar, B. R., 1891-1956—Philosophy. 3. Religion—Philosophy. 4. Ethics. 5. Social sciences—Philosophy. 6. Political science—Philosophy. I. Title.

DDC 300.1 23

CONTENTS

Introduction

Comparative philosophy is a distinguishable field of inquiry in philosophy. When interpreted as a branch of philosophy, it stands alongside with those which pertain to the philosophy of science, the philosophy of religion, the philosophy of social science, the philosophy of language, the philosophy of art. Comparative philosophy has its own methods, presuppositions, activities and frameworks which set it apart from the others. When interpreted as a discipline which takes comparison as its central concern, however, it lapses into the whole itself of which it is supposed to be a part. For philosophy, the whole which comprises its parts is an activity which is always involved in comparing different views about various issues. Socrates philosophized via dialogues in which views held by others were constantly scrutinized and compared with his own; Confucius began his work by refining wisdom previous to his time and in this transformation lays an implicit comparison[1].

Comparative philosophy is a subfield of philosophy in which philosophers work on problems by intentionally setting into dialogue sources from across cultural, linguistic, and philosophical streams. The ambition and challenge of comparative philosophy is to include all the philosophies of global humanity in its vision of what is constituted by philosophy. Comparative philosophers most frequently engage topics in dialogue between modern Western (American and Continental European) and Classical Asian (Chinese, India and Japanese) traditions, but work has been done using materials and approache's from Islamic and African philosophical traditions as well as from classical Western traditions (Judaism, Christianity, Islam)[2].

This approach distinguishes comparative philosophy from several other approaches to philosophy. First, comparative philosophy is distinct from both area studies philosophy (in which philosophers investigate topics in particular cultural traditions, (Buddhism) and world philosophy in which philosophers construct a philosophical system based on the fullness of global traditions of thought. Second, comparative philosophy differs from more traditional philosophy in which ideas are compared among thinkers within a particular tradition; comparative philosophy intentionally compares the ideas of thinkers of very different traditions, especially culturally distinct traditions.

The unique approach of comparative philosophy also comes unique difficulties and challenges that are not as characteristic of doing philosophy within a particular tradition. Such difficulties to be avoided include descriptive chauvinism (recreating another tradition in the image of one's own), normative skepticism (merely narrating or describing the views of different philosophers and traditions, suspending all judgment about their adequacy), incommensurability (the inability to find the common ground among traditions needed as a basis for comparison), and perennialism (failure to realize that philosophical traditions evolve, that they are not perennial in the sense of being monolithic). Furthermore, since comparative philosophy involves an approach that is not dominant in academic philosophy, it has been somewhat neglected by the mainstream of the profession.[3] However, comparative philosophy is fairly early in its developmental stages.

World philosophy may be thought of as an effort at constructive philosophy that takes into account the great variety of philosophical writings and traditions across human cultures and endeavors to weave them into a coherent world view. As such, it is an extension of comparative philosophy, because comparison is fundamental to the constructivist task. But comparative philosophy need not become world philosophy. The comparative philosopher may be working on isolated topics, or with two or more philosophers, just for the sake of gaining clarity on some specific issue. Likewise, those wanting to construct a world philosophy often find a place for the thought of other traditions in the system they construct, but it is fair to wonder whether they really allow the voice of the other to express itself in its strongest form.

The main understanding is that morality and religion both considered very close to the essential nature of philosophy. Generally human activities precisely contain attitudes, judgments towards certain given circumstances. The explanations of human activity of rejecting or receiving with normative claim necessarily presuppose norms. Religion and Morality precisely are attempts to describe the acts or crave of human which clearly includes the normative claims. Religion can be visualized as normative claim in the sense it is an attempt to visualize the ideal concepts. And morality mainly discusses about the ideal values. Altogether philosophy is an attempt to sketch the normative ideas in the realm of knowledge, reality, ethics, aesthetics, religion etc, in justified manner. And philosophical analysis of religion and morality tell us that how justifiably we can talk about the ideal values and concepts. In the realm of religion and morality normative idea is almost identified with ideal nature. But what is the problem with the ideal nature is ideality often loses it s relevance because it always considered as a kind of leap from the empirical realm. And only a philosophical analysis can reveals that how much so called ideal systems are necessary for the life or how much problematic the duality of empirical and ideal or how much each contribute one another.

However, philosophical analysis provides adequate justification for ideas in the systems of religion and morality. Analysis of Western religion and morality reveals that it is mainly anthropocentric; it mainly revolves around the human relation. God is constituted in the position of father and human are considered as son or daughter of the father. And all other specification is worked out by developing this model. Morality is worked by looking on the idea of how children should behave to parents. It mainly emphasizes that human, all other creatures are the creations of God, and the supremacy of one absolute God over the all creation emphasized in the Semitic religions.

In the same way the basis of the socio-political philosophy is that the human being is embedded in the community. There is no being and becoming outside community. As the being and becoming of the individual is dependent on the community every activity of the individual is a political activity. Nothing can explain this political and social philosophical attitude better than their proverbs and aphorisms. "Human beings become human beings through fellow human beings."[4]

The analysis of the socio - political philosophy, we have tried to compare the political and social philosophy of some Western philosophers and that of this does not, however, mean that both philosophies are the same. For example, in the Aristotelian case virtue can be developed within the community, and no one is sufficient for himself unless it is a beast or a god. Moreover, he stresses that state is prior to the individual. All citizens as community determine politics. Moreover, politics, culture and religion are essentially interdependent. As a consequence, any professionalization of these branches is forestalled. Therefore, any universalization of socio-cultural values such as professionalization of politics is rejected.However, even if it seems to be the only socio-political ideology, communitarianism does not completely supersede individual interests. Actually, the preservation of the person and goods of the individual are the implicit but ultimate end.

If we take the first expression, a person exists as long as he/she is accepted by the community, as long as the community does not say bad things about him/her. There is no existence outside of the community. The message that emanates from the community and that goes into the ear of the individual constitutes the existence of the individual. Community is not the goal in itself, rather a means for the individual self-realization within the community. The nature of the community is to make a better individual. Therefore, the becoming and being of the individual is the ultimate goal, not the community as such.

In this context, the main aim of this report is to trace the philosophical perspective of Dewey and Ambedkar with special reference to his philosophical ideas of Religion, Morality and politics, which in turn would pave the way for practical responses to the problem of deferent ideology in the Indian society with comparison of western liberal ideas. Unlike many other social scientists, Dewey and Ambedkar did not reject the role of religion as product of mainstream thinking. They clearly understood how deep role the religion can do in the society. At the same time he understood that how inadequate the religion in its present form to do such role in society. Therefore, Dewey and Ambedkar were attempts to reformulate the religion and morality on the basis of human consideration of the political society.

Never before in history has mankind been so much of two minds, so divided into two camps, as it is today. Religions have traditionally been allied with ideas of the supernatural, and often have been based upon explicit beliefs about it. Today there are many who hold that nothing worthy of being called religious is possible apart from the supernatural. Those who hold this belief differ in many respects. They range from those who accept the dogmas and sacraments of the Greek and Roman Catholic Church as the only sure means of access to the supernatural to the theist or mild deist. Between them are the many Protestant denominations that think the Scriptures, aided by a pure conscience are adequate avenues to supernatural truth and power. But they agree in one point: the necessity for a Supernatural Being and for an immortality that is beyond the powers of nature.

The opposed group consists of those who think the advance of culture and science has completely discredited the supernatural and with it all religions that were allied with belief in it. But they go beyond this point. The extremists of this group believe that with the elimination of the supernatural not only must historic religions be dismissed but with them everything of a religious nature. When historical knowledge has discredited the claims made for the supernatural character of the persons said to have founded historic religions; when the supernatural inspiration attributed to literatures held sacred has been riddled, and when anthropological and psychological knowledge has disclosed the all-too-human source from which religious beliefs and practices have sprung, everything religious must, they say, also go.

There is one idea held in common by these two opposite groups: identification of the religious with the supernatural. The questions we shall raise concern the ground and the consequences of this identification: its reasons and its value. We develop another conception of the nature of the religious phase of experience, one that separates it from the supernatural and the things that have grown up about it.

Any activity pursued in behalf of an ideal end against obstacles and in spite of threats of personal loss because of conviction of its general and enduring value is religious in quality. The question narrows itself to this: Are the ideals that move us genuinely ideal or are they ideal only in contrast with our present state?

The import of the question extends far. It determines the meaning given to the word "God." On one score, the word can mean only a particular Being. On the other score, it denotes the unity of all ideal ends arousing us to desire and actions. Does the unification have a claim upon our attitude and conduct because it is already, apart from us, in realized existence, or because of its own inherent meaning and value? Suppose for the moment that the word "God" means the ideal ends that at a given time and place one acknowledges as having authority over his volition and emotion. The values, to which one is supremely devoted, as far as these ends, through imagination, take on unity. If we make this supposition, the issue will stand out clearly in contrast with the doctrine of religions that "God" designates some kind of Being having prior and therefore non-ideal existence.

In the same way, "Dewey's ethics replaces the goal of identifying an ultimate end or supreme principle that can serve as a criterion of ethical evaluation with the goal of identifying a method for improving our value judgments. Dewey argued that ethical inquiry is of a piece with empirical inquiry more generally. It is the use of reflective intelligence to revise one's judgments in light of the consequences of acting on them. Value judgments are tools for enabling the satisfactory redirection of conduct when habit no longer suffices to direct it. As tools, they can be evaluated instrumentally, in terms of their success in guiding conduct. We test our value judgments by putting them into practice and seeing whether the results are satisfactory whether they solve the problems they were designed to solve, whether we find their consequences acceptable, whether they enable successful responses to novel problems, whether living in accordance with alternative value judgments yields more satisfactory results"[5] In the two Sources of Morality and Religion Dewey made the case that without fraternity; the other two components of the revolutionary slogan face the danger of disintegration. Liberty and equality, inherently vague and open to interpretation as they are, can be so transformed that they no longer serve the public good. In their application, humans are tempted to move them.

John Dewey's approach leads to a radical reconstruction of the definition of morality on the bases of human action. Emile Durkheim as a founder of sociology and an exponent of social facts proposes the transformation of a religiously bound morality to a secular morality. Whereas Dewey prescribes a process of scientific inquiry and democratic communication in communities, accordingly to his focus on human life (and moral) activity, Durkheim distinguishes the 'elements of morality', which he takes as social facts deriving from the collective conscience, societies form. Whereas 'discipline' for example presents one element of morality in Durkheim's approach, Dewey thinks that discipline appears only as an element of morality because we have developed customs of dominance and oppression which we take now as a sort of "natural order", although it is only a custom, we might change in the future. Morals according to Dewey do not have a distinct character to other customs we develop in associated living, and do not reflect a "truth" outside of present life activity in a specific group. They are subject to negotiation and change in just the same way other customs are, and they fulfill a practical task in the longest course of time. Moral elements according to Durkheim are social facts, and as such they go beyond individual utility. We can study them scientifically, and so contribute to a necessary transformation-process from a religiously bound morality to a rationally formulated morality.

Ambedkar understood that the attempts of Buddha were also in the similar lines. For Ambedkar, morality is the basic need of humanity, and of the healthy society. And he criticized Hinduism for de-linking their religious ideas from the moral basis. Hinduism does not consider the religious and moral ideas as corrective force against the evils of society. Instead Hinduism often joins with the illness of society and often produces new illness of inequality. Buddhism considers Morality and religion as firmly rooted on equality and humanity which stems of human mind.

Dewey interpretations of Morals are connected with actualities of existence, not with ideals, ends and obligations independent of concrete actualities. The facts upon which it depends are those which arise out of active connections of human beings with one another, the consequences of their mutually intertwined activities in the life of desire, belief, judgment, satisfaction and dissatisfaction. In this sense conduct and Hence morals are social: they are not just things which ought to be social and which fail to come up to the scratch. But there are enormous differences of better and worse in the quality of what is social. Ideal morals begin with the perception of these differences. Human interaction and ties are there, are operative in any case. But they can be regulated, employed in an orderly way for good only as we know how to observe them. And they cannot be observed a right; they cannot be understood and utilized, when the mind is left to itself to work without the aid of science. For the natural unaided mind means precisely the habits of belief, thought and desire which have been accidentally generated and confirmed by social institutions or customs. But with all their admixture of accident and reasonableness we have at last reached a point where social conditions create a mind capable of scientific outlook and inquiry. To foster and develop this spirit is the social obligation of the present because it is its urgent need. But special ways of expressing the communal sense have been established. They have been limited to a select social group; they hate hardened into obligatory rites and been imposed as conditions of salvation.

Dewey's political philosophy is also precisely this radical character. His vision of democracy, as indicated above, does not exclusively refer to specific institutional arrangements and political procedures. They are important, and he often mentions those institutional features most conducive to democratic life. But such arrangements, he explains, do not exhaust the meaning of democracy. For him, then, democracy implies an *ethos* that "extends to matters of the mind, heart, and spirit." Dewey describes democracy as an ethical ideal he means to highlight a cultural orientation that views power as always already located in a space of conditionality, the result of which contributes to and protects human growth.

In Dewey's estimation, the creative potential of a democratic community is constitutively connected to contestation as the community revises and develops its institutional structures and values. Here he extends his philosophical outlook his anti-foundationalism, experimentalism, and contextualism to elucidate the importance and value of democracy. In other words, the legitimacy of democracy partly derives, he believes, from the extent to which it allows the widest application of inquiry to the problems that confront collective organization. His vision of participation should therefore not be reduced to a minimalist view of democracy that is confined exclusively to voting, reliance on experts and elites, or some adversarial view of politics. He resists all such accounts as primary descriptions of democracy.

Dewey liberalism and modern democracy are closely related and he often yoked the two together, it is a mistake to see them as involving the same logic. Liberalism, he maintains, involves a deep appreciation for liberty and the individual, and is specifically concerned to constrain the use of state power. Liberalism's origins are located in a desire to make the state and its officials responsive to the needs of the people a view quite contrary to the outlook that defined monarchial, ecclesiastical, and totalitarian regimes throughout human history. Democracy, however, emphasizes the equality of individuals before the law, the shared political identity of the rulers and the ruled, and views the people as not merely a group to which authority must be responsive, but as the source of political authority itself.

For Dewey, power may often function without our explicit involvement or control. Nonetheless, the ends to which power will be put cannot be of such a nature that they block the future contestability of how that power functions. Managing political power then is not merely about the range of choices that may exist at any given moment for human beings, but more significantly the ability to initiate change to expand the area in which choice is made possible. To the extent that this possibility is open, freedom remains secure. This implies caution about how our institutions function, but not perpetual doubt. The first of these is healthy for a democracy because it guards against our natural tendency to see our political order as settled a position that will seduce us into believe that existing inequalities and injustices are conditions to which we must resign ourselves rather than overcome. Yet, the second of these perpetual doubts can only have a corrosive effect on how we see our political institutions.

Ambedkar was not a purely speculative and idealistic political philosopher, in the conventional sense, like Plato and Aristotle. Nevertheless, he developed his own social and political ideals, which were deeply rooted in real human problems and issues, and vital human affairs. His political philosophy attempted to bridge the gulf between theory and practice, materialism and spiritualism. Out of his sense of dejection with the inhuman treatment meted out to his community by the caste Hindus, his mission for the total emancipation of the servile classes from the clutches of the privileged caste Hindus, his total engagement with the predicament of Indian society, evolved Ambedkar's political ideology. The book aims to juxtapose Ambedkar's political philosophy and its impact on Indian society and polity with reference to man and society, state and government, nation and nationalism, democracy, socialism, security, social justice, education and emancipation of the downtrodden. However, other aspects of Ambedkar's Political Philosophy and his charismatic personality are also incidentally covered.

The political philosophy of Ambedkar may help in renegotiating the crisis of western political theory in particular and leading the struggles of the masses in general. One can see Ambedkar's association with the grand political streams such as liberal, radical or conservative through his writings. At same time he differentiates himself with these three dominant political traditions. Ambedkar's philosophy is essentially ethical and religious. For him, social precedes the political. Social morality is the central to his political philosophy. He is neither fierce individualist nor conservative communitarian. His conceptions of democracy internalises the principles of equality, liberty, and fraternity in its true spirit. Though there are many attempts but one may find difficulty in locating him in dominant political traditions. Often this may leads to misunderstanding of the essence of Ambedkar. Ambedkar's political thought demands new language to understand the complexity of his thought.

The First Chapter deals with the Dewey and Ambedkar's comparative study on religious philosophy. Dewey idea of that "God" represents a unification of ideal values that is essentially imaginative in origin when the imagination supervenes in conduct is attended with verbal difficulties owing to our frequent use of the word "imagination" to denote fantasy and doubtful reality. But the reality of ideal ends as ideals is vouched for by their undeniable power in action. These considerations may be applied to the idea of God, or, to avoid misleading conceptions, to the idea of the divine. The idea is, as Dewey has said, one of ideal possibilities unified through imaginative realization and projection. But this idea of God, or of the divine, is also connected with all the natural forces and conditions including human associations that promote the growth of the ideal and that further its realization. We are not in the presence of ideals completely embodied in existence nor yet of ideals that are mere rootless ideals, fantasies, utopias. For there are forces in nature and society that generate and support the ideals. They are further unified by the action that gives them coherence and solidarity. It is this *active* relation between ideal and actual to which Dewey would give the name "God." Dewey would not insist that the name *must* be given.

Ambedkar firmly considers that religion is quite necessary for the social life. One hand he denies the existence and need of the supernatural ideas but at the same time he affirms the necessity of religion. From this point it is clear that for him, God is not the centre of religion. *Dhamma* or Moral principles are the centre of religion and implementation of moral principles in this social life is the crux of the necessity of religion in social life. It builds up the person. It is a powerful driving force for human activity and it instills hope. Only religion can satisfy the human being who is not satisfied with material things. In addition, Ambedkar notes that not all the religions have the same kind of moral principles. Some are liberative and oppressive. *Oppressive* religion always will be with irrational elements. Only a rational religion can provide a *liberative* outlook.

The second Chapter deals with the Dewey and Ambedkar's comparative study on morality philosophy. Dewey concept of morality deals with conduct. Ethical theory Offers a systematic view of our choices in conduct with respect to their moral import good, bad; right, wrong. Human conduct has two broad aspects: the psychological (the inner meaning and purpose of life) and sociological (the outward social existence).

Conduct has three levels: 1) impulse-driven, 2) group-imposed, and 3) individual reflection. Ethical progress consists in choosing more rational and social conduct because we value such behavior as good. Moral acts begin when any one asks, "Why should I act this way, and not some other way? Why is this way right and that way wrong?" Moral theory arises only when certainty about the right and wrong has been equivocated by confronting paths that promise opposed goods and each course seems morally justified. Dewey cannot understand how any realization of the democratic ideal as a vital moral and spiritual deal in human affairs is possible without surrender of the conception of the basic division to which supernatural Christianity is committed. Rather Dewey would suggest that the future of religion is connected with the possibility of developing a faith in the possibilities of human experience and human relationships that will create a vital sense of the solidarity of human interests and inspire action to make that sense a reality.

Whereas, Ambedkar's conceptions of morality, is mainly construed on the basis of Buddhist principles. His attempts end up in the reinterpretation of Buddhism, which is depicted in Buddha and *Dhamma. Dhamma* is the main conception of Buddhism. Ambedkar qualifies it as and *Saddhamma.* Thus Morality in Buddhism is converges the social and individual aspects in coherent manner. Ambedkar makes clear that Belief in *Ishwara* (God) is not essentially part of *Dhamma,* and the *Dharma* based on Union with Brahma is a false *Dhamma.* According to Ambedkar, the Hindu social order lacks the spirit of solidarity. For Ambedkar, the social order of Hinduism does not contain any principle of social change.

The Third Chapter deals with the explaining and analysing the John Dewey's and Ambedkar's Comparative Study on socio-political philosophy. Dewey's mature thought in socio-political theory is not only intimately linked to the theory of knowledge in its founding conceptual framework and naturalistic standpoint, but also complementary to it in its emphasis on the social dimension of inquiry both in its processes and its consequences. In fact, it would be reasonable to claim that Dewey's theory of inquiry cannot be fully understood either in the meaning of its central tenets or the significance of its originality without considering how it applies to social aims and values, the central concern of his ethical and social theory.

Dewey's socio-political philosophy focused on the worth of the individual in the context of the collective, and aimed to empower the judgments of the common people. Scientific enquiry was favoured because it represented a method of deliberation that provided provisional answers to situational or emergent problems. These emergent problems comprised the main focal points for enquiry. To Dewey, problems were always seen as opportunities for growth and improvement. He believed that by subjecting the problems of the present to a method of enquiry, humanity could reconstruct and improve itself.

Ambedkar was not a purely speculative and idealistic political philosopher, in the conventional sense, like Plato and Aristotle. Nevertheless, he developed his own social and political ideals, which were deeply rooted in real human problems and issues, and vital human affairs. His political philosophy attempted to bridge the gulf between theory and practice, materialism and spiritualism. Out of his sense of dejection with the inhuman treatment meted out to his community by the caste Hindus, his mission for the total emancipation of the servile classes from the clutches of the privileged caste Hindus, his total engagement with the predicament of Indian society, evolved Ambedkar's political ideology. The book aims to juxtapose Ambedkar's political philosophy and its impact on Indian society and polity with reference to man and society, state and government, nation and nationalism, democracy, socialism, security, social justice, education and emancipation of the downtrodden. However, other aspects of Ambedkar's Political Philosophy and his charismatic personality are also incidentally covered. For Ambedkar, social and political theories are the basic need of freedom for the downtrodden people, as it would create a powerful community and nation building. Ambedkar said that social equality was a force which promises equal opportunity to all.

Reference

1. Raju, P. T. *Introduction to Comparative Philosophy*. Reprint ed. Delhi: Motilal Banarsidass, 1997.
2. Masson-Oursel, Paul. *Comparative Philosophy.* London: Routledge, 2000.
3. Deutsch, Eliot. *Introduction to World Philosophies.* Upper Saddle River, NJ: Prentice Hall, 1997.
4. Aristotle, 1998. *Politics, Book 1*, Indianapolis: Hackett *Publishing* Co., p.10.
5. John Dewey, 1995. *Religious Faith and Democratic Humanism,* Philosophy Education Society, Inc. University of New York Press, New York.p.278.

Chapter-I

John Dewey and Ambedkar's Comparative Study on Religious Philosophy

The main aim of this progress is to trace the philosophical perspective of Dewey and Ambedkar with special reference to his philosophical ideas of Religion, which in turn would pave the way for practical responses to the problem of deferent ideology in the Indian society and western society. Dewey's idea that 'God' represents a unification of ideal values that is essentially imaginative in origin when the imagination supervenes in conduct, is attended with verbal difficulties, owing to our frequent use of the word 'imagination' to denote fantasy and doubtful reality. But the reality of ideal ends as ideals is vouched for by their undeniable power in action. An idea is not an illusion because imagination is the organ through which it is apprehended.[6] In other words, God does not exist except as the projection by our imagination of those non-objective ideals which guide our human conduct. While the idea of God is not real, therefore, since it is created by the fantasy, it is not illusory because it serves the purpose of idealizing our hopes and desires.

Consistent with this doctrine of atheism, Dewey inveighs against the idea of religion any religion which pretends to represent man's relations with an objective and personal Deity. He introduces a distinction between religion and religious which has since become famous. Projected ideals of conduct are religious, but there is no warrant for religion, since there is no extra-mental God for religion to worship. 'Any activity,' according to him, "pursued in behalf of an ideal end against obstacles and in spite of threats of personal loss because of conviction of its general and enduring value is religious in quality."[7]

If I have said anything about religions and religion that seems harsh, I have said those things because of a firm belief that the claim on the part of religions to possess a monopoly of ideals and of the supernatural means by which alone, it is alleged, they can be furthered, stands in the way of the realization of distinctively religious values inherent in natural experience. For that reason, if for no other, I should be sorry if any were misled by the frequency with which I have employed the adjective "religious" to conceive of what I have said as a disguised apology for what have passed as religions. The opposition between religious values as I conceive them and religions is not to be abridged. Just because the release of these values is so important, their identification with the creeds and cults of religions must be dissolved.[8]

Unlike many other social scientists, Ambedkar did not reject the role of religion as product of mainstream thinking. He clearly understood how deep role the religion can do in the society. At the same time he understood that how inadequate the religion in its present form to do such role in society. Therefore Ambedkar attempts to reformulate the religion and morality on the basis of humanity. Ambedkar understood that the attempts of Buddha were also in the similar lines. According to Ambedkar, morality is the basic need of humanity, and of the healthy society. And he criticized Hinduism for de-linking their religious ideas from the moral basis. Hinduism does not consider the religious and moral ideas as corrective force against the evils of society. Instead Hinduism often joins with the illness of society and often produces new illness of inequality. Buddhism considers Morality and religion as firmly rooted on equality and humanity which stems of human mind.

Ambedkar while tracing the relation between philosophy and religion opined that the philosophy is something that is universal whereas the religion is specific and defined. He says that "religion is something definite, there is nothing definite as to what is to be included in the term philosophy."[9] Ambedkar's view of Religion is very much essential to the existence of mankind. He says that "some people think that religion is not essential for society. I do not hold this view. I consider the foundation of religion to be essential to the life and practices of society."[10] "He had strong religious sentiments regarding the formation of religion, but he had no faith in Hinduism as he hated hypocrisy that existed in it."[11] In his opinion, Religion in India acts as a social force in the lives of people and most of the decisions are influenced by the Religion. Ambedkar desired a religion, which instructs people to establish a society based on liberty, equality and social order in which men live with moral values. This will be the science in which we shall be using the term Religion in the following discussion.

According to Ambedkar's analysis of religion, every religion contains primarily a system of ideal scheme and means to attain the same. Every religion proposes an ideal scheme to its followers as the good to be achieved as the sacred goal and divine ultimate aim in life. All religions may not stress equally all values and some may even neglect essential values. Even if some religions were to emphasise the same ideals, it means that they often would differ. This method of studying and analysing the religions can easily be extended also to the ideologies such as Marxism. Theologian, R. Panikkar, and Liberation theologian, J.L. Segundo, have employed a similar method to the study of religions and ideologies.[12]

The questions regarding religion, which haunt and taunt the social activists and the militants involved in the fight for human rights, or the liberation of the oppressed poor, have been satisfactorily answered by Ambedkar by his own life and clarified in his writings. He has demonstrated beyond doubt that religion has a role to play in the liberation of untouchables or Dalits and the non-persons existing in Hindu culture. Religion and revolution need not be opposed to each other; rather religion can serve as the motivation force for revolutionary struggles. Those who deem religion to be the opium of the masses, a projection of the human desires and needs, an infantile fixity or a superstitious hang over the savage past, have a good guide in the writings of Ambedkar, who dispels their doubts about its necessity and importance. Many social scientists have confirmed the revolutionary potential of religion.[13]

Ambedkar has shown the vital need of religion for the individual as well as for the society at large. By presenting sacred ideals and humane values, and by reinforcing them in the society, religion helps the development of the persons and the progress of the society. Religion thus preserves, protects, and promotes life.[14] Conservation of life by religious consecration is the law of life. Hence, religion is not a burden enforced by the supernatural powers, be they God or his prophets, and heavenly revelations. It is a vital role arising out of the need for protecting the weak in the society, and for maintaining peace among the various groups, tribes, classes, races and castes. Religion is, therefore, nothing but morality that is based on the law of love, which is the law of life.[15]

Whereas Dewey's metaphysical aspects of God, as the perfect Personality or Will is the only Reality, and the source of all activity. It is therefore the source of all activity of the individual personality. The Perfect Will is the motive, source, and realization of the life of the individual. He (the individual) has renounced his own particular life as an unreality; he has asserted that the sole reality is the Universal Will, and in that reality all his actions take place.[16]

A clear and intense conception of a union of ideal ends with actual conditions is capable of arousing steady emotion. It may be fed by every experience, no matter what its material. In a distracted age, the need for such an idea is urgent. It can unify interests and energies now dispersed; it can direct action and generate the heat of emotion and the light of intelligence. Whether one gives the name "God" to this union, operative in thought and action, is a matter for individual decision. But the *function* of such a working union of the ideal and the actual seems to me to be identical with the force that has in fact been attached to the conception of God in all religions that have a spiritual content; and a clear idea of that function seems to me urgently needed at the present time.

One reason why personally Dewey think it fitting to use the word "God" to denote that uniting of the ideal and actual which has been spoken of, lies in the fact that aggressive atheism seems to me to have something in common with traditional supernaturalism. I do not mean merely that the former is mainly so negative that it fails to give positive direction to thought, though that fact is pertinent. What Dewey has in mind especially is the exclusive preoccupation of both militant atheism and supernaturalism with humanity in isolation. For in spite of supernaturalism's reference to something beyond nature, it conceived of this earth as the moral centre of the universe and of human beings as the apex of the whole scheme of things. It regards the drama of sin and redemption enacted within the isolated and lonely soul as the one thing of ultimate importance. Apart from humanity, nature is held either accursed or negligible. Militant atheism is also affected by lack of natural piety. The ties binding us to nature that poets have always celebrated are passed over lightly. The attitude taken is often that of our living in an indifferent and hostile world and issuing blasts of defiance. A religious attitude, however, needs the sense of our connection, in the way of both dependence and support, with the enveloping world that the imagination feels is a universe. Use of the words "God" or "divine" to convey the union of actual and ideal may protect human beings from a sense of isolation and from consequent despair or defiance. A humanistic religion, if it excludes our relation to nature, is pale and thin, as it is presumptuous, when it takes humanity as an object of worship.[17]

Were the naturalistic foundations and bearings of religion grasped, the religious element in life would emerge from the throes of the crisis in religion. Religion would then be found to have its natural place in every aspect of human experience that is concerned with estimate of possibilities, with emotional stir by possibilities as yet unrealized, and with all action in behalf of their realization. All that is significant in human experience falls within this frame.

The things in civilization we most prize are not of ourselves. They exist by grace of the doings and sufferings of the continuous human community in which we are a link. Ours is the responsibility of conserving, transmitting, rectifying and expanding the heritage of values we received that those who come after us may receive it more solid and secure, more widely accessible and more generously shared than we have received it.

Here are all the elements for a religious faith that shall not be confined to sect, class, or race. Such a faith has always been implicitly the common faith of humanity. It remains to make it explicit and militant.

Where as Ambedkar's theology is based on his own personal understandings in life. He did bear the stigma of Untouchability and its insults. He was the victim of exploitation of the caste system. He was refused place to stay, water to drink, vehicle to travel, just because he was born in a particular community.

Though a scholar of repute abroad, he had to bear the insults of the ignorant, in his home state just because he was a Dalit.[18] He, like Moses, forsaking the positions that could have been his, opted to lead his people into the land of freedom. Unto the last, he struggled for this mission. His theology/philosophy was therefore pathos-praxis based. His commitment to the liberation of Dalits prompted his critical reflection, motivated and inspired all his studies and writings. He was no armchair philosopher/theologian; praxis-reflection was his methodology.

In his Theology *"wisdom meets love"*, which explains to enlighten as well as empower us, to serve and struggle with detachment and compassion.[19] His theory is not only in its integral synthesis of Christian love and Buddhist wisdom. But there is also an integration of the secular scientific enlightenment of the East and West; where in the modern rational enlightenment and the ancient Buddhist religious enlightenment were happily married.

This is a new paradigm highly recommended to the Indians of secular democracy.[20] The dualisms between science and religion, secular and sacred, politics and spirituality, involvement and detachment, action and contemplation, material and spiritual, works and faith, social reality and the divine Kingdom, do not exist in Ambedkar's new integral holistic theological paradigm.[21]

Dewey and Ambedkar's perspective of Religious Philosophy

Dewey's view is the reconciliation of the inherited traditions of our culture with the progressive revelations of scientific method, such a reconstruction of the tradition. The reconciliation of religious tradition with scientific method is obviously an extremely difficult undertaking. Many products of the religious tradition express sensibility that is remote from scientific methodology. So many efforts at the rationalization of religious views or artificial reconciliation have taken place that any such reconciliation suggests a compromise with intellectual honesty.

Yet since the rise of modern science, from Spinoza through Matthew Arnold and john Stuart Mill, there have been continuous efforts to reinterpret religious belief in a manner compatible with scientific method and scientific knowledge. This efforts usually required a redefinition of the nature of religious belief, or God, or of religious knowledge. In read defining fundamental aspects of religion, however, the philosophers concerned believed that they had preserved continuity with certain vital future of the religious tradition.

Dewey envisages that the religious binds all humanity and presents both a universal and humanistic vision of faith. Thanks to this newly-built faith, Dewey emphasizes that many individuals unable to accept or participate in historic religions would be able to subscribe to the new faith and derive religious experience from it, and that the proposed faith would increase the range of religious experience, since it would enable the extraction of religious experience from many activities and endeavors not commonly recognized as being sources of such experience, and that the proposed faith, because it is rooted in nature, is essentially more religious in quality than faith in the supernatural. In that way, Dewey's faith is very modern and "visionary" because he anticipated the challenges religions were to face during the whole of the 20th century and also the gap that would grow up between religion and science (for Edward A. White, professor at Stanford, "Dewey's work has led to the 20th century rift between religion and science") and between different trends inside religions themselves (fundamentalism/liberalism), and because in consequence he proposes a non-doctrinal and universally acceptable new faith.

Dewey's philosophy of religion follows in this path of what has been termed "religious naturalism" or "religious liberalism" Dewey's sense of the philosophical agenda drew him to a concern with the reconciliation between our inherited views on social, political, and moral question s and the methods of science, rather than to the problems science poses for religious belief. Essentially, his contribution in this area was one small volume, *A Common Faith* (1934).

A Common Faith is a coherent and thoughtful formulation of religious naturalism. Religious belief, it claims, can be consistent with the adoption of scientific method as the only reliable way to knowledge if it is prepared to abandon any assertion of supernatural or transcendental entities or experience.

After such surrender, there remain all those aspects of religious belief and religious experience that involve the imaginative construction of an unification of ideal ends, called God. Further, the celebration or commemoration of the possibility of those ends being realized in the world of our experience has not been abandoned.[23]

Many naturalists and pragmatists found in Dewey's willingness to sanction the use of the term 'God' an evasion of the implications of his consistent naturalistic point of view in metaphysics or theory of knowledge. It is the associations of the term 'God' not only with the supernatural, but also with the conception that there is a guarantee for the outcome of natural and historical process that suggest that a naturalistic use of the term is equivocal. For many philosophical naturalists the introduction of a naturalist conception of God violated the canons of semantic parsimony.

Many religionists and theologians argue that conceptions of a naturalistic or limited divinity ignore the centrality of the transcendent and the irrational for the theory and practice of religion. They believe, accordingly, that works that reconcile religious tradition with scientific method do not do justice to the richness of that tradition in its own settings.

Dewey had set for himself a limited goal in *A Common Faith.* Within the context of the effort to develop a contemporary religious liberalism or religious naturalism, Dewey sought to formulate a statement of that religious option. For Dewey, is the way in which it fulfils its social function? Dewey believed that those philosophical scenarios, in which a completely isolated human being resolves the ultimate questions about the nature of things or of self, of god or of the right, are conceptually incoherent. Philosophy is an activity born out of the conflict of opinions and disagreements about methods of inquiry in a specific culture. Its function of the disagreements about intellectual method. Abstracted from social context, there could be no philosophical discussion.[24]

These general considerations concerning the social basis of all philosophical thought led Dewey to a analysis of the role of philosophy in the contemporary social context. Thus documents taken from that analysis illuminate the recurrent themes in Dewey's reflection on the social and religious problems of our time.[25] Consequently, it is not man alone but man in union with nature who achieves whatever may be the goal of his existence; and the goal in question is quite attainable, since it modestly ambitions nothing beyond the natural and temporal goods of earth.

Whereas Ambedkar's Philosophy of Religion at the outset of his book, Philosophy of Hinduism, takes up the argument on the meaning of "Philosophy of Religion."[26] Due to two facts, he confesses that he is unable to get a clear idea about it. Firstly, there is nothing unambiguous about what is incorporated in the term philosophy. Secondly, philosophy and religion have been adversaries and hostile to each other which makes the unhappy choice of the title, "Philosophy of Religion" confusing. Ambedkar, in his The *Buddha* and His Dhamma describes the accepted perception of religion held by common people and advocated by European theologians, who hold Religion that connotes "belief in God, belief in soul, worship of God, curing of the erring soul, propitiating God by prayers, ceremonies, sacrifices, etc."[27] He shows that the origin of religion was never fixed. From time to time the word, "religion", is an imprecise word with no unchanging meaning: "It is a word with many meanings. This is because religion has accepted through many stages. The impression has not had the same meaning which it had at the prior stage or is likely to have at the succeeding stage."[28]

Ambedkar's reinterpretation of religion, Buddhism and the Philosophy of Religion reveal his hermeneutical skills. His hermeneutical suspicion went beyond the Marxian suspicion, which failed to grasp the evil consequences of caste oppression and caste alienation. His reinterpretation of Buddhism, in accordance with modem scientific principles and socialistic revolutionary thrust is remarkable.[29] Ambedkar's thinking and interpretation was also highly critical. He insisted that Philosophy of Religion should not only be descriptive but also critical. His Dalit Critical Principle was radical in its depth and extent. It sought the root causes of the problem, without stopping the diagnosis at the level of symptoms. And in its extent, the critique of Ambedkar targeted all the political parties, ideologies, religions, social reform movements and the eminent social and political activists, even if they are popularly hailed as mahatmas, freedom fighters and social reformers.[30] The theology of Ambedkar is based on the principles of love and wisdom, which is like two wheels of his theological caravan. He emphasizes the necessities of both the Buddhist discerning wisdom and Christian loving service.

In similar way, Dewey is not satisfied with denying the foundations of religion by substituting his conceptual ideals for a personal God. He goes out of his way to oppose what he calls the suicide of reason and human effort which consists in revelation and the belief in divine grace to supplement the weakness of man. Man is quite capable of himself to attain all the knowledge that he needs and achieve all the ambitions he desires. If there must be faith, let it be men's faith in each other and in their mutual co-operation. 'Faith,' he says, "in the continued disclosing of truth through directed co-operation of human endeavor is more religious in quality than is any faith in a completed revelation."[31] A cardinal principle of Dewey's naturalism is the rejection of any kind of fixed doctrine or creed, based on revelation, and therefore stultifying the progress of human science which must be independent of such chains.

Some fixed doctrinal apparatus is necessary for a religion. But faith in the possibilities of continued and rigorous inquiry does not limit access to truth to any channel or scheme of things. It does not say first that truth is universal and then adds that there is but one road to it. It does not depend for assurance upon subjection to any dogma or item of doctrine. It trusts that the natural interactions between man and his environment will breed more intelligence and generate more knowledge, provided the scientific methods that define intelligence in operation are pushed further into the mysteries of the world.

Here we have a definition of faith, based not on the authority of God's revelation but on the autonomy of man's own reason. 'There is such a thing,' says Dewey, "as faith in intelligence becoming religious in quality a fact that perhaps explains the efforts of some religionists to disparage the possibilities of intelligence as a force. They properly feel such a faith to be a dangerous rival."[32]

So much for knowledge, the same holds true in action and achievement. "Men have never fully used the powers they possess to advance the good in life, because they have waited upon some power external to themselves and to nature to do the work they are responsible for doing. Dependence upon an external power is the counterpart of surrender of human endeavor."[33] Dewey sees only one objection to this deification of man's ability to perfect himself. He answers the objection: Nor is emphasis on exercising our own powers for good an egotistical or a sentimentally optimistic course. It is not the first, for it does not isolate man, either individually or collectively, from nature. It is not the second, because it makes no assumption beyond that of the need and responsibility for human endeavor.... It involves no expectation of a millennium of good.[34] Consequently, it is not man alone but man in union with nature who achieves whatever may be the goal of his existence; and the goal in question is quite attainable, since it modestly ambitions nothing beyond the natural and temporal goods of earth.

Another facet of the Ambedkar Philosophy of Religion is that "to know the ideal scheme for which a religion stands"[35] which follows logically from Ambedkar's elucidation of religion. To define what is fixed, everlasting and foremost part in the religion of any society and to separate its essential character from those, which are expendable, is often very complex. Distinguishing between the primitive religions and the positive religions, he adjudicates that the task is not so difficult in case of the latter. The primary characteristic of positive Religions is that they have not grown up like primitive religions under the action of cataleptic forces operating silently from age to age, but trace their derivation to the teaching of great religious innovators who wrangle as the organs of a divine revelation. Being the result of conscious formulations, the philosophy of a religion which is positive is unchallenging to find and easy to state. He argued for the reorganization of Hindu religion, and listed out the following the necessary items. According to him, there should be one and only one standard book of Hindu Religion, acceptable to all Hindus and recognized by all Hindus. This of course means that all other books of Hindu religion such as Vedas, *Shastras and Puranas*, which are treated as sacred and authoritative, should end to be so, and the preaching of any doctrine, religious or social that are restricted in these books should be penalized.

No ceremony performed by a priest who does not hold a *sunad* shall be deemed to be valid in law and it should he made penal for a person who has no *sunad* to officiate as a priest. A priest should be the servant of the state and should be subject to the disciplinary action by the State in the matter of his morals, beliefs and worship, in addition to his being subject along with other citizens to the ordinary law of the land. "The numeral of priests should be limited by law according to the requirements of the State as is done in the case of the Christianity."[36] Ambedkar required Hinduism based on a set of moral principles, which are appropriate equally to all the participants of the society. And only these moral principles would sustain the society.

Ambedkar argues that the Hindu religion, its concept of God and its allied religious principles and customs that tend to preserve the caste system intact. Religious doctrine made the untouchables, presently called as Dalits, to believe that they are born to be slaves and that they are fit only to the menial jobs. For him, a Hindu means a caste and his responsibility and loyalty is restricted only to his caste. The Virtue and moralities have become caste bound and there is no possibility for sympathy, charity and appreciation of the deserving. The untouchables or Dalits were not allowed to get the same status with others in the Hindu religion. Ambedkar finds significance of religion only in their principles but condemns the religion, which is guarded by its rules and codes. He feels that Hindu religion is meaningless to the untouchables because of its rigidity. Hindu religion has got several codes of conduct. For the untouchables some were strictly adhered. Violating them by the untouchables led to severe punishment and excommunication.

The philosophy of Hinduism as a part of the philosophy of Religion it is necessary to examine the *Upanishads*. The philosophy of the Upanishads has been well summarized by Buxley. He says that the Upanishad philosophy agreed that, "supposing the existence of a permanent reality, or 'substance', beneath the shifting series of phenomena, whether of matter or of mind."[37] The substance of the cosmos was 'Brahma' that of the individual man *'Atman'*; and the latter was separated from the former only, if I may so speak, by its phenomenon envelope, by the casing of sensations, thoughts and desires, pleasures and pains, which make up the illusive phantasmagoria of life. This the ignorant, take for reality; their *'Atman'* therefore remains eternally imprisoned in delusions, bound by the fetters of desire and scourged by the whip of misery.

Lala Hardyal says that, "The Upanishads claim to expound' that, by knowing which everything is known."[38] This quest for 'the absolute' is the basis of all the spurious metaphysics of India. The treatises are full of absurd conceits, quaint fancies, and chaotic speculations. And we have not learned that they are worthless. We keep moving in the old rut; we edit and re-edit the old books instead of translating the classics of European social thought. Indian pundits and graduates seem to suffer from a kind of mania for what is effete and antiquated. Thus an institution, established by progressive men, aims at leading our youths through Sanskrit grammar to the Vedas via the Six *Darshanas*. According to Ambedkar it is a false move in the quest for wisdom.

Ambedkar's Religion is concerned with the love of truth, where as Philosophy is stagnant and Religion is dynamic. These differences are merely two aspects of one and the same thing. Philosophy is static because it is concerned only with knowing of truth.

Religion is dynamic because it is concerned with love of truth. Unless religion is dynamic and begets in us the emotion of love for something, then it is better to be without religion; as religion is a perception of truth and if our perception of truth is not accompanied by our love for it, then it is much better that the religion is not seen at all.

This is the outcome of all transcended philosophies which have no influence on the way of life. As Blake said, "Religion is philosophy and philosophy is Brotherhood. Philosophy must become Religion i.e., it must become a work Ethic."[39] It must not remain mere metaphysics. As Mr. Plowman says, "If religion were a Metaphysic and certain, it would never be the concern for men. To keep it wholly in the realm of Metaphysic is to make nonsense of it. Believing in religion as something which is not directly and vitally effective in politics is ultimately belief that is strictly speaking idiotic; because in the effective sense such a belief makes no difference, and in the world of time and space 'what makes no difference does not exist."[40] It is for these very reasons that the philosophy of the Upanishads proved so ineffective.

According to Dewey, Man possesses no soul or mind in the traditional sense of these terms. The doctrine of organic de-development has eliminated the dualism of soul and body. A spiritual vital principle is rejected because "the independently existing soul restricts and degrades individuality, making of it a separate thing outside of the full flow of things, alien to things experienced and consequently in either mechanical or miraculous relations to them."[41] Although the mind is not spiritual, it can still acquire knowledge in Dewey's hypothesis through what he calls the medium of experience. There are no objective norms of truth or morality because "human experience consciously guided by ideas, evolves its own standards and measures, and each new experience constructed by their means is an opportunity for new ideas and ideals."[42]

The specific instrument by which ideals are to be discovered and the court of last appeal in their prosecution is the scientific method. Dewey recognizes three names by which this theory of scientism may be denominated. Viewed in terms of the specific end or goal of human knowledge, whether this-worldly human utility or divine and extra-mundane, it is pragmatism; viewed in terms of the method by which knowledge is gained, whether by deduction from fixed principles or by experimentation through the scientific method, it is experimentalism; and viewed in terms of the immediate function which thought is to serve, whether to acquire knowledge of truths and finally of Truth or merely as an instrument to 'more vital living,' it is instrumentalism.

The Philosophy of Religion of Ambedkar also, in the same stratum, proposes justice and social welfare as the criterion to judge the religions. Paul Knitter, a liberation theologian of religion, has taken up the debate on the need for a criterion, to evaluate religious practices. He has, in dialogue with Liberation Theology, proposed the critical principles. While Knitter's suggestion still remains a proposal, Ambedkar's dalit critical principle had been put to use and proved to be effective as the criterion to judge religions and ideologies. The promotion of justice to the dalits and the oppressed is the best criterion to judge religions, ideologies or political and social events and activities.

The third dimension in the Philosophy of Religion is the criterion to be adopted for judging the value of the ideal scheme of divine governance for which a given Religion stands. Religion must be put on assessment. That leads to the description of the norm. Of the three dimensions, this third one is the most difficult one to be ascertained and defined."[43] Ambedkar disagrees with those who hold that this dimension is not a part of Philosophy of Religion. D.S. Adam makes it clear that some students of the Philosophy of Religion seem to regard the first two dimensions only in the field of Philosophy of Religion. They do not identify the third dimension as part of the study of the Philosophy of Religion. He disagrees with this view. The difference is probably due to the fact that he regards the Philosophy of Religion as a normative study and as a reminiscent study.[44]

Moreover, the basis of Dewey's philosophy of life is an unmitigated naturalism. In 1925 when Santayana, himself a confirmed materialist, accused Dewey of cowardice in his profession of naturalism, Dewey defended himself in a spirited article entitled 'Half-Hearted Naturalism,' in which he clarified his position to make it very certain that he wanted to be considered 'a whole-hearted naturalist. "While this should be evident from the reading of his numerous works, it is significant that he went out of his way to remove every doubt on this point.

He calls himself an empirical naturalist who allows no break or discontinuity between nature and social man. There is no 'gulf between nature of man and social and conventional man.' Any other concept is 'reminiscent of supernatural beliefs.... To me human affairs, associative and personal, are projections, continuations, complications of the nature which exists in the physical and pre-human world. There is no gulf, no two spheres of existence, and no `bifurcations.'"[45] There is only a 'thorough-going continuity' between man and nature, a fact which is demonstrated by the progress of physical science.

Religion as a Social Liberation

Religion as a social conscious and concerned with the human being in nature. For Dewey views of social idea is rejection of traditional speculations. Traditionally in Christendom the church, a very tangible institution in, but conceived as not entirely of the society,[46] was the home of the intellectuals. The church in this respect was roughly analogous to the university in our society. For those who lived during the centuries of Catholic Christendom, as for the Puritans of early Massachusetts Bay, theologians played the role in society that Parsons and Shills designate as the role of intellectuals in any society.[47] Further, they were expected to give guidance to rulers and people, in minute detail if necessary, for they were the recognized interpreters of the proper application of the general standards to specific issues. In this social-cultural structure 'salvation' was inextricably bound to right conduct in every area of life from birth to last rites.

With the fragmentation of the transnational church by the Reformation, and the establishment of religious pluralism, this unified authoritarian structure was destroyed and Christianity was thereafter incarnated in many different and highly competitive institutions, each legitimated by its absolutes parochial interpretation of the common gospel. Each Established church that resulted made for its place in its nation the same sort of claims that the universal Catholic Church had made for its ubiquitous transnational authority. In other words, the new nations reverted to tribalism, and an Established church was the institutionalization of the nation's tribal cult.[48]

In this situation no substantive difference was made between church and common wealth. Both were merely ways of looking at the same body of people. This was evidenced in the legal structure by the merging of monarch into God, legitimated by some forms of the doctrine of the divine right of kings' In this context the role of the theologian of an Established church was that of a true intellectual of and for his nation-society.

When the American Revolution was completed, let us say with John Adams by around 1815,[49] not only had the Established Church of England been rejected, but, more important, the very idea of Establishment had been discarded in principle by the new Constitution. For the first time in Christendom there was legal *religious freedom* as distinct from toleration in a commonwealth.[50] Church and state could no longer be seen as coextensive functional institutionalized authorities as merely two ways of looking at the same society. A church became a voluntary association within the commonwealth, in competition with perhaps hundreds of others. Loyalty to God, symbol of the highest ideals and standards (cultural system), could now be distinguished from loyalty to monarch or state, symbols of nation (social system), and it was possible to conceive that the two might be in conflict. This development is what John Adams meant by 'the Revolution' the change that took place "in the minds and hearts of the people" which he described as "a change in their religious sentiments of their duties and obligations.".[51]

The Revolution of the theologian, who had lost his transnational perspective with the Reformation, lost also his national perspective, and became the intellectual for but one of the multitude of competing sects. Now his primary role was to construct a solid defense of his sect's peculiar species of Christianity against all the other sects making the same absolutistic claim. Because the one thing all Christians held in common was the authority of Scripture, all such defenses were erected on this foundation. This meant that even while ostensibly defending the authority of the Bible against skeptics, infidels, and atheists, each sect was actually contending against all other Christian groups for sole possession of the revelation by right of having the only, or most nearly, correct interpretation of it. Meantime the Revolution meant that all their sectarian claims had been made completely irrelevant to the individual's status and rights as a citizen, and to the being and well-being of the commonwealth in which they lived. Thus the competition between the sects undermined belief in the distinctive beliefs of all of them. For in the minds of Mr. and Ms. John Q. Public the strident claims of the sects simply cancelled each other out, as their Republic was teaching them that no sect's distinctive had a bearing on their rights as citizens.

Meantime the new kind of commonwealth that had emerged in Christendom found cosmic legitimating in Enlightenment theology the cosmopolitan perspective that induced Benjamin Franklin to pray that God would "grant, that not only the Love of Liberty, but a thorough Knowledge of the Rights of Man, may pervade all the Nations of the Earth, so that a Philosopher may set his Foot anywhere on its Surface, and say, 'This is my Country.'"[52] The same sentiment prompted Alexander Hamilton to suggest in the first Federalist Paper that in the new kind of nation being born philanthropy (love for mankind) must always temper patriotism (love for country), which is to say that 'national security' is not necessarily always the ultimate consideration.

It was this cosmopolitan theology that the Christian denominations almost universally rejected during the course of the revivals that swept across the nation following the 1790s. In doing so they turned back to pre-eighteenth-century theologians, or to the theologians of Europe's Established churches, for the framework of their intellectual structures, while the meaning system that informed and legitimated the social, economic, political and judicial systems of the nation followed in the tradition of Enlightenment thinking. It was this development that institutionalized the separation of 'salvation' from the convert's responsibility for the structures of his society.[53]

One of the most extensively documented historical generalizations is that Enlightenment was driven underground by social opprobrium and character assassination of the infidel, but that its meaning system (to use Parsons' terms) was never examined for its intellectual merits and refuted by Christian theologians.[54] The Enlightenment meaning system continued, of course, to have its more or less able defenders. But most of them might rightly complain with Thomas Paine that his Christian opponents confounded 'a dispute about authenticity with a dispute about doctrines,' that is, in answer to his questioning of the authority of the Bible as sole revelation of God for teaching man his duty, they quoted Scripture to refute him.[55] This suggests what "I suspect was the case, that the great majority of clerical leaders and theologians did not recognize the real issue or realize the nature of the revolution in thinking that was taking place. Each in his denominational stockade tended to absolutes and universalizes his parochial species of Christianity, while sharing with those in his Christian opponent's ghettoes the common abhorrence of 'infidelity.' The 'infidel' was on everyone's enemies list."[56] This meant, to repeat my thesis, that every ardent defense of sectarian Christianity, however unintentional, was by implication an attack on the mainspring of the Republic,[57] Consequently the intellectuals the unofficial 'theologians' of the Republic explaining, defending, acting upon, and in-fusing the values of the commonwealth were commonly anathema to the leaders of institutionalized Christianity. Either that or and this was done by Robert Baird, who published his *Religion in America* in 1844 -45 they were posthumously metamorphosed into his species of good sectarian Christians.

This development meant the emergence in the common-wealth of two disparate, even competing culture systems, inculcating different conceptions of a proper social system, each with its own kind of intellectuals. Many theologians of the sects continued to talk as if they were the exponents of the normative culture system of the commonwealth, while actually they represented only that of, at best Christianity in general, at worst their exclusive sect. Meantime the intellectuals of the commonwealth, e.g., Jefferson, Franklin, Lincoln, and even Eisenhower, naturally found no real religious home in any existing sect. And many sensitive persons squirmed to have the best of both worlds, usually in the end by giving each a separate but equal compartment in their minds.

The question of the place of sectarian theologians in the commonwealth was solved by default. For with the general erosion of belief noted above, they lost even their vocation as defenders of what the Parson Thwackums among them have called denominational distinctive against both those of the other Christian sects and unbelievers. They became, at their best, defenders of the theologically amorphous but highly moralistic species of Christianity-in-general represented in recent decades by *The Christian Century,* at their worst pugnacious and powerful sectarian isolationists like the Rev. Carl McIntire. In either case, having usually been programmed in their theological schools to confuse the cosmopolitan Enlightenment theology with worship of the state, they have found it hard to find a plausibly significant role to play in the society.[58]

In the similar fashion, Ambedkar suggests that a philosophy of a religion must be judged, based on its revolution because the mother of Philosophy is revolution. So Ambedkar held the view that, "As for myself I think it is safe to proceed on the view that to know the philosophy of any movement or the institution has undergone. Revolution is the mother of philosophy and if it is not the mother of philosophy, it is a lamp, which illuminates philosophy. Religion is no exception to this rule. The best method to ascertain the criterion of which to judge the philosophy of (any) religion is to study the Revolutions which religion has undergone. That is the method I propose to adopt."[59] Further he says "To me the best method to ascertain the criterion by which to judge the Philosophy of Religion is to study the Revolutions which religion has undergone."[60]

Ambedkar says that the religion must be taken seriously because, through that a proper socio- political and cultural change can be brought about only through a cultural-religious revolution. Ambedkar not only insists that social and religious problems have a suggestion to politics but also persuasively demonstrates that political revolutions are brought about, or at least proceeded by, socio-religious revolutions which first guide in a cultural revolution. For instance, the Religious Reformation started by Luther was the forerunner of the political liberation of the European people. In England, Puritanism led to the establishment of political liberty which later on led to the foundation of a new world. It was Puritanism which had won the war of American Independence and Puritanism was a religious movement. The same is true in the case of Muslim Empire. Before the Arabs became a political power they had undergone a thorough religious revolution started by the Prophet Mohammad. Even the Indian History supports the same termination. The political revolution led by Chandragupta was preceded by the religious and social revolution of Buddha. The political revolution led by Shivaji was preceded by the religious and social reform brought about by the religious reformers of Maharashtra. The political revolution of the Sikhs was preceded by the religious and social revolution led by Guru Nanak. However, the Gautama Buddha is the first social revolutionary in history claims Ambedkar.

By taking these historic instances Ambedkar says that the emancipation of the mind and the soul is a necessary preliminary for the political expansion of the people.[61] Religion is needed to wage any kind of revolution in the society, since it mentally engineers the minds of the people. Religion, thus, plays no inconsequential role in the emancipation of the mind and soul of the people, which is a preliminary requisite for the socio-political transformations of society. According Ambedkar, revolutionary social change needs religion as an important motivating, concretizing, empowering and energizing factor.

Ambedkar reminds us of great prophets like Buddha, Jesus and his predecessors like Amos, Isaiah who condemned religious practices that exploit the poor and smack of hypocrisy. Ambedkar lashes out at wrong concept of religion and said, "Our religion today has neither God nor morality. I have no doubt that this is a much degenerated state of human mind; and it is a task for the future generation to restore religion in the purer and nobler form."[62] He proceeds to enumerate the stages of its degeneration: He added that in his day in India there was no religion except the worship of idols, whether they were of *Sadhus. Saints,* or miracle-makers. Ambedkar attacked the real character of the Hindu Religion, in short, "so long as we remain in a religion which teaches a man to treat another man as leper, the sense of discrimination on account of caste which is deeply rooted in our minds cannot go. For annihilating castes and untouchability from among the untouchables, change of religion is the only antidote."[63] "I tell you, religion is for man and not man is for religion. If you want to organize, consolidate and be successful in this world, change the religion."[64]

Ambedkar, by captivating support from Robertson Smith and Crawley, analyses the differences and similarities in the norms between the savage and the civilized society which he again divides in to antique society and Modern society. It is consequently clear that savage and civilized societies agree upon one aspect. That is, in both the societies, the inner interests of religion, namely, the life processes by which individuals are preserved and the race maintained are the same. There is no real difference between the two. At the same time they are different in two other important respects. In a savage society, God comes in the scheme of Religion, and in a civilized society, morality becomes consecrated by religion.[65] To determine the norm of judging the Philosophy of Religion, Ambedkar takes up a chronological survey of the 'ruling concepts of religion' as a scheme of divine governance, centuries down from the ancient society to the modern society. He also analyses the important revolutions.

And the character of these revolutions is of dual nature. One is an external revolution, caused by the scientific revolutions such as the Copernican revolution, and the Darwinian revolution caused by the emergence of sciences like Medicine and Psychology, which shattered the empire of religion bit by bit restraining its field and authority. It was a revolt of science against the extra territorial jurisdiction assumed by Religion over a field, which it did not belong. The second one is internal revolution, which was a real Revolution or may be compared to any other political Revolution such as the French

Revolution or the Russian Revolution, "which involves a constitutional change. By these kinds of Revolutions, the scheme of divine governance came to be distorted, amended and reconstituted."[66]

The internal revolution must be paid more attention in order to determine the model for judging the philosophy of religion for it "touches the nature and content of ruling of perceptions of the relations of God to man, of society to man and of man to man. How great this revolution was can be seen from the differences which divide savage society from civilized society."[67] From the analysis of religious revolutions, Ambedkar ends with a note that individual justice and social utility must serve as the norms for judging the value of the varied ideal schemes of divine governance proposed by different religions. The religion that helps greater promotion of individual justice and equality, presents itself with the divine and spiritual religious ideals, and also maintains a moral social order which intern promotes social utility and progress, that kind of religion should be judged as the better religion.

For as John Dewey noted that we cannot observe religion-in-general, but only genera and species of the family.[68] This is to say that outsiders, for whom religion is as religion does, can produce only biographies of the species or genera of religion. And if Jonathan Edwards was, and if Arthur S. Link is, right, the communication gulf between insiders and outsiders is impassable. To the outsider the insider's autobiographical argument is unconvincing or meaningless because he lives in a different world of reality in which the insider's claim is an obscurantist refuge for all the species of privatized religiosity. Ruth Benedict delineated the contrast between the two perspectives, as only an Outsider could do, in her contrast between open and closed groups:

The distinction between any closed group and outside peoples becomes in terms of religion that between the true believers and the heathen. Between these two categories for thousands of years there were no common meeting-points. No ideas or institutions that held in the one were valid in the other. Rather all institutions were seen in opposing terms according as they belonged to one or the other of the very often slightly differentiated religions: on the one side it was a question of Divine Truth and the true believer, of revelation and of God; on the other it was a matter of moral error, of fables, of the damned and of devils. There could be no question of equating the attitudes of the opposed groups and hence no question of understanding from objectively studied data the nature of this important human trait, religion.[69]

Dewey have argued that "the experience of the old Christianity in the New World resulted in the internalizing of Christianity with the consequent separation in principle of one's 'salvation' from a sense of responsibility for the social, cultural and political life of his society. The nature of this separation can also be delineated in contemporary sociological language, and my interest in consensus induces me to try to do so."[70]

In applying this definition to an understanding of our America, it is natural to suppose that the religion (meaning-system) that legitimates America's social, political, and cultural system is Christianity as given institutionalized form in the many denominations. This we have come to believe is a mistake. My thesis that the internalization of religion beginning with the eighteenth-century revivals effectively separated assurance of *'salvation'* from a sense of responsibility for the institutions of the convert's society.[70] This is to say that the species of religion incarnated in the denominations, with their massive institutional inertia, is not the religion that actually sets and legitimates the norms for our society that the theology of the denominations does not legitimate the political and legal structure of the commonwealth.[72]

It follows that it is not very profitable to go looking for the real theology of our Republic in the dusty historical attics of the institutionalized ostentatious piety of our contemporary society. Certainly it is not profitable to look only there. Recognition of this separation was always implicit, for example, in those educators who, while holding that the public schools inculcated the moral and spiritual values of the democracy, were very careful to divorce those values from all species of the religion institutionalized in the nation's sects.

In the same sense, purpose of savage society, Ambedkar's religion is without God, and its morality is self-governed by the religion. The change that has occurred in the civilized society is the first stage in the internal religious revolution. The second stage of Religious Revolution would take place within the Civilized Society. As a result of which the civilized society was split into Antique and Modern Society. This second stage of revolution is far greater than the first, as it brought about prominent differences in the conceptions regarding the relations between God, Society and Man. Ambedkar demonstrates about ten differences in the relationship between God and Man, Society and Man, and Man and Man which was very much evident in the Antique and Modern society. Quoting from R. Smith, he finally sums it up saying, "By this Revolution, God has ceased to be merely the protector of society and social interests, in gross, he has also ceased to be the center of the divine order. Society and man have distorted the places which were the centers of this divine order. It is man who has become the center of it."[73]

Ambedkar sums up his historical survey of the norms by quoting that, 'we began with the distinction between Antique and Modern society, which differed in the type of their divine governance that they accepted as their Religious ideals. At the one end of the Revolution, first it was antique society where in, its primary focus was on society as part of its religious ideals. At the other end, during the period of modern society, the main focus was over individual as part of its religious ideals. To put the same fact in terms of norms, it can be said that the norm or the criterion, for judging a particular act 'right and wrong' in the Antique Society was utility, while the norm or the criterion for judging 'right and wrong' in the Modern Society was justice. Thus "the Religious Revolution was not a revolution in the religious organization of Society, if it results in the shifting of the center from society to the individual. It was a revolution in the norms."[74] Here Ambedkar explains his meaning of justice, "I want to explain what I mean by the principle of justice, if all men are equal, all men are of the same essence and the common essence entitled them to the same fundamental rights and to equal liberty. In short, justice is simply another name for liberty, equality and fraternity."[75] For Ambedkar, Fraternity and liberty are really derived notions. The basic and fundamental conceptions are equality and respect for human personality. Fraternity and liberty take their roots in these two fundamental conceptions. Equality is the original notion and respect for human personality is a reflection of it.

Is there an intimate relationship between the two norms of justice and utility chosen by Ambedkar to judge the religions? Here he brings out their interrelationship and connection relying on the significance of justice given by J.S. Mill who has pointed out, "there is no obligatory antagonism between justice and utility. In other words what is unjust to the individual cannot be useful to society."[76] Ambedkar uses to pass judgment concerning a religion by ascertaining whether a meticulous religion is a religion of rules or of principles. According to him, a religion that does not lay stress on the principles and has developed into only a set of rules has already degenerated. He considers this principle to judge religions to be important, and so he explains the same with minute details, viewing why the religion of principles is better:

The imperative may be right but the act is automatic. A religious performance May not be an accurate act but must at least be an accountable act. To permit this task, religion must chiefly be a matter of principles only; it cannot be a subject of rules. The moment it degenerates into rules, it ceases to be a Religion, as it kills responsibility, which is the real meaning of a religious act. A religion of rules must give way to the religion of principles. A religion like Hinduism which according to him advocates the ancient rules of life must reinstate them with a religion of principles. The principles that must replace the rules are again the identical principles, which are resultant from justice, which is also one of the norms for judging the religions. They are liberty, equality and fraternity, in short, democracy.[77]

For Ambedkar, religion is not a worship of God by man, or a relationship between God and man, nor is it the deliverance of soul after life. For him, religion is a social institution of ethics that sanctifies the proper association between the individuals in the society, and the welfare of the individual and preservation of the egalitarian society. This constitutes the important aspect of Ambedkar's philosophy of religion. Yet, some people claim that religion is a relationship between God and the human beings. It cannot be accepted that "all religions are equal," in the giving of this goal and the ability to attain the same. Hence, we still need a measure to evaluate religions. Ambedkar strongly disagrees with the affirmation that all religions are equal and hence "equal respect" is to be paid to all religions. "Ambedkar strongly advocated that one must give a new doctrinal basis to religion-a basis that will be in consonance with liberty, equality and fraternity and democracy."[78]

According to Ambedkar a religion should be a matter of principle only but shouldn't be a matter of rules. When it degenerates into rules it ceases to be a religion because it destroys the responsibilities of the true religion. He added that the caste has almost disorganized and demoralized the Hindus. Another reason for Ambedkar to find problem with Hindu Religion is its dual role. On the one hand for Hinduism the principles of Freedom, Equality and Fraternity are irrelevant. On the other hand he finds that Hindu religion divides the people permanently because of its inbuilt character of caste stratification. He wanted a religion, which is not duplicitous in the name of religion and teaches his followers to relate with others on the basis of liberty and fraternity. But there is no fraternity or equality among the Hindus and the caste system continued to exist. According to Ambedkar, the outcast is a by-product of caste system and there will be outcastes as long as the caste system exists. So nothing can redeem the outcaste except the annihilation of caste system.

Assuming the aim of religion is to reach God. Every road is that sure to lead him which will perfect religion that is still to be discovered. But the fact is that religions are not all true and hence, the adherents of one faith have a right, indeed a duty, to tell their erring friends what they conceive to be the truth. This argument again appears in another essay of Ambedkar titled, "Away from the Hindus" that discusses the reasons for conversion and disproves the objections raised against the move. The second objection for conversion is that it is not needed since all religions teach the same truth, namely, to seek for the goodness. Granting that all religions may teach to adhere to the "good", yet, they hold opposing views in what they propose as good. Ambedkar perceives that, "Religions may be alike in a way that they all teach that the meaning of life is to be found in the pursuit of 'good'. But religions are not alike in their answers to the question,

'What is good?' In this they certainly differ. One religion holds that brotherhood is good, another caste and untouchability is good. Some religions advocate the method of violence while others absolutist non-violence. This shows that all religions are not the same."[79] Ambedkar says that there are three important characteristics, which form the subject matter of a philosophical analysis of religion both in natural and social theology. They are (a) The existence of God (b) God's providential government of the universe and (c) God's moral government of mankind. For him the philosophy of Religion needed to be seen in terms of three perspectives, "its doctrine of God and of the divine as an integral part of its theory of nature; the ideal scheme for which a religion stands; and the specification of the criterion to be adopted for judging the ideal scheme of divine governance portrayed by a religion."[80] As far as Ambedkar is concerned philosophy of religion is normative science and regarded the specification of a set of criteria for judging the philosophy of a particular religion and by implication of all religions. After this basic explanation Ambedkar attempted to specify the meaning of Religion.

Ambedkar measured religion as a system of values and as a science of social reconstruction. He said that the foundations of religion were indispensable to life and practices of life. He regarded religion as an essential one for single-minded human relationship. His view of religion in terms of character of his community could be understood from his fear of so-called denationalization of the depressed classes. He felt that the acceptance of Buddhism by his community would raise its politico-cultural status and bring them on par with the Hindus. He discarded the Hindu religion because of moral incoherence and also on the grounds of logical incoherence. He looked at the religion not as a road to salvation but as the basis for social interaction.

Ambedkar holds a perception that the religion is a vital force, a scheme of moral governance and foundation for human society. He also says "While I condemn a religion of rules, I must not be understood to the opinion that there is no necessity for a religion. It is the foundation of society, the basis on which all true civil governments rest and both their sanction. Consequently, "when I urge that these ancient rules of life be annulled, I am anxious that a Religion of principles, which alone can claim to be a true Religion, shall take its place."[81] For Ambedkar, religion is necessary as a system of values and as a science of social reconstruction. Religion is necessary for the overall development of an individual and it is a system of such socio-cultural values, which would carry all the individuals on equal plane and would create an equal status for all communities. He looked at the religion not as a road to salvation but as the basis for social interaction. Ambedkar wanted a religion, with morality in order to build up nationalism with the association of Indian culture. He always wanted a religion with complete Indian culture and nature. He also emphasized that a religion should be free from exploitation, and true religion does not justify exploitation.

Moreover what Dewey have been criticizing is the identification of the ideal with a particular Being, especially when the identification makes necessary the conclusion that this being is outside of Nature, and what I have tried to show is that the ideal itself has its roots in natural conditions; it emerges when the imagination idealizes existence by laying hold of the possibilities offered to thought and action. There are values, goods, actually realized upon a natural basis the goods of human association, of art and knowledge. The idealizing imagination seizes upon the most precious things found in the climacteric moments of experience and projects them. We need no external criterion and guarantee for their goodness. They are had, they exist as good, and out of them we frame our ideal ends.[82]

Ideal ends, for Dewey then, emerge from verifiable aspects of reality as the product of imagination which visualizes them as the possibilities which may be made to grow out of existing conditions. As these ends are strived for in the framework of existing conditions, the ideals are tested and the conditions are at the same time modified. This process, observes Dewey, is descriptive of all human progress and cultural refinement. In other words, Dewey emphasizes here, as he does so very often, that all human advances in art and knowledge are natural emergent of art and knowledge previously established in the society; that progress is made as new possibilities are imaginatively seen to exist as improvements in or elaborations upon existing art and knowledge. Dewey comments as follows upon the possible effectiveness of a faith in the power of existent natural and social forces to generate and accomplish the imaginatively perceived ideal ends obtaining potentially in existing conditions: When the vital factors in this natural process are generally acknowledged in emotion, thought and action, the process will both be accelerated and purified through the elimination of that irrelevant element that culminates in the idea of the supernatural. When these factors attain the religious force that has been drafted into supernatural religions, the resulting reinforcement will be incalculable.[83]

Since there are actual, observable forces present in nature and society (e.g. artistic and intellectual endeavor, education, fellowship, friendship, and mental and physical growth) which produce humanly experienced goods and which evince capabilities of accomplishing envisioned ideal ends, Dewey would identify the functioning relationship between the actual forces and ideal ends as being 'the divine.' In his own words he says, "It is this active relation between ideal and actual to which I would give the name God."[84] Such a conception of God or the divine would not, he points out; omit the element of natural piety as do the concepts of the super naturalists and the militant atheists, nor would it exclude man's relation to nature as does the concept of the purely humanistic religionists. It would embody instead a clear recognition of man's essential relationship, in terms of both dependence and support, with the rest of nature. In thus providing a basis for man's achievement of a sense of connection, unity, or harmony with the whole of nature, says, Dewey, the proposed concept would serve better than any of the more traditional ones to promote a genuinely religious attitude and produce genuinely religious experience-for religious attitude and religious experience are characterized chiefly by a sense of purposive oneness with the whole of things.

By way of pointing out the superiority of the proposed basis of faith in the "active relation between the ideal and the actual"[85] over faith in the supernatural, Dewey has thus far prominently emphasized: that many individuals unable to accept or participate in historic religions would be able to subscribe to the new faith and derive religious experience from it,[86] that the proposed faith would widen the range of religious experience, since the new faith would permit the extraction of religious experience from many activities and endeavors not commonly recognized as being sources of such experience, and that the proposed faith, because it is rooted in the natural., is essentially more religious in quality (for reasons just discussed) than is faith in the supernatural.[87]

In the Same manner the Philosophy of Religion, as Ambedkar defines it, differs much from the comparative Religion. All the religions are equally true and good, but not in the field of Ambedkar's 'Philosophy of Religion'. In his view Philosophy of Religion begins where the Comparative Religion ends. He accuses comparative Religions for creating the impression that all religions are equally good and true, and that there is no need of discerning between them. According to him, this belief is positively and perceptibly wrong and there is no greater error than this. He also elaborates that Religion is an uncertain phenomenon, it can be constructive or harmful, it can help to promote the good of society or it can bring adversity, it can also be liberative or oppressive. For instance, particular religion is more ready to lend a hand than others, or a religion can cause more harm compared to the others. It is a fact of experience, and it is to determine this fact properly that we need a norm to judge the value of various religions. To dismiss the false ideology that all religions are good and to point out that religion can also be harmful or helpful. Ambedkar quotes Prof. Tiele's vivid survey of the progress as well as destruction caused by a religion.[88] A force which shows such a strange difference in its result can be accepted as a good religion without examining the form it takes and the ideal it serves. It all depends upon what kind of social ideal that a given religion, as a divine scheme of governance, holds out. This is a question, which is not answered by the science of comparative religion. Indeed, it begins where comparative religion ends. "The Hindu is simply trying to avoid it by saying that although religions are many, they are equally good"[89] "Ambedkar strongly condemns this ideology that all religions are true."[90] On the question of God's existence and the role of religion and morality, Ambedkar says that the religion is necessary for man and society to manage the secular and moral affairs of mankind, but to hold the view that, all religions are equally true and good is to cherish a wrong belief. Most of the existing religions are theistic and metaphysical; but to maintain that God is an essential element of a religion is also to nourish a mistaken faith. Religion, according to Ambedkar, wish to develop the social systems of their own choice to bring men together in peace for progress; but to bestow a divine governance over them so as to prevent the growth of an open society. The Religions must preserve their Textbooks for guiding the people in right direction; but to believe in their infallibility and divine authority is to mar the growth of free inquiry and critical reason. The eternal soul is unknown and unseen, a mere metaphysical speculation and to say that an individual's aim of life is to achieve its salvation *(Moksha)* is to escape the social responsibility bestowed on him as a member of society.

All the religions develop some sort of prayers and pilgrimages, rituals and ceremonies, as religious duties for men, simply being certain appendages to a religion; but the most integral part of a religion is the Morality it professes for the welfare of mankind. The center of Religion and Man, the base is Morality, the aim is the secular welfare of Mankind, and the means is the righteous conduct embedded in social responsibility that all human beings owe towards their fellow-beings living in human society. And lastly, the test of Justice and Utility must be applied to judge the relevance of a Religion, and that consists in the trinity ideal of Liberty, Equality and Fraternity to effect the necessary change in its social norms of cruel and dynamical nature"[91]

For Ambedkar the function of religion is to provide legitimacy to the set of values and rules that would help establish a moral order among human beings. These values and rules could be particularistic, relatively arbitrary and community specific when the communities were small and isolated. Concepts of local deities and of behavioral norms that were thought to please them were an adequate base for a semblance of social order so long as they served the interests of the power elite in the community. But with the changes in technology, in the means of production and the means of communication, isolated human groups were forced into contact with one another, and the need arose for new values and rules which were more universal. Thus what were needed were a more universal morality and more universal concept of Godhood.

Ambedkar reiterates that the religion is a social force and stands for a scheme of divine governance. The scheme becomes an ideal for society to follow. The ideal may be non-existent in the sense that it is something, which is constructed. But although non-existent, it is real. For an ideal it has full operative force which I inherent in every ideal. Those who deny the importance of religion not only forget this; they also forget to realize how great the potency is and sanction that lies behind a religious ideal as compared with that of a purely secular ideal. A religious ideal has a hold on mankind, irrespective of an earthly gain; this can never be said of a purely secular ideal. A religious ideal never fails to work so long as there is faith in that ideal."[92] For Ambedkar, God who permits the survival of immoral social divisions in the society like caste is no God. Ambedkar objects the worship of God who permits the existence and survival caste system. Advocating Buddhism he discarded the *Shastras,* and also their authority as did by the Buddha.

Dewey assumes that the theologians are the intellectuals of a community of faith or belief. Dewey using the word 'intellectual(s)' in the sense developed by Shils and Parsons in the articles noted above. In Parsons's terminology, the intellectual is "expected to put cultural considerations above social,"[93] his function being to define and, presumably, to articulate and disseminate the meaning system (or 'value orientation') of his society. Shils spelled this out in clearer fashion. He assumed, as noted above, that communities are "bound together by the acceptance of a common body of standards"[94] which are internalized and "continually applied by each member in his own work and in the institutions which assess and select works and persons for appreciation or condemnation."[95]

What Dewey have described as the separation of 'salvation' from social responsibility, in the terminology of Parsons and Shils could be described as a separation of the cultural system and value orientation professed in a community from the actual social system, or the divorce of religion from what George Herbert Mead called "the political and social-cultural activities which were fundamental in American life."[96]

Dewey says, a new basis for faith emerges. Instead of a faith founded upon ideals guaranteed to exist by supernatural authority, there would be faith in ideals apprehended by the imagination as being intrinsically valuable possibilities or ends inherent in the natural relationship existing between man and his environment. This latter type of faith, says Dewey, is moral faith, and, as such, it represents "The authority of an ideal over choice and conduct..., not of a fact, or a truth guaranteed to the intellect, not of the status of the one who propounds the truth."[97] The faith in ideal possibilities inherent in man's relations with man and with the rest of nature proposed by Dewey would take cognizance of the dynamism present in nature.

It would repudiate the idea that the ideals to which it is dedicated are supernaturally pre-established in the framework of things. It would embody an insistence upon the necessity and "...upon the capacity of mankind to strive to direct natural and social forces to humane ends."[28] It would not rely upon the assertions of absolutistic credos that ideal ends are supernaturally fixed in a universal scheme of things. This faith, says Dewey, would be characterized by a natural piety that would ...rest upon a just sense of nature as the whole of which we are parts that are marked by intelligence and purpose, having the capacity to strive by their aid to bring conditions into greater consonance with what is humanly desirable. Dewey goes on to emphasize that faith in ideal ends on the proposed basis is faith in ideal ends rooted practically in existing conditions. In this connection he says:

Before concluding Dewey discussion, however, Dewey outlines still another important consideration relating to the superiority of the proposed basis of faith over that of the traditional supernaturalism when he states: The objection to supernaturalism is that it stands in the way of an effective realization of the sweep and depth of the implications of natural human relations. It stands in the way of using the means that are in our power to make radical changes in these relations. It is certainly true that great material changes might be made with no corresponding improvement of a spiritual or ideal nature. But development in the latter direction cannot be introduced from without; it cannot be brought about by dressing up material and economic changes with decorations derived from the supernatural. It can come only from more intense realization of values that inhere in the actual connections of human behaving with one another. The attempt to segregate the implicit public interest and social value of all institutions and social arrangements in a particular organization... i.e., a particular religion...is a fatal diversion.[99] In proposing his new basis for a religious faith, Dewey effectively counters the objections of others who also oppose faith in the context of typical supernatural religions. Lord Russell, for example, has said: Christians hold that their faith does good, but other faiths do harm. At any rate, they hold this about the Communist faith. What I wish to maintain is that all faiths do harm. We may define 'faith' as a firm belief in something for which there is no evidence. When there is evidence, no one speaks of 'faith'. We do not speak of faith that two and two are four or that the earth is round.

We only speak of faith when we wish to substitute emotion for evidence[100] To such assertions as these Dewey replies in essence, "I too reject the super naturalistic view of the universe and of man which cannot be supported by fact. I affirm that what we know is a natural universe of which man is a part. I advocate faith in human intelligence which, in interaction with other real forces in the universe, has the power to promote 'good' that may be known and evaluated pragmatically. Furthermore, I contend that man, by applying his intelligence to the pursuit of his ideals (that which he perceives to be (good), may know experience which is truly religious. Finally, because my proposed faith has human welfare as determined by human experience as its cornerstone, it will focus men's attention on harmonizing their efforts rather than leading them into disputes" Thus, it will enable them to avoid the conflicts that are generated when they place their faith in various (supernaturally revealed and 'infallible' creeds."[101] Robert Enger does not believe that Dewey's 'ideal ends' constitute a completely satisfactory universal ethic. (Men's ideas of what is 'good', even on an empirical basis too often differ.) Taken as a whole, however, Dewey shows clearly in A Common Faith the necessity for and the superiority of his kind of faith.

Dewey argued that the problem of achieving a more democratic society may be insoluble in terms of the relationship between an entity described as "the individual" and the entity of 'society' as such. It becomes open to creative solution if we shift to an investigation of the social conditions that enhance the development of certain kinds of individuality.

Dewey and Ambedkar's Concept of True Religion

According to Dewey to the field of religion are results on the properties of the rich features and dynamic properties of the process through experience. Specific analysis, experience, practices and understanding of the process is the process of unity, is a continuous interactive process, in the context of rational thought processes. Experience in Dewey's view of the system has a rich and content, he makes the field of religious experience and used the experience into direct experience and indirect experience, direct experience is the personal experience gained through personal activities, and indirect experience is the knowledge of the results of others. Concepts and classifications can be seen from the previous results and more from the perspective of Dewey is also a way of thinking and reflection.

And Dewey more dynamic and process from the point of view to explain the experience, experience with the process attributes. In the experience of the process, he is not valued in this process, the experience is the main role in things, and things are acting on the main process of interaction, but also in the interactive process, not the subject of the passive to the environment, into the experience is the experience of reflection, rational experience, experience includes rational use of past experience to guide the main body to undergo a new experience, or a in summary, experience the unity of practice and understanding of the process is a continuous interactive process, in the context of rational thought processes. One is experience and understanding of practice and the process of experience.Experience the process of practice. Practice refers to people of all activities of transforming the objective world, is a social person (the principal) a conscious role in the objective world (objects) of various forms of activity, simply put, is actually to experience also means Dewey stressed that from the Dewey that Therefore, Marxist philosophy that the understanding of the process is perceptual knowledge to rational knowledge from the process is continuous distillation process. Is the initial stage of perceptual knowledge, foundation stage, rational knowledge is knowledge of the advanced stage, there is no more difficult to rise to a rich perceptual rational knowledge; there is no deep theoretical understanding?[102]

Therefore, in the process of understanding, we must first reserve a large number of rich perceptual knowledge. Limited understanding of a rational understanding of the book, too much emphasis on book knowledge, learning, emphasizing rational understanding, it will deny perceptual knowledge, thus undermining the understanding of the law of development. This can have a profound theoretical understanding, cannot make their own access to real development.

In the same way Ambedkar's ideal of religion always wins over the secular practical ideal. This shows how great the difference in the force and sanction of these two ideals over the human mind. A religious ideal never fails to work so long as there is faith in that ideal. There is a criticism against Ambedkar that says that Ambedkar was against religion and wanted to destroy the religion, in contrary, one should remember that he called for the destruction of religion of rules and not of principles.[103] On such principle, he tries to impress upon the necessity of religion. Thus he condemns a religion of rules. Here, Ambedkar agree with Burke that, 'True religion is the foundation of society, the basis on which all true civil government rests, and both their sanction"[104]

Ambedkar deems religion to be essential to personal as well as social life. Religion exercises a great pressure of moral power over a person's heart and mind, builds up the person's character, it is a powerful driving force for human activity and it instills hope. According to Ambedkar religion can only satisfy the human being who is not satisfied with material things. A liberative religion alone can renovate the human minds of those who are socio-culturally enslaved. Ambedkar pertinently illustrates "the dominion which religion exercises over the minds of men"[105]

Ambedkar says that the true religion holds together society based on the moral force that exercises over the members. Its ethical power prevents social evils, crimes and atrocities, thus religion alone can cultivate equality, liberty and fraternity and the enforcement of justice and order. Thus religion is an important governing principle in the society. For Ambedkar "That which governs people is Religion. That is the true definition of Religion."[106]

For him, religion is also an important source of power in the society. Ambedkar recognized the influence of religion over people and its function as effective power-source in Indian society. And, he rejects the view that the religion to be idiosyncratic worship of God for the salvation of one's soul. His idea of religion is basically social and, it is defined in terms of moral and social order based on its ideal and principles. Consequently, the perception of Ambedkar on religion is based on principles, values and ideals where a society is governed by both individual and society that are preserved, promoted and sanctified.

The final rejection of all religions and "religion" as such. as understood in the theistic sense, took place when Ambedkar chose the non-theistic Buddhist *Dhamma* as the true religion. In his book that he wrote for the Neo-Buddhism titled, The Buddha and His *Dhamma,* denounces "religion" and contrasts it with the *Dhamma* of Buddha which is not considered a "religion" by all the European theologians. Here by religion he means a theistic religion: "This is what Religion has come to be and this what it connotes-belief in God, belief in soul, worship of God, curing of the erring soul, propitiating God by prayers, ceremonies, sacrifices, etc."[107] Stating that Pradanya and Karuna are the corner stone's of Buddha's *Dhamma,* Ambedkar explains the difference between the subject matter of religion and the subject matter of *Dhamma:* "The two are poles apart. The purpose of Religion is to explain the origin of the world. The purpose of *Dhamma* is to reconstruct the world."[108]

Dewey writes, "The experimental logic when carried into morals judges every quality as good to the extent to which it contributes to the resolution of existing ills"[109] Thus he disputes the sharp distinction we are accustomed to make between natural science and moral inquiry. The sciences help us recognize particular problems and develop plans to reduce their severity. For example, they pinpoint the presence of carcinogens in the products we consume or in the pollutants in the atmosphere. They enable us to know how much junk we are getting in our food and give us pointers about how to avoid it. In effect, they enable us to decide with some chance of success what steps to take, individually and collectively, to deal with problems created, increasingly, by our own industrial solutions of former problems.

In Dewey's approach, the sciences of fact become part of the apparatus of moral inquiry. Isolated and by itself, discussion of moral values often seems shrill or nagging or pedantic. But when natural science can be combined with ethical concerns, the combination loses these off-putting qualities and is much harder to ignore. It is to the benefit of both scientific and ethical practice when science is pursued for its social relevance and its vital importance in life.[110] Thus Dewey advocates the destruction of what he calls "the greatest dualism which now weighs humanity down, the split between the material, the mechanical and the scientific (on the one side) and the moral and ideal (on the other)."[111] A focus on concrete problems goes hand in hand with the destruction of this dualism. The split can be maintained only if we insist on operating with high abstractions or forget that abstractions are justified only as tools for solving problems. When attention is focused on *'diversified concretes'* we realize the need to use all available intellectual tools to solve special cases.

For Dewey, inquiry and discovery have essentially the same place in moral matters as they do in the sciences of nature. Ideas are tested in experience. What happens as a result of acting in accord with an idea becomes a measure of its worth. Reason in ethics, he says, takes flesh "in the methods by which needs and conditions, obstacles and resources, of situations are analyzed in detail, and plans for addressing problems worked out".[112]

Failing to do this we fall back on a few abstract ideas which promote the drawing of hasty conclusions. Bad consequences occur, but instead of recognizing that the fault lies in policies that are too simpleminded, we deplore these results as arising from inborn perversity of human nature or "inhospitable destiny" or simply the limitations of the human condition. But when we focus on the concrete situation, inquiry and alert observation of consequences become duties. All value ideas, all notions of things that are held to be valuable, are revisable, in Dewey's view, in the same sense that a scientific theory or hypothesis is regarded as revisable. A purpose must be considered a working hypothesis until results confirm it. Mistakes are to be expected, but, for Dewey, they are not accidents to be mourned or sins to be expatiated. Rather, they are "lessons in wrong methods of using intelligence and instructions as to a better course in the future."[113]

In the same way Ambedkar equates *Dhamma* is with morality. He regrets that in non-*Dhamma* religions morality is not given prominence nor is it effective. He asks the question that what the place of morality in Dhamma is and gives the simple answer that morality is *Dhamma* and Dhamma is morality. In other words, in *Dhamma,* "morality takes the place of God although there is no God in *Dhamma.* In Dhamma there is no place for prayers, pilgrimages, rituals, ceremonies or sacrifices"[114] Morality is the essence of Dhamma, without it there is no Dhamma. "Morality in Dhamma arises from the straight necessity for man to love man. It does not involve in the sanction of God. It is not to please God that man has to be moral. It is for his own good that man has to love man."[115]

The rational and scientific principle is the other pillar on which Buddha-Dhamma of Ambedkar needs to be stressed and substantiated. Being a man of science and a philosopher, who was influenced by secular scientific rationalism that swept the West, Ambedkar, was cautious to avoid anything that would smack of superstition, and verge on the border of the irrational. Nothing that cannot be proved rationally and argued logically can be part of his philosophy. The influence of Western Philosophy on his modern scientific mind was great. Not solely a single school of thought, but various trends in philosophy such as the secular humanism of Renaissance and Enlightenment, Socialism, Marxism, Positivism, Liberalism, Utilitarianism, engaged his attention and left their marks on his mind.[116] In the light of all these, Ambedkar strove hard to make his new religious sect thoroughly rational. He hinges his arguments unshakably in the Buddha's rational epistemology of "dependent origination", that is, things are related to each other in cause and effect relationship in the ceaseless change of reality. Accordingly, the speculative and supernatural beliefs in God *(Brahman)* or the eternity of the Soul (Atman) or heaven (Moksha) do not enter his scheme. Dhamma is not a belief in the supernatural being but the striving for a moral humane fraternal social life. Dharma in the Vedic Brahminic religion was to offer sacrifices *(Yagnas)*, rituals and prayers to worship God *(Brahman)*. These praises, offerings and sacrifices are offered in order to gain heavenly benefits hereafter, along with the earthly gains.

Ambedkar lays stress on the Buddha's reinterpretation of *Dhamma* as morality and his rejection of Brahminic understanding of *Dharma* as sacrifices and prayers. Thus, Ambedkar comes to reject all the theistic religions and the age-old Hindu beliefs, the existence of God *Brahman* is an *Atman*, Soul, *Samsara* theory of transmigration, the Karma theory of the effects of past, affecting the present life, and the Moksha theory of life after death. Infallibility of Vedas is not accepted and Upanishadic thought is considered pure imagination.

Further, Ambedkar, while accepting the *Buddha* and his *Dhamma,* presents him as the most rational and enlightened of human beings, and his *Dhamma* as the most scientific system, at least as Ambedkar understands and interprets it. The Buddha is presented as one who did not force his followers, but who gave complete freedom of thought. He rejected the infallibility of sacred books, divine authority and the revelation. The Buddha, emphasizes Ambedkar, unlike the other founders and innovators of religions like Moses, Jesus, and Mohammed does not claim to be of divine origin, nor receiver of divine revelation as a divine prophet. The Buddha claimed to be only in 'Enlightened' human being who, in turn, is a *Marga-data*, the finder and giver of the way, and not, as others have claimed to be, a *Moksha-data,* giver of salvation.[119] Finally, according to the rational scientific principle, Ambedkar tries his best faith all the intellectual calibre that was at his disposal in great store, to clarify and reinterpret some of the accusations against Buddhism, which he calls "misunderstandings." He gives scientific explanations for the same and proves them to be useful to the society.

Ambedkar affirmed the inevitability of a religion. He said that "a man made with hunger did not resort to theft not feared the legal consequences, but because of pressure his religion exercised over his mind". Religion had a direct connection with the laws based on the reason. He often said that whatever good he had in him were the fruit of religion, he also emphasizes that, he wanted religion, but did not want hypocrisy in the name of religion. To him, "religion is the driving force for human activity. Man cannot live with bread alone. Since he has a mind it needs food for thought. He considered the foundations of religion to be essential to the practices of society."[21] Ambedkar's personal philosophy of life and political involvement was based on religion.

His whole philosophy was based on the fundamental principles of liberty, equality and fraternity which borrowed from the teachings of his master, the Buddha.[122] Herbert Spencer describes religion as "the weft, which everywhere crosses the warp of history."[123] This is true in every society. But religion has not only crossed everywhere the warp of Indian history, In fact it forms the heart and soul of the Hindu mind. From his birth to death, the life of Hindu is influenced by his religion in relation to his food, dress, occupation, marriage, etc. Another reason why Ambedkar lays stress on religion as a social force is that it provides the people with the motivation to realize the same religious ideals that are more powerful than the practical secular ideals.

Religion, social status and property are all sources of power and authority, which one man has, to control the liberty of another and also leads to legitimacy.[124]

Ambedkar insists that "The primary things in religion are the usages, practices and observances, rites and rituals and theology is secondary, its objective is to rationalize them."[125] In the same way, religion should also be distinguished from what is considered to be supernatural. It is not to think religion as though it was super-natural. It is not right to view religion as an individual, private and personal matter, nor is it to be mistaken as the zenith of the special religious instinct inherent in the individual nature. The correct view is that the religion, like language is social for the reasons that either it is essential for social life or individual has to have it because without it's involvement he cannot participate in the life of the society.

Mean while, Dewey's religious experience means experience, which means personally seen and done, contact, suffered, etc., true religion discount, experience is the main role of the outside world, the outside world and the main reaction in the process, in this process, it provides a rich emotional understanding. In addition, the experience or the experience of reflection, experience includes a reason, so the experiences also provide a rational understanding. We would be said that experience is a scientific understanding of the process of the process.

Religious experience is the process of unification of practice and understanding of the process, in line with the laws of human cognition. Dialectical materialism that: the dialectics of human knowledge is the practice, knowledge, again practice, more knowledge, the cycle ad infinitum. Knowledge and theory only in the experience to get a deep understanding of the activities. Dewey said, an experience, a very meager experience, to produce and contains any quantity of theory (or intellectual content), but left the experience of the theory is not even certain to be understood as a theory.

Secondly, the experience is a continuous interactive process. Experience the process is interactive process. Dewey experience in real terms as the main interaction between environment and mutual influence on each other, the main action to impose on the environment, true religion online; impact the environment at the same time counter in the main, the principal impact. In this process, those are experiencing the main action, but also bear the consequences of action. Religious experience includes an active element and a passive element. In the active, the experience is the attempt; in the passive, the experience is to bear the consequences.[126]

In Dewey's classic case, a child put his hand into the flame is to try, is active, the child feels pain is to bear the consequences, is a passive aspect of the experience gained is that children reach into the flame of a pain, it is active and passive connection, the operation itself and the link between the results of operations. Experience the process is a continuous process. Because the so-called experience to have continuity of John Dewey, true religion. Empirical process is continuous interactive process. Continuity of experience also means that every experience both adopted from past experience something on; he somehow changed the nature of future experience. Thus, restructuring and reform.

Third is experience in the context of rational thought process. Experience the process of rational thinking process. Dewey's experience against the experience of reason and the opposition, he mentioned the experience of experience is not without reason, and that experience is the experience of thinking, experience includes the rational, free thinking, no, no rational experience, not a factor in thinking it is impossible to have a meaningful experience. The value of the experience level of experience depends on whether this is connected.[127]

Religious experience is in the process of context-specific process. Dewey experience as the interaction between subject and environment. And here's our objective in life all the time world, and the objective external world constitutes the environment, but does not constitute a situation. Environment and situation are two different but linked concepts. Environment for the individual, it is purely objective, different individuals can be in the same environment, the situation is the unity between objective and subjective, each individual being always in a certain situation. General sense of the environment only through the individual work situation fishes, only when the objective conditions have some experience of the individual subordinate to mind the situation, then the environment can be called context. Between the situations can only interact with people, which can have a real sense of the experience. So we experience the process of being in a particular context, in particular the occurrence and development context. Experience the process of rational thought in the context of the process.

In the same way rational thoughts of Ambedkar spells out its functions: Firstly, from the savage society to our present day the main social function of religion is concerned with life, life processes and the preservation of life. The religious ceremonies are related with the stages of life with events like birth, puberty, marriage, death, sickness, war, drought, pestilence or concerned with the cultivation of food grains and cattle that furnish to human social life. God's place in religion is only as a means for the conservation of life and that the end of religion is the end of conservation and sanctification of social life. In the same way this is true for the present society also, though this essence of religion is hidden or forgotten. "The life and the preservation of life make up the essence of religion even in the present day society are beyond question."[129]

Secondly, Ambedkar asserts that the best statement regarding the purpose of religion given by Charles A. Ellwood who had written that, "Religion projects the essential values of human personality and of human society into the universe as a whole. It unavoidably arises as soon as many tries to take up a valuing attitude towards this universe, no matter how small and mean that universe may appear to him... What the reason does for ideas, religion does then for the feelings. It universalizes them; and in universalizing them, it brings them into harmony with the whole of reality.[130] As C.A. Ellwood understands 'social values are universalized and also continued to be spiritualized by religion for the realization of a specific social purpose'.

Ambedkar says that Religion emphasizes, universalizes social values and brings them to the mind of the individual who is required to be familiar with them in all his acts in an order that he may function as an approved member of the society.[131] Thirdly, maintaining the social control and social order is the significant function of religion. Religion acts as an organization of social control by prohibiting the individual's beliefs and practices that go divergent to the good of the larger group. Thus religion is an influential way of social control, more powerful than the Law and Government. Ambedkar again quotes Ellwood to strengthen his argument, "Without the support of religion, Law and government are bound to remain a very insufficient means of social control. Religion is the most powerful force of social gravitation without which it would be impossible to hold the social order in its orbit."[132]

Though, different religions given different theistic explanations about the purpose of Religion, Ambedkar rejects them all and offers his own formulation. According to him, the purpose of religion is "To make the world a Kingdom of Righteousness." What does he mean by the Kingdom of Righteousness? What does it entail? What are the means to realize this ideal scheme? Can this goal be reached at all? Ambedkar clears all these doubts in the following verses, which he puts in the Buddha's mouth: To the question "What is the purpose of religion?"

The Buddha's answer is very different. He did not tell people that their aim in life should be to reach some imaginary heaven. The kingdom of righteousness lies on earth and is to be reached by man by righteous conduct. What he did was to tell people that to remove their misery each one must learn to be righteous in his conduct in relation to others and thereby make the earth the kingdom of righteousness.[134]

In addition, two other purposes were also added, they are, the training of man's mind, instincts and dispositions and the courage to stand by what is right, even alone. A religion that does not have as its core, morality essential for social order and progress, is anathema for Ambedkar. His religion of Neo-Buddhism is nothing else but the way, the *Marga,* which would realise not the kingdom of God here on earth or in the otherworldly heaven, in *Moksha,* but a religious path that would usher in the just, moral "Kingdom of Righteousness."[136]

The Dhamma would not only enforce morality by detachment,[137] it would purify the mind and cleanse it of all the passions bring forth harmony; cater to the growth of all the individuals in the society without discrimination, thus fostering equality and fraternity. It would establish proper human relationships essential for happiness, with karuna and maitri and thus remove sorrow (Dhukka).[138]

It would in a special way protect the weak leading their liberation, and stop the class-caste conflicts resulting in a class-casteless society.[139] Psychological revolution is brought about by shedding of the ego and the desires through detachment and enlightenment. But one cannot stop with this. He/she must continue with the social revolution to remove the causes of *Dukkha. Love, karuna with Maitri,* demands this. Liberation of the oppressed and poor people is the task of the En-lightened persons.

Dewey concept of God and evil is unknown thought and also some philosophers used to spend enormous effort on the problem of evil: how do we square the goodness of God, or the universe, or life, with the existence of evil? Dewey urges that were conceive the problem of evil as "the practical problem of reducing, alleviating, as far as may be removing the evils of life."

In[104] his view, it's not the job of philosophy to explain away evils or justify them. Philosophy's job is to contribute to methods that will help us discover what causes the ills that beset humanity. If he were alive today, we think it had replace *'humanity' with 'planet'* since ecological science has shown us the interdependence of all life forms on earth. Dewey, suspect, would have been a big fan of ecology, since it is the natural science which takes most seriously one of his recurring philosophical themes, the interaction of living creatures with their environment.

Dewey rejects any description of happiness as a fixed attainment, even if it is called bliss and assigned to the afterlife. The notion of such bliss he describes as "an insipid tedium, a millennium of ease and relief from all struggle and labour could satisfy only the most delicate of mollycoddles."[141] He risks being misunderstood when he says that happiness is 'found only in success'. But he does not understand success as making a lot of money or getting elected to high office. For him success is "the overcoming of obstacles, the elimination of sources of defect and ill."[142] Beauty, i.e., aesthetics sensitiveness and enjoyment, is a part of his conception of happiness. But he regards aesthetic enjoyment as linked to the consummator phase of all well-executed solutions, and not the exclusive province of the fine arts.[143]

The consequence of Dewey's approach is an attack on the traditional distinction between instrumental goods, which are means to something else, and intrinsic goods, which are desired in them. The distinction, of course, is a very old one. We find an early version of it in Plato's Republic. Instrumental goods, when they are purely instrumental, are desired only for the sake of something else, not for their own sakes. An example often given is that of unpleasant medicine which one swallows for the sake of health. Most people, says a character in Plato's Republic, think of justice like that, as something desirable not for its own sake but for the sake of the rewards or benefits one acquires when people think you have it. Plato himself argues that justice is, in fact, desirable for its own sake (though he does not deny that there are often advantageous side-effects of being just). For Plato and Aristotle, contemplation of truth is the best example of a human thing desirable in its own right.

Religion as Modernity and Culture

John Dewey religious modernity has been subjected to misinterpretations that portray both traditions in a way that depletes them of the full force of their critical insight. The source of these misinterpretations is in many cases an attempt to squeeze the philosophical projects of pragmatism and genealogy into the mold that shapes the thought of most participants on both sides of the modernity debates. This mold can usually be traced back to the work of the influential sociologist, political economist, and philosopher Max Weber. One unfortunate residue of the subtle dominance of Weberian concepts in contemporary debates over modernity is that many thinkers who operated largely outside of these concepts cannot be brought into these debates without filtering their thought through this conceptual prism.

In the case of Dewey and Foucault, their contributions to our understanding of the basic problems of modernity are widely misunderstood due to being filtered through Weberian concepts that simply were not central in Dewey's or Foucault's thinking.[144] By distancing Dewey and Foucault from Weber as concerns their interpretations of modernity a significant point begins to emerge: a hitherto unnoticed convergence between pragmatism and genealogy. This convergence is significant because comparative analyses of pragmatism and genealogy, like those of these two traditions and Weber described above, generally tend to miss the important points of resonance which prove these traditions much closer than is commonly thought. After explicating Weber, Dewey, and Foucault will conclude discussion by considering briefly the attractive philosophical possibilities of combing Dewey's work on inquiry as reconstructive problem-solving with Foucault's work on critique as genealogical problematisation.

The same thought, Ambedkar regarded that religion is necessary for nationalism, since religion is the essence of cultural heritage and value system that are very much necessary for the formation of a civil and political community and, necessary factor for building a powerful nation. Ambedkar was not in favour of the depressed classes converting themselves into Islam or Christianity, as both these religions are alien to Indian culture and therefore they cannot provide the foundations of a political and social community. Ambedkar's theory of religion based on this concept is expressed as, "If the depressed classes join Islam or Christianity they not only go out of the Hindu religion but they also go out of the Hindu culture. On the other hand, if they become Sikhs, they remain within the Hindu culture. This is by no means a small advantage to Hindus. What the consequences of conversion will be to the country as a whole is well worth bearing in mind, Conversion into Islam or Christianity will denationalize the depressed classes. If they go to Islam, the number of Muslims will be doubled and the danger of Muslim domination also becomes real."[145]

Ambedkar opens up a big problematic territory here. It had touched the many issues related to the concepts of religion, culture and nation. Ambedkar has evaluated each one of these concepts from the marginalized interest point of view. One might wonder about the Ambedkar's differentiation of the terms 'Hindu religion' and 'Hindu culture'. His coinage of the term Hindu culture seems to be, thoroughly equivalent to Indian culture. Scholars ought to differ from Ambedkar's equation of Hindu culture with that of Indian culture. But we may accept with his implied view that culture is a broader category than religion. The second issue dealt by Ambedkar is the question of conversion. While preferring conversion into Indian religions such as Buddhism and Sikhism, Ambedkar discards conversion into Islam and Christianity on the ground that they are not Indian in origin.

Here Ambedkar's option could be named as soft moderate or limited conversion. The reasons behind this limitation may be his nationalistic concern and his fear of alienation of the Dalits that he did not want to leave his followers with the risk of losing their national identity. Even after clarifying these aspects, Ambedkar's conclusion remains debatable. It clearly implies that he considered both religion and culture as constituent element of nationalism. That is why he was searching for such a religion within the Indian culture. His concept of religion became not only highly political but came very closer to social living.

The religion can also be tested by yet another set of criteria that Ambedkar has outlined in his article, 'Buddha and the Future of His Religion.' B.A.M. Paradkar gives an astute summary of these criteria in his essay, 'The Religious Quest of Ambedkar': Apart from the classification of religion into a 'Religion of Principles' and a Religion of Rules, Ambedkar maintained four essential criteria as the ways of testing the utility of a religion. Firstly, a society in order to hold itself together, it must have either the endorsement of the law or the sanction of morality. But the part played by law in this respect is very small. It is proposed only to keep the minority within the range of social discipline. "The majority is left out and has to be left out, to sustain its social life by the postulates and sanction of morality. Religion, in the sense of morality must therefore remain the governing principle in every society"[146]

Secondly, in order to function, Religion must exist with reason, which is merely another name for science. In other words, an understanding between science and religion should not be preposterousness. Thirdly, moral code is not enough for religion, but its moral code must recognize the essential canons of social life, namely liberty, equality and fraternity and finally, religion must not consecrate or ennoble poverty. Ambedkar said, 'Renunciation' of riches by those who have, it may be a blessed state but poverty can never be. To announce poverty to be a blessed state is to misrepresent religion, to perpetuate vice and crime, to consent to make earth a living hell.[147] These social functions can also serve as the criteria to judge the value of a religion. To some extent, a particular religion is able to fulfill the social function of a religion, only to that extent, it can be deemed to be good religion. Ambedkar himself favourably uses this criterion and questions the usefulness of Hinduism. He asks whether it acknowledges the personal dignity and equality, strives for justice and promotes the social advancement.

Dewey too contributed much on the construction of a democratic society which is based on liberty equality and fraternity. he foundation of democracy is faith in the capacities of human nature; faith in human intelligence and in the power of pooled and cooperative experience. It is not belief that these things are complete but that if given a show they will grow and be able to generate progressively the knowledge and wisdom needed to guide collective action. Every autocratic and authoritarian scheme of social action rests on a belief that the needed intelligence is confined to a superior few, who because of inherent natural gifts are endowed with the ability and the right to control the conduct of others; laying down principles and rules and directing the ways in which they are carried out. It would be foolish to deny that much can be said for this point of view. It is that which controlled human relations in social groups for much the greater part of human history.

And also Dewey's democratic faith has emerged very, very recently in the history of mankind. Even where democracies now exist, men's minds and feelings are still permeated with ideas about leadership imposed from above, ideas that developed in the long early history of mankind. Belief in equality is an element of the democratic credo.[148] It is not, however, belief in equality of natural endowments. Those who proclaimed the idea of equality did not suppose they were enunciating a psychological doctrine, but a legal and political one. All individuals are entitled to equality of treatment by law and in its administration. Each one is affected equally in quality if not in quantity by the institutions under which he lives and has an equal right to express his judgment, although the weight of his judgment may not be equal in amount when it enters into the pooled result to that of others. In short, each one is equally an individual and entitled to equal opportunity of development of his own capacities, be they large or small in range. Moreover, each has needs of his own, as significant to him as those of others are to them. The very fact of natural and psychological inequality is all the more reason for establishment by law of equality of opportunity, since otherwise the former becomes a means of oppression of the less gifted.

While what we call intelligence is distributed in unequal amounts, it is the democratic faith that it is sufficiently general so that each individual has something to contribute, whose value can be assessed only as enters into the final pooled intelligence constituted by the contributions of all. Every authoritarian scheme, on the contrary, assumes that its value may be assessed by some prior principle, if not of family and birth or race and colour or possession of material wealth, then by the position and rank a person occupies in the existing social scheme. The democratic faith in equality is the faith that each individual shall have the chance and opportunity to contribute whatever he is capable of contributing and that the value of his contribution be decided by its place and function in the organized total of similar contributions, not on the basis of prior status of any kind whatever.

Ambedkar religion is a religion of humanity, a religion at the service of humans to understand the humanness.[149] It is very much contextual and cultural. He would not accept wholesale, the imported Marxian theory, which does not take into account caste and religion, which are very powerful and influential factors in the Indian context and culture.[150]

He rejected also Islam and Christianity that are foreign and were attached to the anti-national and imperialistic countries. By the revival of Buddhism, Ambedkar did a great service to the downtrodden people. The return of Buddhism not only gives identity and explanation to the downtrodden, it has also revived the non- Brahminic *"Indian"* culture, whose ancient religion was Buddhism. It has exploded the myth of Hindus, who equate Indian culture with Hindu-Hindi culture, and India with Hindustan.

Ambedkar reveals that his address towards religion is not a mere crave towards addressing a religion as a social institution but it was very deep that concentrated on the structure of social system in its wholeness. Ambedkar holds a perception that the religion is a vital force, a scheme of moral governance and foundation for human society. In Ambedkar's sense, religion is necessary as a system of values and as a science of social reconstruction. He looked at the religion not as an instrument for the individual salvation but as the basis for social interaction. He redefines the purpose of the religion. This redefinition is what makes him to embraces of Buddhism.

Religion is not an end in itself. It meant for the preservation of life and human welfare. Hence, religion is not the one that has the final say; it is not infallible, absolute, inflexible nor permanent. Ambedkar stressed that religion is for humans and not humans for religion. For him, man and morality must be the centre of religion. Religion instills hope in man and drives him to activity. Hindu religion has watered down the enthusiasm of the downtrodden. Ambedkar says that Religion emphasizes, universalizes social values and brings them to the mind of the individual who is required to be familiar with them in all his acts in an order that he may function as an approved member of the society. The concern for the universal well-being is the main consideration of Ambedkar's scheme of morality.

Ambedkar emphasises that the human existence is not to be treated solely in the physical sense alone, but it has to be valued in the sense of something higher than that. According to which every human being has a spiritual super-existence through knowledge and love. According to Ambedkar, three important kinds mark the principle of a reconstructed social order. Human society is to be built on the foundation of freedom or liberty, equality and fraternity. These values are based on the notion that an individual is not a means but an end itself. While the notion of liberty emphasizes the inviolability of the human person, the concept of equality insists the right of the individual to be treated as an equal and to be respected as a complete member of the society irrespective of his attainments. According to Ambedkar, fraternity is the "disposition of an individual to treat men in reverence and love and dignity and the desire to be in unity with other fellow beings."[151] It strengthens the society and it gives vigour for the individuals to commit for the welfare of all. According to Ambedkar the Hinduism comprises of caste social order is an order of graded inequality. 'Sanskritisation'[152] is impossible that one cannot change his caste and fraternity must also be sacrificed as the proper climate for the change of caste status, merely by adopting the behavioral development of personality"[153]

For Dewey, from the standpoint of the individual, it consists in having a responsible share according to capacity in forming and directing the activities of the groups in which one belongs and in participating according to need in the values which the groups sustain. From the standpoint of the groups, it demands liberation of the potentialities of members of a group in harmony with the interests and goods which are common.[154]

Full liberation of an individual's potentialities can only be achieved in a democratic social order, one in which social conflicts are treated as the subject of social inquiry. Dewey's argument that the experimental character of democracy renders it desirable should not merely be interpreted instrumentally, then. He is not only saying that democracy allows a clearer view of social problems and how to address them. His suggestion is also that individuality can only be properly expressed if the individual participates in democratic practices, since social inquiry is a constitutive part of the individual good. And this is a claim about individuality in the specific ethical sense in which he develops the notion in his critique of classical liberalism.

Reference

6. John Dewey, 1934. *A Common Faith.* New Haven, Yale University Press, New York. p.43-44

7. John Dewey, 1934. *A Common Faith.* New Haven, Yale University Press, New York.p.27

8. Ibid, p.27-28

9. Moon, Vasant. Vol.III, 1987. (ed.), *Babasaheb Ambedkar's: Writings and Speeches,* Dept. of Education, Govt. of Maharastra, Bombay. p.8

10. Dhananjay Keer, 1991.Dr. *Ambedkar Life and Mission,* Popular Prakashan, Bombay.p.259

11. Ambedkar, B.R. 1998. *Ambedkar's Philosophy of Religion,* INA Shree Publishers, Jaipur.p.76

12. Panikkar and A. Koothothil, *Man and Religion,* Jeevadhara Publications, New Delhi, 1981 and Segundo,J. L., *Faith and Ideologies,* Orbis Books, New York, 1977. p.7-11
13. Otto Maduro, *Religion and Social Conflicts,* New York, Orbis Books, 1982.p.224
14. Ibid, p.223
15. Thumma Anthony Raj, Wisdom of the Weak: Foundations of People's Theology, ISPCK, New Delhi, 2000.p.33
16. Christopher1997. *"Reconstructing Dewey",* Cornell University Press, Berlin, p.9
17. Steven Rockefeller, 1995. *John Deey: Religious Faith and Democratic Humanism,* Columbia University Press, 1994. Columbia, p.232
18. Keer, Dhananjay. 1991. *Dr. Ambedkar Life and Mission,* Popular Prakashan, Bombay.p.1-2
19. Pieris, *A. Love Meets Wisdom: A Christian Experience of Buddhism,* Orbis Books, New York, 1988. p.54
20. Paulos Gregorios, 1989, *"East and West : pointers in the quest for India's secular identity"* B. R. Publishing House, New Delhi.p.151
21. Jatava, D.R.1965. *The Social Philosophy of B. R. Ambedkar,* Phoenix Publishing Agency, Agra.p. 256-260
22. John Dewey, 1934. *A Common Faith.* New Haven, Yale University Press, New York.p.52
23. Ibid, p.235
24. John Dewey, 1934. *A Common Faith.* New Haven, Yale University Press, New York.p.236
25. Ibid, p.183
26. Ambedkar, B.R. 1998. *Ambedkar's Philosophy of Religion,* INA Shree Publishers, Jaipur..p.3
27. Ambedkar, B. R. (1957),1991, *The Buddha and His Dhamma,* Siddharth Publications, Bombay. p.226
28. Ambedkar, B. R. (1957),1991, *The Buddha and His Dhamma,* Siddharth Publications, Bombay. p.225
29. Keer, Dhananjay 1991. *Dr. Ambedkar Life and Mission*, Popular Prakashan, Bombay. p.53 & 64
30. Jatava, D.R.1965. *The Social Philosophy of B. R. Ambedkar,* Phoenix Publishing Agency, Agra.p.6

31. John Dewey, 1934. *A Common Faith.* New Haven, Yale University Press, New York.p.26
32. John Dewey, 1934. *A Common Faith.* New Haven, Yale University Press, New York.p.26-27
33. Ibid, p.46
34. Ibid
35. Ambedkar, B.R. 1998. *Ambedkar's Philosophy of Religion,* INA Shree Publishers, Jaipur.p.4
36. Moon, Vasant, (ed.), *Babasaheb Ambedkar's: Writings and Speeches,* Vol. VII, Dept. of Education, Govt. of Maharastra, Bombay, 1989. p.76-77
37. Moon, Vasant, (ed.), *Babasaheb Ambedkar's: Writings and Speeches,* Vol. III, Dept. of Education, Govt. of Maharastra, Bombay, 1989.p.85
38. Ibid
39. Moon, Vasant, (ed.), *Babasaheb Ambedkar's: Writings and Speeches,* Vol. III, Dept. of Education, Govt. of Maharastra, Bombay, 1989. p.85
40. Ibid
41. John Dewey. (1910a/1978). *How We Think. MW16, Southern* Illinois University Press. Carbondale, IL.p.268
42. John Dewey.1929. *Religious Faith and Democratic Humanism,* Philosophy Education Society, Inc. University of New York Press, New York.p.168
43. Moon, Vasant, 1987. *Why go for Conversion?*, trans, Dalit Sahitya Akademy, Bangalore. p.8
44. Moon, Vasant, 1987. *Why go for Conversion?,* trans, Dalit Sahitya Akademy, Bangalore. p.8
45. John Dewey, 1925. *"Experience and Nature," LW1* Southern Illinois University Press, Carbondale.p.121
46. George, Lawrence, 1966. (Trans) *A common Faith,* New York: Harper & Row, , Part II, chap. 2, p.51-53
47. Roger, Williams.1967. *"Separation of church and state."* John Milton's publisher,United States p.68

48. John Neville Figgis 1965. *"Religion and Society"* Rand McNally & Co., Chicago.p.77

49. Koch, Adrienne. 1965. *"Pragmatic Wisdom and the American Enlightenment,"* Vol. 18, No. 3 in JSTOR, p. 228- 229

50. Saul K. Padover. 1943. *Religious freedom* Duell, Sloan and Pearch, Inc., New York.p.945

51. Niles. 1818. *"The American Revolution"* Samuel and *John Adams* Publisher, Baltimore,p.228

52. Franklin & David Hartley. 1789. *"The Love of Liberty"* Poor Richard's Almanack and The Pennsylvania Gazette. United States.p.107

53. John Herman Randall Sr and Jr .1929. *"Religion and Modern World"*, Stokes Co., New York. p. 23-44

54. Mary Kelley. 1975. *Religion and American Revolutionp..* Seabury Press, New York p.342-45

55. Thomas Paine, 1794. *The Age of Reason,* preface to Part II, Dell *Publishing* Co., New York. p.53

56. Martin B. Marty, 1961. *The Infidel; Free Thought and American Religion,* World Pub. Co.'s Meridian Books, Cleveland. p.376

57. Nathaniel William Taylor, 1942. *"A Connecticut Liberal,"* Chap IV&VI,University of Chicago Press, Chicago.p.189

58. Bernard Murchland.1967. *"The Meaning of the Death of God"* Random House, New York.p.138

59. Moon, Vasant, 1987. *Why go for Conversion?*, trans, Dalit Sahitya Akademy, Bangalore, .p.6

60. Ibid

61. Moon, Vasant, *Why go for Conversion?*, trans, Dalit Sahitya Akademy, Bangalore, 1987. p.43-44

62. Keer, Dhananjay,1990. *Dr.Ambedkar: Life and Mission,* Sangan Books, London,p.452

63. Moon, Vasant, 1987.Why go for Conversion?, trans, Dalit Sahitya Akademy, Bangalore, p.17

64. Keer, Dhananjay,1990. Dr.Ambedkar: Life and Mission, Sangan Books, London,p.275

65. Moon, Vasant, 1987. *Why go for Conversion?,* trans, Dalit Sahitya Akademy, Bangalore, .p.11-12
66. Moon, Vasant, 1987. *Why go for Conversion?,* trans, Dalit Sahitya Akademy, Bangalore. p.21
67. Moon, Vasant. 1989. *B.R.Ambedkar, Writings and Speeches,* Vol.III, Govt of Maharastra, Bombay. p. 9
68. John Dewey, 1934. *A Common Faith.* New Haven, Yale University Press, New York.p.10
69. Benedict.1927, Divine Truth,Ignatius Press and the Vatican's *Publishing* House,San Francisco. p.8
70. Ibid, p.9
71. John Herman Randall Sr and Jr .1929. *"Religion and Modern World"*, Stokes Co., New York. p. 112
72. Robert M. Brown, 1967 "In Conscience I Must Break the Law" M. *Ryan, editor*, New york. p.307
73. Moon, Vasant, 1987, *Why go for Conversion?,* trans, Dalit Sahitya Akademy, Bangalore. p.9
73. Ibid, p.21-22
75. Ibid, p.21-22
76. Ibid, 25
77. Moon, Vasant, 1987. *Why go for Conversion?.* trans, Dalit Sahitya Akademy, Bangalore. p.66
77. Moon Vasanth, 1989. *B.R.Ambedkar, Writings and Speeches,* Vol.III, Govt of Maharastra, Bombay.p.420-421
78. Gore, M.S, Social *Context* of an ideology: *Ambedkar's Political and Social Thought,* Sage publications, New Delhi, 1993.p.237
79. Moon Vasanth, 1987. *B.R.Ambedkar, Writings and Speeches,* Vol.III, Govt of Maharastra, Bombay.p.405
80. Gore, M.S. *"Social Context of an ideology: Ambedkar's Political and Social Thought,"* Sage publications, New Delhi, 1993.p.231
81. Moon Vasanth, 1987. *B.R.Ambedkar, Writings and Speeches.* Vol.III, Govt of Maharastra, Bombay.p.73

82. John Dewey, 1934. A Common Faith. New Haven, Yale University Press, New York.p.48-49
83. John Dewey, 1934. *A Common Faith.* New Haven, Yale University Press, New York.p.50
84. Ibid, p.51
85. Ibid,p.1
86. Ibid,p.2
87. John Dewey, 1934. *A Common Faith.* New Haven, Yale University Press, New York. p.3
88. Moon, Vasant, 1987. *Why go for Conversion?,* trans, Dalit Sahitya Akademy, Bangalore. .p.24
89. Ibid
90. Ambedkar, B.R, 1987.*The Buddha and His Dhamma,* Siddharth Publications, Bombay. p.203
91. Keer, Dhananjay,1991. *Ambedkar: A Memorial Album,* Popular Prakasan, Bombay. p. 494-495
92. Moon Vasanth, 1987. *B.R.Ambedkar, Writings and Speeches,* Vol.III, Govt of Maharastra, Bombay.p.68
93. Roger. Mead, 1967. *"social and cultural continuity"* International Publishers, New York.p.382
94. Ibid, p.383
95. Ibid
96. David W. Noble.1965. *"The American Political Tradition",* University of Minnesota Press, Minneapolis.p. 5
97. John Dewey, 1934. *A Common Faith.* New Haven, Yale University Press, New York.p.21
98. Ibid, p.24
99. John Dewey, 1934. *A Common Faith.* New Haven, Yale University Press, New York.p.80
100. Robert E. Enger (ed.), Bertrand Russell's Best, The New American LibraryPress, New York.p.34

101. Ibid, p.35
102. John Dewey, 1990. *"Experience and Nature"* Southern Illinois University Press. Carbondale, IL.p.434
103. Moon, Vasant, (ed.), 1989. *Babasaheb Ambedkar's: Writings and Speeches,* Vol. III, Dept. of Education, Govt. of Maharastra, Bombay.p.75
104. Ibid, p.76
105. Moon, Vasant, (ed.), 1989. *Babasaheb Ambedkar's: Writings and Speeches,* Vol. III, Dept. of Education, Govt. of Maharastra, Bombay,p. 77
106. Moon, Vasant, *Why go for Conversion?,* trans, Dalit Sahitya Akademy, Bangalore. 1987.p.27
107. Ambedkar, B.R, 1991. *Slavery and Untouchability: Which is worse?,* Dalit Dayal, New Delhi. p.226
108. Ibid, p.227
109. John Dewey, 1990. *"Experience and Nature"* Southern Illinois University Press. Carbondale, IL.p.434
110. John Dewey, 1934. *A Common Faith.* New Haven, Yale University Press, New York.p.178-179
111. Ibid, p.179
112. John Dewey, 1934. *A Common Faith.* New Haven, Yale University Press, New York.p. 179
113. *John Dewey,* 1934. *A Common Faith.* New Haven, Yale University Press, New York.p.180
114. Ambedkar, B. R. 1987. *The Buddha and His Dhamma,* Siddharth Publications, Bombay.p.230-231
115. Ibid, p.231
116. Jatava, D. R. 1965. *The Social Philosophy of B. R. Ambedkar.* Phoenix Publishing Agency, Agra, p.41-43 and 267-268
117. Ambedkar, B. R.1987. *The Buddha and His Dhamma,* Siddharth Publications, Bombay. p.247
118. Lederle.M, 1976. *"The Untouchables' Claim to Human Dignity,"* Journal of the University of Poona, Humanities Section, Off-Print, Poona,. p.71-72

119. Keer, Dhananjay, 1991. *Dr.Ambedkar: Life and Mission,* Sangan Books, London.p.151-157

120. Kuber, W.N, 1990. *B.R. Ambedkar,* Publication Division, Ministry of Information and Broadcasting, Government of India, New Delhi. p.80

121. Ibid

122. Keer, Dhananjay, 1991. *Dr.Ambedkar: Life and Mission,* Sangan Books, London.p.459

123. Moon, Vasant, 1987. *Why go for Conversion?,* trans, Dalit Sahitya Akademy, Bangalore. p.22

124. Moon, Vasant, 1987. *Why go for Conversion?,* trans, Dalit Sahitya Akademy, Bangalore. p.45

125. Moon, Vasant, (ed.), *Babasaheb Ambedkar's: Writings and Speeches,* Vol. III, Dept. of Education, Govt. of Maharastra, Bombay. 1989. p.407

126. John Dewey, 1925/2004. *"Experience and Nature,"LW1* Southern Illinois University Press,Carbondale.p.4

127. Ibid

128. Moon, Vasant, (ed.). 1989. *Babasaheb Ambedkar's: Writings and Speeches,* Vol. III, Dept. of Education, Govt. of Maharastra, Bombay. p.408-409

129. Ibid, p.407

130. Ibid, p.409

131. Moon, Vasant, (ed.), 1989. *Babasaheb Ambedkar's: Writings and Speeches,* Vol. III, Dept. of Education, Govt. of Maharastra, Bombay p.409

132. Moon, Vasant, (ed.), 1989. *Babasaheb Ambedkar's: Writings and Speeches,* Vol. III, Dept. of Education, Govt. of Maharastra, Bombay. p.411

133. Ibid.201-202

134. Ibid.201

135. Ibid.201-203

136. Moon, Vasant, (ed.), 1989. *Babasaheb Ambedkar's: Writings and*

Speeches, Vol. III, Dept. of Education, Govt. of Maharastra, Bombay, p.200-202

137. Moon, Vasant, (ed.), 1989. *Babasaheb Ambedkar's: Writings and Speeches,* Vol. III, Dept. of Education, Govt. of Maharastra, Bombay, p.179 & 229

138. Ibid, p. 83

139. Ibid,p.232-234

140. John Dewey, 1995. *Religious Faith and Democratic Humanism,* Philosophy Education Society, Inc. University of New York Press, New York.p.181

141. John Dewey, 1995. *Religious Faith and Democratic Humanism,* Philosophy Education Society, Inc. University of New York Press, New York.p.181

142. John Dewey, 1995. *Religious Faith and Democratic Humanism,* Philosophy Education Society, Inc. University of New York Press, New York.p.181

143. John Dewey, 1934. *A Common Faith.* New Haven, Yale University Press, New York.p.5

144. Robert Cummings Nuville, 2002. *'Functions: New Essays in The Philosophy of Psychology'* Oxford University Press, Oxford. P.161

145. Moon, Vasant,1987. *Why go for Conversion?,* trans, Dalit Sahitya Akademy, Bangalore. p.19

146. Paradkar, B. A. M. 1968. *The Religious Quest of Ambedkar,* Ajay Prahaghan, New Delhi,.p.51

147. Paradkar, B. A. M. 1968. *The Religious Quest of Ambedkar,* Ajay *Prahaghan,* New Delhi,.p.51

148. John Dewey, 1995. *Religious Faith and Democratic Humanism,* Philosophy Education Society, Inc. University of New York Press, New York.p.327

149. Moon, Vasant, (ed.), *Babasaheb Ambedkar's: Writings and Speeches,* Vol. III, Dept. of Education, Govt. of Maharastra, Bombay. 1989. p.265-267

150. Jatava, D. R. 1965. *The Social Philosophy of B. R. Ambedkar,* Phoenix Publishing Agency, Agra. p.64

151. Moon, Vasant, (ed.), 1989. *Babasaheb Ambedkar's: Writings and Speeches,* Vol. III, Dept. of Education, Govt. of Maharastra, Bombay. p.97

152. Srinivas M.N, 1988. *Social Change in Modern India,* Orient Longman, Hyderabad. p.67

153. Moon, Vasant, (ed.), 1989. *Babasaheb Ambedkar's: Writings and Speeches,* Vol. III, Dept. of Education, Govt. of Maharastra, Bombay. p.99

154. John Dewey, 1995. *Religious Faith and Democratic Humanism,* Philosophy Education Society, Inc. University of New York Press, New York. p.327-328

Chapter 2

John Dewey and Ambedkar's Comparative Study on Moral Philosophy

The main objective of this chapter is to highlight the John Dewey and Ambedkar's Comparative Study on morality philosophy. Dewey believed that neither traditional moral norms nor traditional philosophical ethics were up to the task of coping with the problems raised by these dramatic transformations. Traditional morality was adapted to conditions that no longer existed. Hidebound and unreflective, it was incapable of changing so as to effectively address the problems raised by new circumstances.

Traditional philosophical ethics sought to discover and justify fixed moral goals and principles by dogmatic methods. Its preoccupation with reducing the diverse sources of moral insight to a single fixed principle subordinated practical service to ordinary people to the futile search for certainty, stability, and simplicity. In practice, both traditional morality and philosophical ethics served the interests of elites at the expense of most people. To address the problems raised by social change, moral practice needed to be thoroughly reconstructed, so that it contained within itself the disposition to respond intelligently to new circumstances. Dewey saw his reconstruction of philosophical ethics as a means to effect this practical reconstruction.

In the similar fashion, Ambedkar, morality is the basic need of humanity, as it would create a just and powerful community. He believed that morality was necessary for the growth of a strong and powerful nation. As Hinduism already became corrupted and degenerated since it separated itself from the key element of morality. The critique is seen in operation in the rejection of religions and ideology, which clearly shows that without the existence of morality sufficient justice, cannot be promoted for the marginalized in the society.

Ambedkar who offered philosophical reasons to reject all religions and his opinion that morality is the central element for any religion. He has reinterpreted the Neo-Buddhism from the original teachings of Buddha that is purely based on the morality. Ambedkar emphasises on the transformation of the marginalized in the ideological terms as well as in the practice. In his view, morality is very much necessary for their 'spiritual ideology reforms' in the society. His quest and struggle for the liberation of marginalised people and his ideological foundation for the egalitarian society remained as the core of his moral philosophy. Indian society has lost the three principles of liberty; equality, fraternity; and values.

On the similar lines, Ambedkar too argued for a radical a reconstruction of moral principles. The underlying moral and logical assumptions of Ambedkar can be understood in terms of technical metaphysical concepts of liberty, equality and fraternity that associated with the philosophical notions of universality and rationality. Further, the inner essence of Ambedkar's intellectual development also can be understood as the attempt to realise his concepts of freedom and fraternity. Thus Ambedkar's main concern shifts from proclaiming the philosophical nature of freedom to ever-deepening interests of the social and historical conditions that produce inequality, exclusion and alienation. Ambedkar's writings are full of moral judgements - implicit and explicit. From Ambedkar's early writings and also from his childhood experience made him to attack on the Hinduism. His analysis on the Hindu religious order with specific reference to the problem of the *caste* and *Untouchability* is potential of providing a viewpoint of liberation. Ambedkar made scathing attack on Hinduism as a philosophy and religious immoral order and how it paved way for a practice of *Untouchability* and social degradation. Ambedkar was fired by outrage, indignation and the burning desire for a better world through the establishment of true *Dhamma.*

Dewey too replaced transcendental principles with concrete, specific concerns. Dewey's ethics replaces the goal of identifying an ultimate end or supreme principle that can serve as a criterion of ethical evaluation with the goal of identifying a method for improving our value judgments. Dewey argued that ethical inquiry is of a piece with empirical inquiry more generally. It is the use of reflective intelligence to revise one's judgments in light of the consequences of acting on them. Value judgments are tools for enabling the satisfactory redirection of conduct when habit no longer suffices to direct it. As tools, they can be evaluated instrumentally, in terms of their success in guiding conduct.[155] .e test our value judgments by putting them into practice and seeing whether the results are satisfactory whether they solve the problems they were designed to solve, whether we find their consequences acceptable, whether they enable successful responses to novel problems, whether living in accordance with alternative value judgments yields more satisfactory results. We achieve moral progress and maturity to the extent that we adopt habits of reflectively revising our value judgments in response to the widest consequences for everyone of living them out. This pragmatic approach requires that we locate the conditions of warrant for our value judgments in human conduct itself, not in any a *priori* fixed reference point outside of conduct, such as in God's commands, Platonic Forms, pure reason, or "nature," considered as giving humans a *fixed telos.* To do so requires that we understand different types of value judgments in functional terms, as forms of conduct that play distinctive roles in the life of reflective, social beings. Dewey thereby offers a naturalistic meta-ethic of value judgments, grounded in developmental and social psychology.

According to Ambedkar, morality is a "form of social consciousness; it is a social institution which regulates the conduct of people in all spheres of their social life. Morality expresses the general social requirements and interests of society through generally recognised injunctions and evolutions that are supported by the people. Ambedkar says that an individual relaying on the moral conceptions produced by society, assimilating them in the process of education, the individual may independently regulates his behaviour to a considerable extent and judge about the moral significance of all developments that takes place around. Thus Ambedkar says that the individual should not only act as the object of social control, but also as its conscious subject. Most of the philosophical, theological, religious, ethical writings of Ambedkar, along with his sociological writings are polemical in character."[156] Even, "*The Buddha* and His *Dhamma,* his most systematic book on religion, contains many passages which are polemic and apologetic, besides the dialectical disputes of the Buddha."[157]

According to Ambedkar's, morality being a complex social formation it concerned with: what are rights, rightness, duty, responsibility, obligation, justice, punishment, virtue, conscience and wisdom? How are customs, public opinion, laws, contracts, authority, self realisation and god or religion is related morality? What actions are accepted in a society, what norms of behaviour are adopted for the people to follow, what part do intentions play in determining rightness, can practical moral problems be solved generally, or do specific problems like caste, race and religion require separate treatment?. All these forms of moral consciousness are united into a logically ordered system which can prescribe, motivate and appraise moral actions. In addition to general human elements morality also incorporates historically transient and class, caste norms, principles and ideals. According to Ambedkar morality is socially constructed, and says that, the morality and moral norms are formed in the moral consciousness of society."[158]

Dewey's mature thought in ethics and social theory is not only intimately linked to the theory of knowledge in its founding conceptual framework and naturalistic standpoint, but also complementary to it in its emphasis on the social dimension of inquiry both in its processes and its consequences. In fact, it would be reasonable to claim that Dewey's theory of inquiry cannot be fully understood either in the meaning of its central tenets or the significance of its originality without considering how it applies to social aims and values, the central concern of his ethical and social theory.

Moral and social problems, for Dewey, are concerned with the guidance of human action to the achievement of socially defined ends that are productive of a satisfying life for individuals within the social context. Regarding the nature of what constitutes a satisfying life; Dewey was intentionally vague, out of his conviction that specific ends or goods can be defined only in particular socio-historical contexts. In the Ethics[159] he speaks of the ends simply as the cultivation of interests in goods that recommend themselves in the light of calm reflection.

Ambedkar points out the intricacy cabled in the order of casteism and inequalities. According to him, the social order of Hinduism does not contain any principle of social transformation. In the caste order, other than the Brahmins, those who occupy the higher caste order aspire to become higher and higher by 'infection by imitation' however in practice such an upward movement is not a possibility. In the order of its hegemonic hierarchy, the upper or middle caste groups do not and cannot have any inclination towards equilibrium or change towards equality and justice.

Ambedkar observes that the Indian Social order tends to deprive moral life of freedom and spontaneity and to reduce it to a more or less anxious and servile conformity to externally imposed rules. There is no loyalty to ideas; there is only conventionality to command. The laws are inequities in that they are not the same for one class as for another. "The laws are made arranged to be the same for all generations. The laws made by certain persons called as the lawgivers. This code has been invested with the nature of finality of fixity."[160] The writings of Ambedkar shows his deeper consideration of the dynamics of an ideal source of the society. It presupposes that a society must include in itself the sources of its own change and transformation without which it cannot promise its forward movement and growth. Ambedkar's assessment of the instant of spontaneity as one of the sources of social dynamics helps him to appraise the Indian social order and come to the conclusion that it lacks such a basis.

From the previous discussion and analysis of Ambedkar, we can record a few and methodological structure of Ambedkar's observations about the theoretical backdrop of his analysis of the Indian social order. For Ambedkar, the Indian social order is grounded in immorality. It is against justice, liberty, equality and fraternity. It is a collection of closed units that enclose themselves leaving no room for relationship and social intercourse. It is an order of self-imprisonment that enslaves the human into the caste prisons. It segregates 'infection by imitation' which in turn affects every consecutive caste groups and eventually. The Indian society is a system that degrades and alienates human labour and labourers. It lacks any social conscience for being in union. Spontaneity and moral freedom is alien to the system of caste social order. Participation and communication for social living is methodically prohibited in it. Its social expression is the social exclusion whose increasing effect is laid very seriously on the shoulders of the broken people.

Unlike Ambedkar, for Dewey, the central issue of ethical concern of the individual; the collective means for their realization is the paramount question of morality in the society. Conceived in this manner, the appropriate method for solving moral and social questions is the same as that required for solving questions concerning matters of fact: an empirical method that is tied to an examination of problematic situations, the gathering of relevant facts, and the imaginative consideration of possible solutions that, when utilized, bring about a reconstruction and resolution of the original situations. Dewey, throughout his ethical and social writings, stressed the need for an open-ended, flexible, and experimental approach to problems of practice aimed at the determination of the conditions for the attainment of human goods and a critical examination of the consequences of means adopted to promote them, an approach that he called the "method of intelligence."[161]

The central focus of Dewey's criticism of the tradition of ethical thought is its tendency to seek solutions to moral and social problems in dogmatic principles and simplistic criteria which in his view were incapable of dealing effectively with the changing requirements of human events. *In Reconstruction of Philosophy and The Quest for*

Certainty, Dewey located the motivation of traditional dogmatic approaches in philosophy in the forlorn hope for security in an uncertain world, forlorn because the conservatism of these approaches has the effect of inhibiting the intelligent adaptation of human practice to the ineluctable changes in the physical and social environment.[162] Ideals and values must be evaluated with respect to their social consequences; either as inhibitors or as valuable instruments for social progress, and Dewey argues that philosophy, because of the breadth of its concern and its critical approach, can play a crucial role in this evaluation.

The social condition for the flexible adaptation that Dewey believed was crucial for human advancement is a democratic form of life, not instituted merely by democratic forms of governance, but by the inculcation of democratic habits of cooperation and public spiritedness, productive of an organized, self-conscious community of individuals responding to society's needs by experimental and inventive, rather than dogmatic, means.

In same manner Ambedkar has a strong backdrop of western clarification of thought that helped him to assess the Indian social structure from the point of view of liberty, equality, and fraternity. When he goes for assessing the structural elements of the Indian society, he looks up into the society from the point of view of individual, as the indispensable unit of the system on the one hand and from the point of view of social whole as the universal aspect of the society. Thus, the individual and the social are the two complimentary vital elements in the theoretical frame of Ambedkar analysis. He is interested not only to define a society or to provide a theoretical discourse of society except basically his intention lies in indicating and providing necessary foundations of a humane society. And for this he strongly believes that that the sources of change and transformation for the forward movement of a society are essential. Such an approach of Ambedkar helps him to assess the Indian society.

Another very significant facet of Ambedkar's method is the social democracy and democratic constitutional feature of his thought. Ambedkar powerfully holds that social democracy is an explanation to relocate the caste social order. Ambedkar criticizes the Hindu social order from a moral direct of view. For him, since the Hindu social order lacks any moral conscience and value basis, he gave an advice that the Hindu society has to be reconstructed on the basis of an ethics of emancipation. For Ambedkar, liberty, equality and fraternity are the values that would offer a viable and humane Indian social order. The purpose of Ambedkar is to establish an alternative to the Hindu social order. Such a task in Ambedkar may be classified in two folds: On the one hand, Ambedkar wanted to establish the identity of the untouchables as an indigenous social religious '(Buddhism) group that resisted caste inequality from its very inception. And on the other, he ignited an ongoing social, educational, political movement, an action for liberation, which would continue to raise the cause of justice in the Indian society, irrespective of the pains and sufferings in its encounter with the orthodoxy.

Dewey too was strong critique of religion especially against moral undemocratic/ unequal structures. For Dewey the vision Democracy was throughout his life the promise of a good life, of which all people should be able to partake. Already the young Dewey mentions the main argument of his later critique of religion: The religious dare not be something separate from all other action. It entails a duty for each person, to share one's own experience with others. The understanding of a shared experience becomes later a central moment of his demand to reconstruct democracy as a just society. The radical separation of religion from society is not just for the atheistic, but already for the believing Dewey an expression of self-righteousness and self-arrogance.[163]

Dewey emphasizes that the way to democracy can only be done through social conscious. The socially-reformed power and the spirit, through which this movement is influenced, are of religious nature. The Social Gospel movement, a group of liberal American theologians which opted for democracy and social justice, convinces Dewey. Here in Chicago he writes his "Religious Confession of Faith", here he demands as most important presupposition of religious nature not only a nominal, but an authentic faith of the existence of moral principles. Dewey's religiosity undergoes a transformation into the social world, which goes parallel with the loosening of bond to the institutions of the Christian religion.

Dewey and Ambedkar's Morality as Important

Dewey ethical theory was invented by the ancient Greeks, particularly Plato and Aristotle. They were responding to the same social crisis that produced the questioning of Socrates. Customary or traditional morality was breaking down, and the philosophers, who in earlier times devoted themselves to the study of nature, were urged to use their skills in responding to this crisis. As Dewey sees it, what happened is that philosophers created an ethical theory which served as a partial substitute or reinforcement for traditional morality.[164] This kind of solution, which was never clearly challenged before Dewey, is in his view the source of philosophy's failure to give ethical inquiry the direction it needs. Philosophers, in his view, substituted an idea of the good or the just for traditional morals. But when they did so, they only created a new standard as fixed and eternal as traditional morals were originally thought to be.

According to Dewey's, the history of all earlier ethical theory is the assumption of a single, fixed ideal pattern of life or a single fixed law or duty. Sometimes the ideal is described as a life of activity in accord with virtue, sometimes as the most pleasant life (as hedonistic thinkers called it), or the life in accord with nature (in the words of the Stoics). Sometimes the single law is to obey God's will, sometimes it is to do unto others as you would have them do unto you, and sometimes to act so as to produce the greatest possible balance of pleasure over pain for everyone affected. Whether the fixed point of morality is an ideal pattern of life or a law, the traditional task of moral philosophy is then to discover it, clarify it, defend it against critics, and proceed to apply it to particular cases.[165]

Ambedkar as a humanist he fight against untouchably or the evil of casteism is not a simply a fight for the downtrodden people. Moreover it is a fight for the moral redemption of the humanity. Existence of *Untouchability* may be only a direct challenge to the downtrodden only. But it is a moral challenge to all humanity. Caste and *Untouchability,* therefore it is crucial problem for humanity in general, rather than an only problem of down trodden. Deconstructing the identity of the untouchables, in the case of Ambedkar, is sill of reconstructing a society, which in turn conceives the possibility of building up a humanized world. Therefore, if the human society requests to be really a social whole, then it should attend to the broken-particular, namely the discriminated. The universal to be universal needs to restore the broken particular if not what is claimed to be universal is pseudo. Such a task he envisaged needs to be carried on at two interlined levels. One at the level of the philosophical or theoretical, while the other at the level of the practical. At its philosophical level of Ambedkar sets example for the need for a clear lucid and serious understanding and analysis of the theoretical foundations of an oppressive system. At the realistic level, he has suggested the need for a continuous discourse and a communication of resistance against any oppressive forces like caste and *Untouchability*.

The major theme of Ambedkars' analysis of morality is that the religious immorality is based on the philosophical and practice of social dominance. The Hindu religious philosophy and its *socio*-cultural appearances are grounded on the belief that human life is unequal and immoral, therefore cannot scream for religious and social equality. Those human beings are pre-determined to be born unequal and therefore cannot lay claim to equality either in terms of their religious-spiritual status or in terms of their social, economic, civic or political status in the community. The morality is also played main role to survive religion to right path. The religion is survived in the wheel of morality in action and the Hindu religious moral ideology always hurting to the depressed people.

This shows the morality of the Hindu is purely social. This means that the level of his morality is merely traditional and customary. There are two evils of customary morality. In the first place there is no surety that it will always be charged with sincerity and purity of motive. For it is only when morality penetrates to the deepest springs of purpose and feeling in' the individual that pretense will cease to find a place in human behavior. In the second place customary morality is an anchor and a drag. It holds up the average man and holds back the man who forges ahead. Customary morality is only another name for moral stagnation. This is true of all cases where morality is only customary morality. But the customary morality of the Hindus has an evil feature that is peculiar to it. Customary morality is a matter of meritorious conduct. Ordinarily this meritorious conduct is something that is good from the general or public point of view. But among the Hinduism the commendable conduct is not concerned with the worship of God or the general good of community. Meritorious conduct in Hinduism is concerned with the giving of presents, of good and of honour to the Brahmins. Hindu Ethics is worship of the superman.

Ambedkar's concept of morality arises from the "direct necessity for man to love man."[166] Ambedkar makes it comprehensible that, "it is not to please God that man has to be moral, rather for his own good qualities that man is to love man."[167] In the struggle for existence the individual's rights may not' be catered for, and at times his or her interests can be, rare by the group. Similarly, "a weak group may also be discriminated by a stronger group, hence the indispensability; ability of the *law of love,* fraternity and brotherhood, which is another name for morality."[168]

Dewey moral judgment and moral responsibility are the work wrought in us by the social environment; signify that all morality is social; not because we ought to take into account the effect of our acts upon the welfare of others, but because of facts. Others do take account of what we do, and they respond accordingly to our acts. Their responses actually do affect the meaning of what we do. The significance thus contributed is as inevitable as is the effect of interaction with the physical environment. In fact as civilization advances the physical environment gets itself more and more humanized, for the meaning of physical energies and events becomes involved with the part they play in human activities. Our conduct t is socially conditioned whether we perceive the fact or not.[169]

The norms devised by Ambedkar, as criteria to assess the ideal scheme of obligations, were mainly to deal a deathblow to Hinduism. He was persuaded that Hinduism badly needed reform, and wanted to expose the oppression it had unleashed and the slavery it had perpetuated on the depressed. He was one of the victims of the social system of Hinduism, and so he should know what Hinduism aimed at. Which of these was Ambedkar attacking? What Hinduism did he condemn and reject? After discussing, various meanings of the word 'Hindu' as denoting a religion, parentage, country and a race. Ambedkar points out that he is dealing with Hinduism in which caste has become indispensable as doctrine, ideology and sanctified social order. Hinduism that is object of his derisive attack is that Bahrainis variety, a Hinduism who's *'care* is the creed 'of *caste'*,' and where "the Manu Smriti must be accepted as the Book of Religion."[170] Ambedkar quotes Max Muller and affirms that his target is, "Modem Hinduism rests on the system of caste as on a rock which no arguments can shake."[171] Ambedkar sees that Hinduism is not a religion for individual justice with equality, fraternity and liberty and it fails to bring social utility of just, free and moral social order as the ideal scheme of divine governance. In the sense Hinduism has failed to lift the depressed.

In the same line Ambedkar arrives at the final judgment of Hinduism: The only answer is that Hinduism is overwhelmed with the fear of contamination. It has not got the power to purify. It has not the desire to serve and that is because by its very nature it is in human and unmoral. It is a misnomer to call it religion. Its philosophy is against to very thing for which religion stands.[172] Hinduism is destined for failing the trial by the first norm of justice. It is found advocating inequality as the dependable doctrine: "This brief analysis of the Philosophy of Hinduism from the point of view of justice reveals in an obtrusive manner how Hinduism is adverse to equality, antagonistic to liberty and opposed to fraternity. Indeed, inequality is the *Soul* of Hinduism."[173]

The second norm of social utility equally fails to free from domination: "If these conclusions are sound, how can a philosophy which disconnects intelligence from labor, which expropriates the rights of man to comfort vital to life and which prevented society from mobilizing resources for common action in the hour of danger, be said to satisfy the test of social utility"[174]

Ambedkar puts the rational and logical question that what difference would it have made if I had taken Hindu Ethics as the basis for deducing the philosophy of Hinduism? Most students of Hinduism do not remember that just as in Hinduism there is no difference between law and Religion so there is no difference between law and ethics. Both are concerned with the same thing namely regulating the conduct of the low class Hindus to subserve the ends of high Caste Hindus. The false pictures of Hinduism in as much as "I have omitted to take into account the *Upanishads* which are the true source of Hindu philosophy."[175]

Ambedkar reiterates that the Inequality is the *Soul* of Hinduism. The morality of Hinduism is only social. It is unmoral and inhuman to say the least. What is unmoral and inhuman easily becomes immoral, inhuman and infamous. This is what Hinduism has become. Those who doubt this or deny this proposition should examine the social composition of the Hindu Society and ponder over the condition of some of the elements in it. It is essential to emphasize the great part played by crime in the general life of these peoples. A boy is initiated into crime as soon as he is able to walk and talk. No doubt the motive is practical, to a great extent, in so far as it is always better to risk a child in petty theft, who, if he were caught, would probably be cuffed, while an adult would immediately be arrested. Women, who, although they do not participate in the actual raids, have many heavy responsibilities, also play an important part. Besides being clever in disposing of stolen property the women of the Criminal Tribes are experts in shoplifting. The only answer is that Hinduism is overwhelmed with the fear of pollution. It has not got the power to purify. It has not the impulse to serve and that is because by its very nature it is *inhuman* and *unmoral*.

Dewey question of religious morality and faith is not his theme of predilection, in *A common faith* he presents a kind of humanistic study of religion where his thoughts concerning logics, his belief in the importance he grants to human experience are in evidence as much as in his other, more famous books. *A common faith* consists in a series of lectures delivered at Yale University (another title of the book is: Dwight H. Terry Lectureship at Yale) collected and first published in 1934. It addresses, over and beyond the issue of religion, the subjects of faith and belief and how they should be apprehended in a changing world where science was still the predominant parameter of thought (the 30s, even if we had tempered this trend, were still marked by the influence of positivism and scientism). In such a context, Dewey presents a faith which simultaneously rejects the total and immediate adherence to an omnipotent God, but also the opposite point of view which considers religion to be archaic and criticizes it in an extreme way.[176] Therefore the issue at stake is to see how far his views, formulated more than seventy years ago, are still relevant for a contemporary approach to religious studies and thus recognize the great modernity and capacity for anticipation of Dewey's ideas.

Dewey provides us with a very new and original approach to faith, especially regarding the context (the United States of the 1930s) where such criticism of organized and traditional religions where not that usual. Giving the definition he found for religion in an Oxford dictionary "recognition on the part of man of some unseen higher power as having control of his destiny and as being entitled to obedience, reverence and worship,"[177] he tries to show us that this way of thinking, though very common, divides humanity into two great camps: those who think that religion can't do without the supernatural, necessary to belief and truth, and those who assert that with the advent of science, it is not only the 'historic religions' which have been discredited, but also the whole field of the 'religious' which has to be eliminated from human thought.[178]

Contrary to those two very distinct, dichotomist visions, Dewey proposes we become emancipated from such positions and promotes a non-sectarian faith, free of the supernatural aspects which are, he agrees, totally irrelevant to the modern world. It is at this point that the philosopher distinguishes clearly between 'religion' and the "religious."

The elements defining a religion morality are, according to Dewey, reduced "to such a low common denominator that little meaning is left": the concepts dealing with the nature of the 'unseen powers' are very diverse, there is no great similarity in the 'obedience and reverence' in the world's religions and the moral motivations for 'worship' are not the same for everyone. Dewey thus observes that there is only a multitude of religions and not one religion which can be confined to a special class, race or culture. His preference goes to enhancing the universality of the 'religious', a 'religious' which has gotten rid of the 'encumbrances' of 'religion' (meaning the supernatural aspects established religions are made up of, by their very nature.[179]

Quoting John Locke's definition of faith as 'assent to a proposition on the credit of its proposer', Dewey then makes a distinction between 'speculative belief' and 'justifying faith', showing that religions were born with the fear original human beings felt, and have remained so since that time and, for that reason, are obstacles to human actions, because people prefer to rely entirely on an 'unseen power' instead of acting for themselves, thanks to the power of their own imagination and experience. For Dewey, any activity pursued on behalf of an ideal and against obstacles or any threat is deeply 'religious in quality' and doesn't require any institutionalized entity, because any daily human attitude can be 'religious' in the way he's defining. The Religious is more a way of living and behaving, with the help of imagination and experience, in order to convert ideals into action, rather than a special system of beliefs and practices institutionally established and never questioned.[180]

Mean while Ambedkar's morality is not only with rightness, but also with rights. This is more often associated with political and legal philosophy, since people seem to be more concerned about their legal than their moral rights. According to Ambedkar, "rights are real only if they are accompanied by remedies.

It is no use giving rights if they aggrieved person has no legal remedy to which he can resort when his rights are invaded. Consequently when the Constitution guarantees rights it also becomes necessary to make provision to prevent the Legislature and the Executive from overriding them. This function has been usually assigned to the Judiciary and the Courts have been made the special guardians of the rights guaranteed by the Constitution."[181]

Ambedkar says that the "rights are protected not by law but by the social and moral conscience of society. If social conscience is such that it is prepared to recognise the rights which law chooses to enact, rights will be safe and secure. But if the fundamental rights are opposed by the community, no law, no Parliament, no Judiciary can guarantee them in the real sense of the word."[182] Thus the right is the minimum claim upon the services of others, as a duty is the minimum claim of others upon us.

The concepts of rightness and wrongness lie close to the core of Ambedkar's moral thought. His explanation of rightness is in relation to duty, responsibility, ought ness, justice, virtue and wisdom. Acts are right because they produce good results for the most people. Rights consist in acting for the benefit of others; wrong action is one's own benefit. Self-seeking is selfish and selfish is the root of all evils. The cure for this evil is to pursue the opposite course that is love others and promote their good. For Ambedkar democratic form of government is considered right because it is believed to produce the best results for the most people.

Dewey says that there is a peculiar inconsistency in the current idea that morals ought to be social. The introduction of the moral *"ought to"* into the idea contains an implicit assertion that morals depend upon something apart from social relations. Morals are social. The question of ought, should be, is a question of better and worse in social affairs. The extent to which the weight of theories has been thrown against the perception of the place of social ties and connections in moral activity is a fair measure of the extent to which social forces work blindly and develop an accidental morality.

The chief obstacle for example to recognizing the truth of a proposition frequently set forth in these pages to the effect that all conduct is potential, if not actual, matter of moral judgment is the habit of identifying moral judgment with praise and blame. So great is the influence[183] of this habit that it is safe to say that every professed moralist when he leaves the pages of theory and faces some actual item of his own or others' behavior, first or ' instinctively' thinks of acts as moral or non-moral in the degree in which they are exposed to condemnation or approval. Now this kind of judgment is certainly not one which could profitably be dispensed with. Its influence is much needed. But the tendency to equate it with all moral judgment is largely responsible for the current idea that there is a sharp line between moral conduct and a larger region of unmoral conduct which is a matter of expediency, shrewdness, success or manners.

Moreover this tendency is a chief reason why the social forces effective in shaping actual morality work blindly and unsatisfactorily. Judgment in which the emphasis falls upon blame and approbation has more heat than light. It is more emotional than intellectual. It is guided by custom, personal convenience and resentment rather than by insight into causes and consequences. It makes toward reducing moral instruction, the educative influence of social opinion, to an immediate personal matter, that is to say, to an adjustment of personal likes and dislikes. Fault-finding creates resentment in the one blamed, and approval, complacency, rather than a habit of scrutinizing conduct objectively. It puts those who are sensitive to the judgments of others in a standing defensive attitude, treating an apologetic, self-accusing and self-exculpating habit of mind when what is needed is an impersonal impartial[184] habit of observation. *'Moral'* persons get so occupied with defending their conduct from real and imagined criticism that they have little time left to see what their acts really amount to, and the habit of self, blame inevitably extends to include others since it is a habit.

Dewey's Consideration of the form commonly assumed today by self-seeking; namely command of money and economic power. Money is a social institution; property is a legal custom; economic opportunities are dependent upon the status of society; the objects aimed at, the rewards sought for, are what they are because of social admiration, prestige, competition and power. If moneymaking is morally obnoxious it is because of the way these[185] social facts are handled, not because a money-making man has withdrawn from society into an isolated selfhood or turned his back upon society. His 'individualism' is not found in his original nature but in his habits acquired under social influences. It is found in his concrete aims, and these are reflexes of social conditions. Well-grounded moral objection to a mode of conduct rests upon the kind of social connections that figure, not upon lack of social aim. A man may attempt to utilize social relationships for his own advantage in an inequitable way; he may intentionally or unconsciously try to make them feed one of his own appetites. Then he is denounced as egoistic. But both his course of action and the disapproval he is subject to bare facts within society. They are social phenomena. He pursues his unjust advantage as a social asset.[186]

For Ambedkar fraternity is another name for morality. He says that the fraternity is nothing but another name for brotherhood of men and women which is another name for morality. Ambedkar concludes that the "fraternity is the name for the disposition of an individual to treat men as the object of reverence and love and the desire to be in unity with his fellow beings."[187]

According to Ambedkar "fraternity strengthens socialites and gives to each individual a strong personal interest in practically consulting the welfare of others. It leads him tom identify his feelings more and more with their good or at least with an even greater degree of practical consideration for it. Ambedkar argues that with a disposition to fraternity, the individual comes as though instructively to be conscious of him as being one whom ofcourse pays a regard to others. Thus the good of others becomes to him a thing naturally and necessarily to be attended to like any of the physical conditions of our existence."[188]

A society in which fraternity remained a guiding value would do much to rehabilitate the term and the aim of fostering a transformative rather than a merely multi-cultural ideal. Under the umbrella of 'fraternity' the transformative ideal would be one that emphasizes engaged transactionalism rather than the oppositional extremes of homogeneity and fragmentation.[189] Fraternity, however, seems not all that prevalent in either contemporary theory or practice. Even its 20th century philosophy, Dewey most prominently, seem, as we shall soon see, flummoxed about how to characterize it. Such an open embrace of fraternity has deep roots. John Winthrop reminded new colonists how the great divergence of human character was divinely ordained so that 'every man might have need of others, and from hence they might be all knit more nearly together in the Bonds of brotherly affection.'[190]

The exhortation to 'love one's neighbor' suffers from two serious flaws: (1) theoretically, it goes against an honest scientific understanding of human nature, (2) practically, attempts at realizing it come at a high price, finding a common enemy. . What is the best way for people to rally together under slogans like brotherhood and love of neighbor? Freud knew the answer only too well from personal experience: identify a shared enemy. Nothing moves people more effectively toward solidarity within a particular group than concerted focus on a commonly despised foe.

John Dewey praised the slogan 'liberty, equality, and fraternity' as the 'historic formula of the greatest liberal movement of history.' In the same breath, though, he admits the inherent, problematic vagueness of the three key terms.[191] Dewey's approach hinges on how seriously one takes the claim that democracy is a more than just a system of government, that it is a *'way of life.'* Democracy as a political system can be defined in terms of constitutions, legal systems, voting procedures, eligibility to hold office. Important as these are, they are not, for Dewey, sufficient. Democracy is not secure, he claims, until it becomes a way of life, until, that is, it comes to be appropriated in our habitual dispositions.[192]

Still, the question remains why fraternity should be held onto as an ideal for a flourishing community life. Within the context of political democracy, diversity and solidarity take the social ideal about as far as it can go. They recognize the reality and value of a multi-ethnic society, one in which tolerance extends across racial, ethnic, and class lines. What does Dewey offer in this regard? A mixed bag. Wanting to provide a specific, constructive formulation, he characterized fraternity in terms of shared social interactions and goods. "In its just connection with communal experience, fraternity is another name for the consciously appreciated goods which accrue from an association in which all share, and which give direction to the conduct of each."[193] This formulation is minimally helpful. 'Solidarity' would be a more accurate term for what he describes. We're all in it together, he is saying, and by both recognizing our interdependence and sharing in the common good, we will all benefit.

Another formulation gets closer to a more robust notion of fraternity. Fraternity, as an ideal, he says, means taking 'continuity' seriously. It means "association and interaction without limit"[194] In an earlier work Dewey had made clear the criteria which were to serve as "a measure for the worth of any given mode of social life." These took the form of two questions: "How numerous and varied are the interests who are consciously shared? How full and free is the interplay with other forms of association?."[195]

However, Ambedkar's inquiry was substantially different the western kinds of theorization. Ambedkar morality and religion are inseparable and that morality is able to be understood only in the context of religion and it has been at the center of his philosophical discussion. According to Ambedkar, religion must be essentially moral; religion cannot live unless it interacts with other forms of spiritual life as morality, beauty, and truth. Religion is thus when compared with morality it turns out to be at once *infra* and *supra* ethical. The fact that the religion takes as its point of departure human life, for this it provides a goal. Without such a destiny in sight religion cannot exist, provided with it faith passes on far beyond the realm of morality.

For Ambedkar, morality is based on love.[196] Morality is sacred and has taken the place of "God" in his Philosophy. It must not be desecrated even by the mighty, so that it is able to protect the weak in the society. He felt that the foundation of morality is love. The reason for this love is not anything mystical, it arises from man's natural condition, out of the necessity of peaceful coexistence, the need of protecting oneself and the weak, and to bear each other for a happy life on earth.

Dewey says that there is no reasonable basis for this preconceived notion that morality belongs to religion. Throughout recorded human history, many non-religious ethical systems have been proposed. The Golden Rule promoting mutual respect in human relations, for example, originates from several different sources, some of them non-religious. The philosopher Paul Kurtz has this to say about Gould's principle: Religionists have no special competence in framing moral judgments. "I say this because a great effort has been expended in the history of ethics. John Dewey to demonstrate that ethics can be autonomous and that it is possible to frame ethical judgments on the basis of rational inquiry."[197] When we consider that religious dogma is based on irrational beliefs in supernatural phenomena such as god(s), the soul, spirits, demons and angels, heaven and hell, creation, etc., we must ask ourselves: What does such mythology have to do with sound ethical principles? Why should acceptance of these vacuous concepts be a prerequisite for morality? Religious belief systems are human inventions. So-called 'sacred' scriptures were written by human beings. To declare with ostensible certainty that the Bible or the Koran or the *Bhagavad-Gita* is the word of some god is just a pious lie. The fact that some people sincerely believe in the sacredness of scripture does not make the idea any less absurd. Even modern religious tendencies which prefer a very metaphorical interpretation of traditional dogma remain ultimately founded on supernatural principles such as the belief in an omnipotent creator transcending time and space. Every theist is essentially a creationist in the generic sense of the term, even if he or she places that creation billions of years in the past.

Indeed, if we adopt the simple ethical principle of intellectual honesty, then we are forced to confront the following conclusion: As religious systems of morality are based on unfounded beliefs and are thus fundamentally dishonest, they are inherently unethical. For example, if a religious authority declares that lying is sinful because it is contrary to 'God's will', then that authority is guilty of hypocrisy, because even if one were to grant the existence of 'God', we have no way of knowing 'His' will. The author of this article knows as much about the will of 'God' as does any pope or ayatollah, and that knowledge is zero.[198] Humanism maintains that moral values derive their source from human experience. The precepts and mores of a heterogeneous society tend to accord with those of the dominant religious group within that society, but a common ground exists because the society insists upon it, not because it was commanded by God or any other moral authority. Love, kindness, and generosity would still be good things in a world where no religions existed.

Any religious morality that enslaves the minds of the people by fear or force, curtailing their liberation and freedom, that denies justice, equality and democracy that hinders universal fraternity, is no religion at all. Such religious practices, ceremonies and customs are to be rejected, and such doctrines are to be corrected. Even when a single person or small group is oppressed by a religion, a religious person or a religious class, that religion is in need of urgent reform. Domination of the clergy, exploitation of people in the name of devotions, superstitious and magical ceremonies, and outdated and irrelevant practices, over-spiritualization of religious doctrines, and deification of religious figures and saints, distort religion. We need religion for the liberation of humanity, but from the religion that does not liberate humanity we need liberation.

In short, the purpose of the liberative religion is to "teach the virtues of fellow feeling, equality and liberty" [199] and thus build the Kingdom of *Dhamma.* Hence, the urgency for all the religions to purge themselves of the magical practices, outmoded cults and ceremonies, irrelevant institutions and traditions, outdated doctrines and dogmas, and unleash the liberative elements and the revolutionary potential that is present in all of them. Only then can they be effective paths to the Kingdom.

Dewey says, Freedom means the possibility that, in the future, one might become different, even better. One may change habits and become a different self. The self is never finished; it changes because it acts, establishing habits. Established habits have momentum, and resist emendation. They would be static. But new circumstances demand new habits, and the self adapts. "Goodness" is welcoming life's demand for growth. The growing self is dynamic. The moral law may be stated: Become the possible new self demanded by current circumstances. So, morality emerges from the conditions of human life: a) desire perceived leads to foresight, and the quest for wisdom and prudence in making life's purposes inclusive and persevering; b) mankind is social. Mutual demands lead to conceptions of right and obligation; c) approved habits are virtue. Over time, morals change. But morality itself is a human trait, built into the fabric of the human life of activity.[200]

Morality abandons fixed views of virtue. It must do so, because circumstances differ among communities and change within each group over time. Certain traits emerge, upon reflection, as characteristic of human interests that deserve approbation. First, human interests should be whole-hearted (sincere). Our motives are mostly divided, which diminishes them. Whole-heartedness is a goal toward which one works. Second, human interests should be persistent. Desirable human interests persevere in the face of contrary conditions.

Third, human interests should be impartial. One should treat those one loves and those one knows only distantly by the same measures. Iniquity is inequity. We cannot feel equally for those near and that afar. But our interests should press us toward equal treatment. Virtuous interests interpenetrate in individual character. They are not compartmentalized. The classical virtues (wisdom, temperance, courage, and justice) meld into a person's character, in one who is virtuous. Large human societies tend to fragment personal morality.[201] Despite personal efforts at a whole-hearted, persistent, and impartial set of interests, business teaches ruthlessness for personal gain, nations teach hatred and racism and readiness for war. The convictions of personal morality degrade under the onslaught of divergent value structures in great collectives. Ultimate happiness for the individual lies on the path of helping the human community develops its full potential. This end is insulated from frustration because flexible and emerging. The moral life consists in forming habits in oneself that benefit the common life, and oneself within that common life.

Dewey's and Ambedkar's Concept of Science and Morality

John Dewey, also identifies a weakness in the tendency among liberal theologians to reduce religion to a simple foundation. In *A Common Faith* (1934), Dewey writes, "There is much talk, especially in liberal circles, of religious experience as vouching for the authenticity of certain beliefs and the desirability of certain practices. It is even asserted that religious experience is the ultimate basis of religion itself."[202] But whereas Whitehead draws attention to the metaphysical characteristics of a God available to the modern mind, Dewey draws attention to the pragmatic value of a modern notion of God for an increasingly secular culture. Rejecting a supernatural or ontologically prior God, Dewey defines God as the "unity of all ideal ends arousing us to desire and to action."[203] So we must ask: Is Dewey's God available for religious purposes?

The collapse of belief in a traditional God poses a serious dilemma for Western civilization. Dewey observes that a growing number of educated people "think the advance of culture and science has completely discredited the supernatural and with it all religions that were allied with belief in it"[204] (1). The danger here is not the loss of the supernatural: Dewey considers the concept of the supernatural that which stands outside the natural world to be the defining *limitation* of traditional Western faith. Rather, the danger is that everything understood to accompany belief in the supernatural "everything of a religious nature" may also be dismissed by thinking people. As the scientific worldview takes more and more of the world into consideration, the arena for knowledge of the supernatural shrinks first to the world of the purely subjective and private experience of individuals, and eventually into vacuity as psychology and physiology overtakes even this arena. If everything traditionally associated with the supernatural the virtues, the moral traditions, the arts and contemplative sensitivities, indeed, even the institutions of the church and synagogue cannot be liberated from the sinking ship of supernaturalism, then Western civilization will lose much of its depth and vision.

Whereas Ambedkar emphasized that the Buddhist ethics is not a mere rules or guidelines for the individual purity and its sanctity. Certainly Buddhist ethics very much talk about the importance of minds to be cleansed, but that is not confined in it. If we look on the morality of the all other religion we could have find out that all principles are directed towards the individual aspect of ethics. They are narrowed down as some kind of instruction to the individuals. one thing which we have to notice is that it does not mean that socially aspects are totally excluded from it. But social aspects are also included in the frame work of individuality.

The best example of this is Christian dictum "Love thy neighbour as you love yourself."[205] The dictum which can be considered as the paramount of social concern is also exactly a preaching of individual oriented ethics. Actually that principle is also an advice to an individual to change his mind from the selfish motives. Other religions if we look we can find out that certain instruction to an individual which are quite appropriate to keep the current social order. Hinduism is the evident example. But only in Buddhist ethics we can find out the ethical aspects which address society as whole, which emphasizes with the social concerns.

Ambedkar makes out this difference very clearly and emphasizes the social-morality of the Buddhism in *'Buddha and His Dhamma'.* "What is the purpose of religion? Different religions have given different answers. To make man seek after God and to teach him the importance of saving his *Soul* is the commonest answer one gets to this question. Most religions speak of three kingdoms. One is called the kingdom of heaven. The second is called the kingdom of earth and the third is called the kingdom of hell. All the religions preach that to reach this kingdom of heaven should be the aim of man and how to reach it is the end of all."[206] But Ambedkar emphasize that for Buddha, the purpose of religion was entirely different. To the question what is the purpose of religion Buddha's answer was entirely different. "He did not tell people that their aim is life should be to reach some imaginary heaven. The kingdom of righteousness lies on earth and is to be reached by man by righteous conduct"[207]

Ambedkar tries explains that the Buddhism is not related to the concept of God but morality. But what become now evident in Buddhism is that the purpose of morality is defined as to make the earth of righteousness. One should here note that many religions talks about the earth of love, but only Buddhism talks about the earth of righteousness. According to Ambedkar in Buddhism virtue is defined in socially aspects. It is this which distinguishes Buddhism form all other religions.[208]

Moreover what is appealing is that Buddhist ethics is not the denial of the Individual ethics, beyond it, the individual ethics and social ethics both are construed and formed in the critical engagement with each other. May be one wonder that how we can categorically define certain values as social and individual. It is true that this division is not a water tight division. But in emphasis, one can define that certain values are socially oriented and certain others individual oriented. Certainly righteousness is social virtue. It is because righteousness is not merely a person's attitude towards others. This is a virtue which exists in the social relation only. This is not something which resides in one person and expressed towards other, but something which is only evolving in social relation. In certain sense we can distinguish both these kinds of values as follows: Social relation is quite necessary for the definition of the social value. Individual value also most of the time includes social relation, but for the definition of it social relation is not a necessary one.

But at the same time Buddhist ethics are not the denial of individual aspects of ethics. But what we can see in Buddhist ethics is critical engagement between individual aspect and social aspects. In Buddhism both guides each other while in other religions it is only one-way relations. That is individual aspects determines the social aspects. But Buddhism offers the possibility of interaction of both it is evident from following: "Only righteousness can remove this inequity and the resultant misery. That's why Ambedkar said that religion must not only preach but must inculcate upon the mind of man the supreme necessity for being righteousness in his conduct."[209]

Meanwhile Dewey too had careful and rigorous analysis on the religion-society interaction. He proposes two basic reformulations to aid the renewal of the religious dimension in modern life. The first reformulation is a careful analysis of the word 'religion' itself. "There is no such thing as religion in the singular, he writes; there is only a multitude of religions."[210] religion involves its own beliefs, practices, and institutional forms, and each religion describes religious experiences in particular ways with such variety, in fact, that Dewey believes a comparative study will reveal no beliefs, practices, or forms common to all religions. Each religion accommodates or acknowledges only certain experiences as properly religious.

The decay of Christianity and Judaism among educated people is partly due to the fact that these religions "now prevent. the religious quality of experience from coming to consciousness and finding the expression that is appropriate to present conditions, intellectual and moral."[211] Dewey distinguishes a religion (with its specific content and recognizable religious experiences) from the religious, which is an attitude that can characterize any human experience. The distinction is important because Dewey rejects the liberal Christian notion that there is such a thing as a specific kind of experience which is religious experience. Any experience can be religious, not by virtue of its content but rather by "having the force of bringing about a better, deeper and enduring adjustment in life."[212] Dewey clearly approaches the problem of religious experience from the American pragmatist tradition of assessing ideas for their efficacy in life. (William James is of course famous for examining the 'varieties of religious experience,' but he also emphasizes the difference each experience makes instead of emphasizing the conceptual truth or content of those experiences.) This shift from assessing the intellectual content per se to assessing the overall qualitative effect of an idea in life is also characteristic of Dewey's second reformulation.

In the same way Ambedkar proposed the ideal of *Saddhamma* which looks on a better human living in the theorization. For Ambedkar: *"Dhamma* is *Saddhamma* when it makes learning open to all. *Dhamma* is *Saddhamma* when it teaches that mere learning is not enough. It may lead to pedantry. *Dhamma* is *Saddhamma* when it teaches that what is needed is prajna (Pranya). *Dhamma* is *Saddhamma* only when it teaches that Prajna is not enough. Sila must accompany it. Dhamma is Saddhamma only when it teaches that besides Prajna and Sila, what is necessary, is *Karuna. Dhamma* is *Saddhamma* only when it teaches, that more than Karuna what is necessary is *Maitri, Dhamma* to be *Saddhamma* must break down barriers between man and man. *Dhamma* to be *Saddhamma* must teach that 'worth' and not 'birth' is the measure of man.[213] *Dhamma* to be *Saddhamma* must promote equality between man and man." The functions of *Saddhamma* are in the first place to cleanse the mind of its impurities and in the second to make the world a kingdom of righteousness. In order to practice *Saddhamma,* however, *Dhamma* must promote *prajna* or insight, and this it does by making learning open to all, by teaching that mere learning is not enough as it may lead to pedantry, and by teaching that what is needed is *Prajna* or right thinking.

Moreover *Dhamma* as *Saddhamma* only when it teaches that *Prajna* must be accompanied by Sila or right action as well as by *Karuna* or compassion for the poor and helpless and by *Maitri* or love for all living beings. It follows that, in order to *Saddhamma,* Dhamma must break down the barriers between man and man must teach the worth and not birth and must promote equality between man and man. According to Ambedkar the practice of *Saddhamma* includes, to cleanse the mind of its impurities; to make the world kingdom of righteousness; to make learning *(knowledge)* open to all; to teach the relevance of what is learnt in education; to practice moral *virtues* (Sila); to promote mercifulness *(Karuna);* and to promote Maitri or fellowship. As part of negations, for the *Dhamma* to be *Saddhamma* it should involve in breaking away the barriers between men or among human beings. The Dhamma to be Saddhamma must teach worth and not birth as the measure of man. Buddha is against the theory of the supremacy of birth as described in the concept of *Chaturvarna.* Instead, he preached the idea of the worth of man. He says no one is an out caste by birth- and no one is a *Brahmin* by birth and the most important element in the *Saddhamma,* more than *Prajna* is *Sila.* The *Sila* is *Karuna,* love of human beings and *Maitri* which is love of all living beings.[214]

According to Ambedkar, Buddhism demanded living experience and a life divine, attainable there and now; not after death, it was realism and never idealism. It upheld liberty, equality, truth and justice; it emphasized humanity, love and peace. It was dynamic, scientific and all embracing. Its explanation of life and its meaning and purpose of birth and death and its aftermath were very clear, intelligible and logical. Above all, man was the center of his study and examination and not anything outside of him. Ambedkar tried to prove that the untouchables were Buddhists. In his thesis on the origin of *Untouchability* he made it clear that today's *untouchables* were once Buddhists.

"Buddhism could withstand even the severest scientific test and had the power and capacity to direct destines of the modern world. The untouchables would join with the world Buddhist community and thus pave the way for world brotherhood."[125] Ambedkar said that, "Buddhism gives three principles in combination, which no other religion does. Buddhism teaches *prajna* (understanding) as against superstition and supernaturalism, *Karuna* (love) and *samata* (equality)... Neither god nor *Soul* can save the society,"[216] Referring to Marx's philosophy, Ambedkar observed that Man cannot live by bread alone. He has a mind, which needs food for thought. Religion instills hope in man and drives him to activity. Hindu religion has watered down the enthusiasm of the downtrodden. And "I found it necessary to change my faith and embrace Buddhism."[217] Ambedkar says that Religion emphasizes, universalizes social values and brings them to the mind of the individual who is required to be familiar with them in all his acts in an order that he may function as an approved member of the society.

Dewey also reformulates the idea of God. Because the rise of modern science has undermined the credibility of the two great Western faiths, he looks to science for a clue to this new reformulation. Science, he observes, is a method and not a body of doctrine. "There is but one sure road of access to truth the road of patient, cooperative inquiry operating by means of observation, experiment, record and controlled reflection."[218] Any particular conclusion made along the way may be discarded as new occasions demand without challenging the soundness of the method of inquiry. Religious questions, according to Dewey, ought to be also pursued using the explorative methods of science. Our loyalty belongs properly to a method, not to a set of conclusions. This method is cooperative, critical, empirical, experimental, and reflective. It steadfastly rejects a settled content for religious truth. But God remains the object of faith, even though a modern faith as Dewey describes it avoids treating the object of faith like a thing. God is an ideal, or, properly speaking, the "unity of loyalty and effort evoked by the fact that many ends are one in the power of their ideal, or imaginative, quality to stir and hold us."[219]

Dewey does not follow Whitehead in treating ideals as metaphysically real; instead, he simply proposes that the possibilities available to us can take on the quality of the ideal. 'Things unrealized in fact,' which 'come home to us and have power to stir us,' are ideals; the ideal "emerges when the imagination idealizes existence by laying hold of the possibilities offered to thought and action."[220] In other words, as the religious qualities of various experiences yield imaginative ideals that animate life, the imagination also responds to those ideals. This ideal quality of our imaginative ideals, as it were, arouses our hope and excitement and draws us forward through the imagination into new or renewed ways of living. The response to the ideal is worship.

The style of empiricism that enables one to speak of an ideal, non-supernatural, non-ontological God gathers its ideals from a humble test: when people sense that the value of an experience exceeds what has gone before, they also sense the possibility of betterment generally. So long as the lure of continued advance and continued cultivation of human goods obtains, there will be continuing grounds for the idealization of God. Only a breakdown of confidence in the possibility of expanding the good threatens this view.[221]

Ambedkar's attempt to justify morality without reference to transcendental religious beliefs is a first step to make the realm of morality as an autonomous one. The concern for the universal well-being is the main consideration of Ambedkar's scheme of morality. Thus, external considerations are no longer being above moral principles. Ambedkar makes such a morality the basis of religion, which he constructed as *Dhamma.* In this construal, he redefines the centre of religion as morality rather than God. According to Ambedkar, Natural law is the basis of moral order of universe. *Dhamma* for Ambedkar is all-inclusive. The underlying meaning of the *Dhamma* is a message of equality and fraternity. Ambedkar's position is that morality in religion would not be an effective one. In religion, morality is only a wagon which is attached to it. It is attached and detached as the occasion requires. Ambedkar notes that "Morality comes in only wherein man comes in relation to man.

Morality comes into religion as a side wind to maintain peace and order....Be good to your neighbour because you are both children of God....The action of morality in the functioning of religion is therefore casual and occasional."[222] Ambedkar affirms that morality is *Dhamma* and *Dhamma* is morality that is inclusive. Further analysis shows that, Ambedkar's attempt to justify morality without reference to transcendental religious beliefs is a first step to make the realm or morality as an autonomous one. The concern for the universal well-being is the main consideration of Ambedkar's scheme of morality. Thus, external considerations are no longer being above moral principles. Ambedkar makes such a morality the basis of religion, which he construes as *Dhamma.*

And also John Dewey co-opted the name "liberalism" to describe an ideology that was actually "progressive." Dewey described the "old liberalism" as committed to protecting the individual's rights of free speech, religion right, and government economic non-intervention; Dewey considers the "old liberalism" to have lacked the principle of "historic relativity"; this "deficiency" led the "old liberals" to declare their principles immutable natural laws and advocate as an eternal truth the confinement of government to protecting against the infringement of the individual's liberty to action on the part of the others.

Dewey does not share the "old liberals'" belief in the "individual as something given, complete in itself, of liberty as a ready-made possession of the individual, only needing the removal of external restrictions to manifest itself."[223] Rather he claims that this belief has degenerated into "pseudo-liberalism" or the advocacy of a laissez-faire economy and limited government that he opposed in his own day. Dewey's "new liberalism," i.e., progressivism, holds that the individual is "something achieved with the air and support of cultural, physical, legal, and political institutions." The role of governance according to progressivism is not merely to remove active violations of the individual's freedom but to promote and cultivate positive institutions to assist in the development of individuality.

In accordance with the Lord Buddha, Ambedkar also insists that the purpose or religion and spirituality are not mere quest of notion or truth. His analysis shows that this is not a defensible claim. Buddha also analyzes the metaphysical quest as follows; "Morality is justified in theistic religion in terms of reward and punishment give by God to the individual. Atheistic religions justify morality in terms of the doctrine of karma, according to which, morally good or bad lead to consequence, which are pleasant or painful to the agent. Therefore, the ethics in both theistic and atheistic religious lead to a kind of egoistic consequentialism."[224] This implies that the morality and its principles, roughly which can be considered as the benefit of all, is built on the egoistic basis. Morality is defined and prevailed in most religious by looking on the consequence of violation or maintenance, which ego would face. Here, suggests that in Ambedkar's reconstruction of Buddhism, is morality is justified in terms of universalistic consequentalism. A morality which was based on the principles of truth and love. Hinduism, according to Ambedkar, did not recognize the principles of freedom and equality and had not succeeded in evolving a universal morality.

Furthermore, Dewey believes that progressivism is committed to the idea of historic relativity and holds that "the content of the individual and freedom change with time; this is as true of social as of individual development."[225] In this way, progressivism departs from the Founders' understanding of fixed self-evident moral principles such as those expressed in the Declaration of Independence which hold true for all men in all times and places; rather, progressivism adheres to evolving standards of justice, the proper role of government, and the individual itself. The "ends" of Dewey's progressivism are claimed to be the "full freedom of the human spirit and of individuality," which entails "full cultural freedom"[226] to share in "the resources of civilization" an extremely broad aspiration whose content changes and evolves with the times.

Dewey's appropriation of the term "liberalism" to mean advocacy of extensive government intervention in the economy completely reversed that term's prior meaning. In the 19th and early 20th centuries, liberalism stood for limited government, free enterprise, and the sovereignty of the individual in all areas regarding his own life. It is time to return to that ideal and expose "new liberalism" for an unjustified name at the least; while the old liberalism truly empowered and liberated the individual, the "new liberalism" shackles him under an ever-amassing array of state controls.[229]

For Ambedkar Morality is based on the Natural Order of the Physical world. It is evident from the natural phenomena that there is an order of the physical world. There is certain order for the movement of heavenly bodies, regularity for the seasons. These are called *'Niyamas'* in Buddhism. "Similarly there is a moral order in Human society. How is it produced? How is it maintained? Those who believe in God have no difficulty in answering the question. And their answer is easy. Moral order is maintained by Divined dispensation. God created the world and God is the supreme governor of the world. He is also the author of moral as well as of physical law. Such is the argument in support of the view that the moral order is maintained by Divine Dispensation."[228]

Ambedkar contests these arguments. He asks "For if the moral law has originated from God and if God is the beginning and the end of the moral order and if man cannot escape from obeying God, why is there so much moral disorder in this world".[229] According to Ambedkar, Natural law is the basis of moral order of universe. "...God leaves it to Nature to work itself out in obedience to the laws originally given by him."[230] The moral order is maintained by Kamma Niyam and not God which maintains the moral order in the universe. "The moral order of universe rests on man and on nobody else. Kamma means man's action and Vipaka is its effect."[231]

According to Dewey the most important task of the Christian is to reveal God. The truth of faith, however, stands in a special relationship to reality: When the faith is in our consciousness already present, the human being has first through his actions to bring the reality of this truth into the external world. "God's kingdom is in us ...is in our midst."[232] Dewey wants to clarify that both the democratic consciousness and the Christian experience of salvation come out of the same anthropological source: They both come from the social disposition of the human being. His action is always socially oriented: One is the other's brother.

Dewey basic question is that an action right or wrong because God commands or prohibits it, or God commands or prohibit the action because it is already right or wrong? A divine command ethicist takes the position that the standard of right or wrong is the commands and prohibitions of God. According to the divine command theory "an action or kind of action is right or wrong if and only if and because it is commanded or forbidden by God."[233] According to the Natural law theory, the basic principles of morals are objective, accessible to reason, and based on human nature. An action is right if it serves to fulfill human nature and wrong if it goes against human nature. Our human nature includes various inclinations and tendencies. The task of reason is to discover, sort out and order these inclinations in accord with appropriate human fulfillment.

However, in the analysis of Ambedkar's position one can find out that Ambedkar clearly counter the argument for the divine command ethics. Major divine command ethics' arguments are based on the conception that God is the first cause. That is God cannot be causally affected by anything. Therefore it is difficult to claim that God chosen which is already good, that is God is causally affected. All the similar positions already assume the supremacy of God in all senses. This presupposition which Ambedkar denies thoroughly throughout his theological positions and especially in his construal of Buddhism. If certain presupposition are accepted as certain, it itself is obstacle to the critical engagement and analysis. Divine command ethics can be defended only on the ground that it follows from certain beliefs we have about God's nature and status and about the character of the relationship between god and Human beings.[234]

Dewey says that a new basis for faith emerges given the emancipation of religious experience from religions. Instead of a faith founded upon ideals guaranteed to exist by supernatural authority, there would be faith in ideals apprehended by the imagination as being intrinsically valuable possibilities inherent in the natural relationship existing between man and his environment. Religious experience is thus a universal possibility and not restricted to a particular type of believer who excludes other people who don't believe in the same way. This is the point where Dewey expresses his original idea of 'God' (or 'Supreme Being') as the unification of all ideal ends with the imagination, which bestows a power in mind but also in action: "It is this active relation between ideal and actual to which I would give the name God."[235] Such a conception of God or the divine should not, he points out, forget the element of natural piety, as the concepts of the 'super naturalists' and the militant atheists (he rejects them back-to-back) tend to do, nor exclude man's relation to nature as the concept of the purely humanistic religionists does. It would instead embody a clear recognition of man's essential relationship, in terms of both dependence and support, with the rest of nature. He finally discusses the crisis affecting religion in his period and throughout the 20th century, stating that though this is due to the rise of science and knowledge, it doesn't call into question "the religious values of our common experience." This crisis is however somewhat of a bargain, in the sense that it helps us in freeing our ideals from illusions and fantasies, and by telling us we can achieve our goals through acts and not by waiting for some external intervention.

It is important to note that Dewey's empirical faith requires confidence in the ability of human beings to recognize and revere the grand moments in all of human experience, and to carry forward those processes apparent in the accomplishments of the human past. Without a sense of history, all novelty would appear trivial; with a sense of history, however, novelty stands in relation to past accomplishment and can be valued progressively. Because the past yields evidence for the emergence of new value in the continual emergence of artistic creativity, scientific curiosity, and even in new human relationships one may even continue to draw from the religious traditions of the past insofar as one treats their conceptualizations and practices as embodying the process of cultivating the ideal. The past cannot be viewed as the repository of final truths, but as the fertile ground of emergent ideals and accomplishment on which we build. Dewey's method invites modern people to sympathize not with worn-out doctrines but with the sense of something greater-yet-to-come which has enlivened every human accomplishment.[237]

In Plato's *Euthyphro*, Socrates raises the question, "is what is holy because the gods approve it, or do they approve it because it holy."[238] According to Boyd and Vanarragon observe in their article 'Ethics is based on natural law" that "These questions, first posed in Plato's *Euthyphro* have long troubled theists, because each of the obvious question carries with it unpleasant consequences. In other words, these questions appear to introduce a dilemma, as can be seen in the following argument:

- If God's command makes an act right, then morality is arbitrary.
- If God commands an act because it is right, then God's command is not essential to morality.

- Either God's commands makes an act right, or God's commands an act because it is right. Therefore, Either Morality is arbitrary or God's command is not essential to morality."[239]

Ambedkar's position was that the natural order of the universe is the basis of the morality.

Ambedkar interprets the concept of *Karma* as, "the law of *Karma* has to do only with the question of general moral order. It has nothing to do with the fortunes and misfortunes of the world. It is concerned with the maintenance of the moral order in the universe."[240]

Dewey says, the ability of man to cope with his own fate seems to show that one can do without the transcendent instance of "God" and "The Last Judgment". Especially the fearful uncertainty to possibly be delivered to eternal damnation in the life to come is impossible for Dewey to accept. This dogma is in conflict with his humanism; it keeps man in dependence and hinders social progress. Thus the acceptance of a religious transcendence has given way to an inner-worldly religiosity.[241] It pursues with unlimited faith-power the human development of society, whose goal is the social democracy. The "good life" through "shared experience" is the dynamic inner-worldly alternative, based on a steady societal change, over against the transcendent-static religion which promises an afterlife with its paradise.

For Ambedkar, *Dhamma* is social. *Dhamma* is social in the sense that it is all embracing and for all humanity .In other religions, a person leading a secluded life and performing certain rituals is considered to be a religious man but in Buddhism a man's behaviour towards his fellow-beings is the test of his being religious. *Dhamma* teaches righteousness which means right relations between man and man in all spheres of life. Society, therefore, cannot do without *Dhamma.* If *Dhamma* is not social and is not for the welfare of the people then it has no value for suffering humanity. Further, the underlying meaning of the *Dhamma* is a message of equality. Where there is equality, there is hope for individual initiative, progress and attainment of Nirvana, the supreme state of Bliss, the ultimate aim of every Buddhist.

Further, in most religions there is no place for morality but morality is the essence of the *Dhamma.* Without it, there is no *Dhamma.* In *Dhamma* morality takes the place of God although there is no God in *Dhamma.* Then Ambedkar discusses the principle of *Ahimsa* of Buddha. In Buddhism *Ahimsa* is a principle and not a rule. Buddha made a distinction between the 'need to kill' and the *'will to kill'.* Buddha denounced Himsa (Violence) and advocated a ban on the killing of animals for the sake of food, sacrifice, sport or pleasure; but it is wrong to interpret that He banned *Himsa* under all circumstances. But Buddha said that no one should run away from the Army with a view to join *Sangha.* This means that the Buddha was not against killing for the defense of the country. The principle of *'the need to kill'* and the *'will* to *kill'* therefore is correct. To kill is entirely a matter of necessity and personal moral responsibility. Every act has to be guided by man's own *Prajna* and *karuna.* Buddhism in *Ahimsa* means non-aggressiveness; but in self -defense, if anyone needs to fight then he should fight.

Dewey as think that *"there* is a malignant principle at work in traditional theism and supernaturalism."[242] and " left the church in the name of human community, abandoned the idea of special revelation in the name of truth and morality, and eventually rejected the God of the Church theologians in order to overcome humanity's alienation from its own essential goodness and in order to realize the spiritual meaning inherent in ordinary human relations."[243]

Dewey's interpretation of the religious dimensions of life constitutes a "substantial contribution to the development of an American democratic spirituality."[244] It is spirituality whose faith and hope are centered in the secular trinity of modem science as the source of truth, modern technology as the empowering principle for the employment of this truth, and democratic community as they lived realization of this truth and power. Dewey's involvement in the competing currents of thought that dominated the religious scene in America through the twenties and thirties. Dewey's account of the religious quality of experience has "implications for an understanding of reality that are not fully articulated in his metaphysics and idea of the divine."[245] Dewey's own religious experience points "to a depth dimension of reality that is not adequately expressed in his philosophical language."[246] Dewey's naturalism may be able to overcome such shortcomings by reworking its conception of the divine as the union of the ideal and the real.

This union has an affinity to the notion of the "Cosmic Christ . . . [being] the principle of order, creativity, and goodness in the universe," [247] in terms of the non-personal Godhead of the mystical tradition that symbolizes 'a dimension of experience and reality which cannot be fully conceptualized,' and that is "the final source of ultimate meaning and the eternal ground of the Great Yes to life."[248] Dewey naturalism is that it can philosophically accommodate those aspects of religious experience of which Dewey himself is aware, but which seem to escape the nets of naturalism unreconstructed.

Ambedkar tried to find the difference between *religion* and *Dhamma* in relation to their purposes and the way that different terminologies like *karma* and *Ahimsa* or non-killing are interpreted and used. Then he went to explore the relation between Dhamma and religion out of which he asserts that mere "Morality is not enough, but it must be sacred and universal."[249] Morality, he asserts, has no place in religion. Religion is concerned with the relation between man and God and morality is concerned with the relation between man and man. Though every religion preaches morality, morality is not the root of religion, it can be attached if it is needed or detached if it is not needed. The action of morality in the functioning of religion is not a serious one but casual and occasional. After describing the non-closeness of morality and religion Ambedkar takes *Dhamma* for his analysis and say that "Morality is *Dhamma* and *Dhamma* is Morality."

The contradiction between the message of God and the condition of the world is apparent. The solution of this contradiction is a challenge to every person and to the community, to change this situation through practical action. Dewey interprets democratic action and democratic life-style as consequence of the Christian revelation, which is not a one-time act, but which more fully reveals itself the more social barriers, prejudice, and exploitation can be overcome. He views democracy as standard for the liberation of godly truth from its really existing incompleteness caused through man as media of this god-given-truth: "Democracy thus appears as the means by which the revelation of truth is carried on. It is in democracy, the community of ideas and interest through community of action, that the incarnation of God in man (man, that is to say, as organ of universal truth) becomes a living, present thing, having its ordinary and natural sense. This truth is brought down to life; its segregation removed; it is made a common truth enacted in all departments of action, not in one isolated sphere called religious"[257] action is just like religious action in the first place social action. It gains its spiritual power through revelation of the Christian truth. But this truth does not yet really liberate one, if it is only realized individually. Only after the message has first reached the public, the society, becomes it in a real sense true. The only individually recognized message is limited. It brings about no common consciousness.

As per Ambedkar's understanding Morality is the essence of *Dhamma* and the absence of it there is no *Dhamma*. Religion attaches everything to God and man is expected to do every act to appease God. His responsibility himself to serve and save the fellow beings. But *Dhamma* is not ike that everything the man does, is for his own self. He says that the "Morality in *Dhamma* arises from the direct necessity for man to love man. Such morality does not require divine sanction. It is not to please God that man has to be moral. It is for his own good that man has to love man."[252] This morality, which is *Dhamma,* is not to satisfy a particular group but serves to protect the weak from the strong standards, and rules and which safeguards the growth of the individual. It is what makes liberty and equality effective, for if there is liberty for some but not for all and equality for few but not for the majority, what is the remedy? The only remedy lies in making fraternity universally effective. What is fraternity? It is nothing but another name for brotherhood of men, which is another name for morality.

Ambedkar is justified in his reinterpretation of Buddhism; he has left a few gaps unfilled. Firstly, by not linking his community of Neo-

Buddhists to any of the existing Buddhist *Sangha,* he fashioned a gulf between them. He refused to accept the existing forms of Buddhism, as they were not, he deemed, faithful to the original teaching of the Buddha. This shortcoming has not only isolated the Neo-Buddhists depriving them of historical continuity, and a continuous tradition, it also deprived them of a *Sangha* and religious leadership to guide them. The sudden demise of Ambedkar widened this gulf much more.

For Ambedkar, usually science or reason is considered as in rival position of religion or religion bounded morality. The direct difficulty science could pose for religious belief would be direct scientific refutation of essential religious principles. But refutation can emerge only out of genuine conflict and that fact imposes some boundaries. For instance, many believe that science and religion operate in different domains or levels. If such positions are correct, there can be no genuine conflict. Any apparent conflict would represent trespassing or confusion. Furthermore, serious conflict between science and religion is possible only if both purport to be true.

Consequently if moral commitment is non-negative or non-propositional, genuine conflict seems impossible. That's why Ambedkar's position one who takes religion very seriously must approach it with a scientific attitude. Otherwise our religion would be a superstition. Making religion more active or creative or critical is making it scientific. Making it non-scientific is blocking the growth religion; consequently it would become an ideology which advocates intolerance. And as per Ambedkar's position only through the critical engagement with science and reason one can draw the limits of religion. Drawing the limit is never deteriorating the system, it only corroborates it.

The second thing is that "the Buddha never cared to enter into a discussion, which was not profitable for man's welfare. Therefore anything attributed to the Buddha, which did not relate to man's welfare couldn't be accepted to be the word of the Buddha."[254] This test for dealing with the teachings of the Buddha, Ambedkar offers, is to distinguish between those matters in which the Buddha was certain and those in which he was not and so gave only tentative views. Social relevance, that is making the Dhamma relevant to the present Indian context and to the unequal oppressive situation of the down trodden, should be considered the major principle and key to his interpretation. For, the above mentioned second test of the three prescribed by him, to clear the doubts that arise out of confusion and suspicion, again reiterates the use of the principle of existential social utility as important in interpreting the Dhamma. Ambedkar, with other poor people, was in search of a religion with a revolutionary social message and the ideal of equality that enforces the moral social order of a class-casteless prosperous fraternal human society.

According to Dewey, the appeal for a moral better, because socially conscious society, makes clear the enlightened as well as secular aspect in Dewey's understanding of religion, which we can already now outline assuming Dewey's later religious development. The question of truth, which caused him such effort, science answers Dewey is more and more certain. Science has discovered no God; however, it has demythologized religion.

Dewey insists on the role of science in the knowledge of these religious experiences, but not as a new 'religion' that requires worship (as was believed in a certain sense by the positivist movement) but rather as a good method for apprehending 'real' faith. According to Dewey, there has been "a revolution in the seat of intellectual authority."[255] migrating from religion to the scientific and social sciences and this is also for him the origin of the growing gap between fundamentalists and liberals inside churches. But the discredit science has thrown on religion, contrary to what some may think, does not concern the item 'belief' itself: since religious experience is so commonly associated exclusively with particular religions, Dewey points out that there are many people who, because they find it impossible to accept the intellectual and moral implications of established religions, "we are not even aware of attitudes in themselves that, if they came to fruition, would be genuinely religious."[256] It is rather the method of accessing faith that is challenged than belief itself, as science, as a method, is at the same time cooperative, critical, empirical, experimental and reflective, contrary to the settled contents of religious truth. Dewey Traditional moral virtues have lost their power to persuade modern people, who tend to think scientifically. When the teachings of traditional religions either contradict science or are unrelated to science, they become unacceptable to modern people, who tend to place absolute confidence in science.

When we see this collapse of traditional values, we realize that there is a need for a new view of value. This new view of value, first of all, must be able to embrace the fundamental teachings of all religions and thought systems. It must also be able to overcome materialism and atheism. Furthermore, it must be able to embrace and even guide science. This would be a view of value that is centered on the absolute God. Unification axiology seeks to present such a view of value.[257] This new view of value is presented for the sake of establishing our future society. The future society is a society that will be built by people of original nature, whose intellect, emotion, and will are centered on Heart. Accordingly, the future society will be a society where the activities of people's intellect, emotion, and will are carried out in it harmonious way, centering on heart. Here, new values refer to the values corresponding to the original faculties of intellect, emotion, and will. The future society will thus be a society where the values of trueness, goodness, and beauty will be realized; in that society.[258]

In the same line Ambedkar has also deliberately emphasized the social message of the Buddha. Ambedkar and reinterpreted his teaching and projected his personality to bring out not only the enlightened Siddhartha Gautama full of wisdom, *prajna,* but also the compassionate one, full of *karuna* and *maitri.* It is indeed a social gospel of Buddhism. It lays more stress on love and service than wisdom and insight. Doctrines of Buddhism did Ambedkar hold and teach? In the central part of his Bible, Ambedkar dedicates a whole book to summarise the main teachings of the Buddha and the main doctrinal matters regarding the *Dhamma.* He candidly presents what are *Dhamma*, A *dhamma* and *Saddhamma* according to the Buddha. The main titles and points of the book' 'What the Buddha taught' are: What is *Dhamma?* "It is to maintain Purity of Life; to reach Perfection in Life; to live in *Nibbana;* to give up craving; to believe that all compound things are impermanent; to believe that *Karma* is the instrument of Moral Order."[259] What is *Saddhamma?* His answer is that *Dhamma* is *Saddharma* when it makes learning open to all; teaches that mere learning is not enough and may lead to pedantry, that what is needed is *Pradnya,* that *Pradnya* is not enough, but must be accompanied by *Sila,* that besides *Pradnya* and Sila what is necessary is Karuna, and that more than *Karuna* what is necessary is *Maitri. Dhamma* to be *Saddhamma* must break down barriers between man and man, teach that worth and not birth is the measure of man, and must promote equality between man and man.[260]

Ambedkar's views of the Perfection in Ethical and spiritual life comes through a) watchfulness, b) mindfulness and c) right understanding.[261] The virtue of liberty giving is essentially a product of compassion; compassion is the root of Bodhisattva's life. "His enlightenment is nothing but liberality or charity."[262] He thinks thus: "My neighbour suffers his pain just as I suffer mine; why should I be anxious about myself and not about him."[263] The perfection of charity leads to the equivalence of me and my fellow beings. When to me, as to others, pain and fear are unpleasant, there is no special to protect my own person and not others. Compassion is the only virtue to which a saint must apply himself; all other virtues will follow up naturally. Nothing is superior to charity; even the vow of chastity. Liberality consists not only in giving material goods, things of enjoyment, but also in giving spiritual knowledge. Liberty born of compassion is the supreme means of conciliating creatures by alms giving, lovable speech, kind cooperation, and by sharing the joys and woes of beings.

Reference

155. Dewey, John. (1925a/1981). *Experience and Nature.* LW1, Southern Illinois University Press,Carbondale.p. 76

156. Keer, Dhananjay, 1982. *Ambedkar: A Memorial Album,* Popular Prakasan, Bombay. p.3

157. Ambedkar, B.R, 1987. *The Buddha and His Dhamma,* Siddharth Publications, Bombay.p.156-57& 351- 64

158. Ambedkar, B.R, 1987. *The Buddha and His Dhamma,* Siddharth Publications, Bombay. p.370-371
159. John Dewey, 1925. *Science and the Modern World.* Lowell Lectures: Macmillan, New York. p.77
160. Moon, Vasant, (ed.), 1989. *Babasaheb Ambedkar's: Writings and Speeches,* Vol. II, Dept. of Education, Govt. of Maharastra, Bombay. p.118
161. John Dewey, (1927;1984). *The Public and Its Problems* in *The Late Works,* vol. 3. Southern Illinois University Press. Carbondale.p.143
162. John Dewey, 1982. *Reconstruction in Philosophy and Essays 1920,* Southern Illinois University Press, Carbondale.p.171
163. John Dewey, 1983/2008. *"Religion and Morality,"* Southern Illinois University Press. Carbondale, p.46
164. John Dewey, 1983/2008. *"Religion and Morality."* Southern Illinois University Press. Carbondale. p.236
165. John Dewey, 1995. *Religious Faith and Democratic Humanism,* Philosophy Education Society, Inc. University of New York Press, New York. p.25
166. Jatava, D.R.1965. *The Social Philosophy of B. R. Ambedkar.* Phoenix Publishing Agency, Agra.p.231
167. Ibid
168. Ibid, p.233-234
169. John Dewey,1922/ 1983. *Human Nature and Conduct,* Southern Illinois University Press, Carbondale. p.14
170. Ambedkar, B.R, 1987. *The Buddha and His Dhamma,* Siddharth Publications, Bombay, p.487
171. Ibid, p.488
172. Keer, Dhananjay, 1982. *Ambedkar: A Memorial Album,* Sangan Books, London,p.92
173. Ibid, p.66
174. Keer, Dhananjay, 1982. *Ambedkar: A Memorial Album,* Sangan Books, London,p.71

175. Keer, Dhananjay, 1982. *Ambedkar: A Memorial Album,* Sangan Books, London.p.73

176. John Dewey, 1995. *Religious Faith and Democratic Humanism,* Philosophy Education Society, Inc. University of New York Press, New York.p.34

177. Ibid, p.41

178. Ibid, p.43

179. John Dewey, 1995. *Religious Faith and Democratic Humanism,* Philosophy Education Society, Inc. University of New York Press, New York.p.44

180. John Dewey, 1995. *Religious Faith and Democratic Humanism,* Philosophy Education Society, Inc. University of New York Press, New York. p.48

181. Moon, Vasant, (ed.), 1989. *Babasaheb Ambedkar's: Writings and Speeches,* Vol.VI, Dept. of Education, Govt. of Maharastra, Bombay, p.406

182. Moon, Vasant, (ed.), 1989. *Babasaheb Ambedkar's: Writings and Speeches,* Vol.VI, Dept. of Education, Govt. of Maharastra, Bombay. p. 222

183. Dewey, John. (1922/1983). *Human Nature and Conduct.* Southern Illinois University Press.Carbondale.p.320

184. John Dewey. (1922/1983). *Human Nature and Conduct.* Southern Illinois University Press.Carbondale.p.321

185. Ibid, p.318

186. Dewey, John. (1922/1983). *Human Nature and Conduct.* Southern Illinois University Press.Carbondale.p.319

187. Moon, Vasant, (ed.), 1989. *Babasaheb Ambedkar's: Writings and Speeches,* Vol. I I-VI, Dept. of Education, Govt. of Maharastra, Bombay, p.97

188. Ibid, p.97-98

189. Bernabé. 2006. *"Diversity as Fraternity Lite"* El Diario La Prensa, New York City. p.87

190. Winthrop, John 2009. *'A Model of Christian Charity,'* Anchor Books, NewYork.p.79-80

191. John Dewey, 1993, *"Philosophy and Democracy," MW*11, Southern Illinois University Press, Carbondale. p.43
192. John Dewey. (1939/1988). *"Freedom and Culture"*. Southern Illinois University Press. Carbondale, IL. p.155
193. John Dewey, 1927;1984). *"The Public and Its Problems,"* LW3. Southern Illinois University Press, Carbondale. P. 329
194. John Dewey, 1993, *"Philosophy and Democracy,". MW*11, Southern Illinois University Press, Carbondale.p. 46
195. John Dewey.1919 *'Philosophy and Democracy,'* MW11, Southern Illinois UniversityPress, Carbondale.p. 88- 89
196. Jatava, D.R.1965. *The Social Philosophy of B. R. Ambedkar,* Phoenix Publishing Agency, Agra. p. 267
197. Paul Kurtz, 2002 *"Are Science and Religion Compatible? "Skeptical Inquirer* Vol. 26, no. 2, Amherst Publisher, New. York. p. 234
198. Ibid, p. 235
199. Keer, Dhananjay, 1991.*"Dr.Ambedkar"* Sangan Books, London. p. 273
200. John Dewey, (1939;1988). *"Freedom and Culture" LW*13, Southern Illinois University Press, Carbondale. p.99
201. Ibid
202. William James. 1902/1994. *'The Varieties of Religious Experience.'* Longmans, Green, Modern Library, New York. p.102
203. John Dewey, 1934. *A Common Faith.* New Haven, Yale University Press, New York. p. 44
204. Ibid.
205. Billy Graham, 1983. *"The Bible is a Book",* American Bible Society, New york, Verse.27
206. Ambedkar, B.R, 1987. *The Buddha and His Dhamma,* Siddharth Publications, Bombay,. p. 282
207. Ibid,p. 283
208. Ambedkar, B.R, 1987. *The Buddha and His Dhamma,* Siddharth Publications, Bombay,. p.283

209. Ambedkar, B.R, 1987. *The Buddha and His Dhamma,* Siddharth Publications, Bombay,. p. 284
210. John Dewey, 1934. A Common Faith. New Haven, Yale University Press, New York. p. 13
211. John Dewey, 1934. *A Common Faith.* New Haven, Yale University Press, New York. p. 14
212. Ibid
213. Kuber, W.N, *B.R. 1978. Ambedkar,* Publication Division, Ministry of Information and Broadcasting, Government of India, p. 96
214. Jatava, D. R. 1965. *The Social Philosophy of B. R. Ambedkar,* Phoenix Publishing Agency, Agra,p. 301
215. Ambedkar, B. R.1968. *The Buddha and the Future of His Religion,* The Mahabodhi, Bombay. p. 5
216. Ibid
217. Rabb, Peter (ed.), 1993. *Dalit Movements and the Meaning of Labour in India* Oxford University Press, New Delhi,. p. 18
218. John Dewey, 1934. *A Common Faith.* New Haven, Yale University Press, New York. p. 21
219. John Dewey, 1934. *A Common Faith.* New Haven, Yale University Press, New York. p. 22
220. Ibid, p. 23
221. Ibid, p. 24
222. Ambedkar, B.R, 1987. *The Buddha and His Dhamma,* Siddharth Publications, Bombay. p. 322
223. John Dewey, 1934. A *Common Faith.* New Haven, Yale University Press, New York.p. 38
224. Gokhale, Jayasree,1993. *"The Politics of an Indian Untouchable Community,"* Popular Prakashan, Mumbai.p. 127
225. John Dewey, 1934. *A Common Faith.* New Haven, Yale University Press, New York.p. 40
226. John Dewey, 1934. *A Common Faith.* New Haven, Yale University Press, New York.p. 41

227. John Dewey. (1933/1986). *"How We Think"* Southern Illinois University Press. Carbondale, IL.p. 33

228. Ambedkar, B.R, 1991. *Slavery and Untouchability: Which is worse?*, Dalit Dayal, New Delhi, p. 242

229. Ibid, p. 243

230. Ibid

231. Ambedkar, B.R, 1991. *Slavery and Untouchability: Which is worse?*, Dalit Dayal, New Delhi. p. 244

232. John Dewey, 1995. *Religious Faith and Democratic Humanism,* Philosophy Education Society, Inc. University of New York Press, New York. p. 26

233. Ibid, p. 28

234. John Dewey, 1995. *Religious Faith and Democratic Humanism,* Philosophy Education Society, Inc. University of New York Press, New York. p. 29

235. John Dewey, 1995. *Religious Faith and Democratic Humanism,* Philosophy Education Society, Inc. University of New York Press, New York.p. 30

236. Ibid

237. John Dewey, 1995. *Religious Faith and Democratic Humanism.* Philosophy Education Society, Inc. University of New York Press, New York. p. 31

238. Janine Marie Idziak, 1978. *Divine Commands are the foundation of Morality,* Oxford, Clarendon Press, p. 290-299

239. Craig. & Raymond. 1987. *Morality and Religion"* Simon & Schuster Publishers, New York. p. 94

240. Craig. & Raymond. 1987. *Morality and Religion"* Simon & Schuster Publishers, New York. p. 95

241. John. Dewey, 1892/1997. *Christianity and democracy. In: early works of John Dewey.,* vol. 4.Southern Illinois University Press, Carbondale, IL. p. 32

242. John Dewey, 1995. *Religious Faith and Democratic Humanism,* Philosophy Education Society, Inc. University of New York Press, New York. p. 378

243. Ibid, p. 216
244. Ibid, p. 489
245. Ibid, p. 531
246. John Dewey, 1995. Religious Faith and Democratic Humanism, Philosophy Education Society, Inc. University of New York Press, New York. p. 532
247. Ibid, p. 536
248. John Dewey, 1995. Religious Faith and Democratic Humanism, Philosophy Education Society, Inc. University of New York Press, New York. p. 537
249. Kadam K.N, 1993. *Ambedkar: The Emancipator of the Oppressed,* Sangam Books, London. p. 105
250. Ibid
251. John Dewey, (1919; 1988). *'Philosophy and Democracy,'* in The *Middle Works,* vol. 11. Southern Illinois University Press, Carbondale. p. 97
252. Kadam K.N, 1993. *Ambedkar: The Emancipator of the Oppressed,* Sangam Books, London, p. 105
253. Asghar Ali Engeneer, ed., 1984. *Islam and Revolution,* Ajanta Published, New Delhi. p. 27
254. Keer, Dhananjay, 1987. *Dr. Ambedkar: Life and Mission,* Sangan Books, London. p. 254-255
255. John Dewey, 1995. *Religious Faith and Democratic Humanism,* Philosophy Education Society, Inc. University of New York Press, New York. p. 64
256. Ibid, p. 68
257. John Dewey, (1952). *'The Impact of Science on Society'.* London: George Allen &Unwin.p.178
258. John Dewey, (1952). *'The Impact of Science on Society'.* London: George Allen &Unwin. p. 179
259. Ambedkar, B.R, 1991. *Slavery and Untouchability: Which is worse?,* Dalit Dayal, New Delhi. p. 229-233.

260. Paradkar, B. A. M. 1968. *The Religious Quest of Ambedkar,* Ajay Prahaghan, New Delhi.p. 69
261. Joshi Lal Mani, 1977. *Studies in the Buddhistic Culture of India,* Motilal Banarasidass, New Delhi. p. 101
262. Ibid, p.102
263. Joshi Lal Mani, 1977. *Studies in the Buddhistic Culture of India,* Motilal Banarasidass, New Delhi. p. 102.

Chapter. 3

John Dewey and Ambedkar's Comparative Study on Socio - Political Philosophy

The main objective of this chapter is to explaining the John Dewey's and Ambedkar's comparative Study on social and political philosophy. For Dewey's mature thought in social theory is not only intimately linked to the theory of knowledge in its founding conceptual framework and naturalistic standpoint, but also complementary to it in its emphasis on the social dimension of inquiry both in its processes and its consequences. In fact, it would be reasonable to claim that Dewey's theory of inquiry cannot be fully understood either in the meaning of its central tenets or the significance of its originality without considering how it applies to social aims and values, the central concern of his ethical and social theory.

Dewey's political philosophy has not only benefited as a by-product of serious philosophical (and, it should be said, historical) attention to his work as a whole. Some have read him as a precursor of recent concerns about the relationship between liberal individualism and the social setting in which the individual is embedded. Indeed, Dewey sometimes reads like a forerunner not of Rorty but of a writer such as the Canadian philosopher Charles Taylor, who is keen to marry a doctrine of a socially embedded self with a historically and culturally self-conscious form of liberalism. Dewey has also been seen as a source of inspiration for notions of participatory or deliberative democracy and sometimes he reads like a forerunner of the German philosopher and social theorist Jürgen Habermas, who views autonomy and a particular talk-centred conception of democracy as mutually sustaining ideals for modern societies.

In the same way, Ambedkar, social and political theories are the basic need of freedom for the downtrodden people, as it would create a powerful community and nation building. He believed that liberation was necessary for the growth of a strong and powerful nation. Ambedkar said that social equality was a force which promises equal opportunity to all. The aim of this chapter is to explain the His quest and struggle for the liberation of marginalised had aimed to enter into the *Hindu* temples and his ideological foundation for the egalitarian society remained as the core of his social philosophy. Hinduism has lost the three principles of liberty; equality, fraternity.

Some people are born great, some have greatness thrust upon them and some achieve greatness. To the last category, Bhimrao Ramji Ambedkar belongs. Ambedkar was a great nationalist, political thinker, reformer and revolutionary and prolific writer with prodigious ideas. He stood for all scientific and social activities which enhanced the cause of human progress and happiness. His contribution in the making of the Constitution of India was phenomenal. He defiantly fought for the betterment of the oppressed classes. And in this struggle, he showed rare crusading spirit, carving out in the process an important place for himself among the prominent architects of modern India.

Dewey and Ambedkar's Ideas on Social Philosophy and Action

Dewey's liberal thought in social theory is not only intimately linked to the theory of knowledge in its founding conceptual framework and naturalistic standpoint, but also complementary to it in its emphasis on the social dimension of inquiry both in its processes and its consequences. In fact, it would be reasonable to claim that Dewey's theory of inquiry cannot be fully understood either in the meaning of its central tenets or the significance of its originality without considering how it applies to social aims and values, the central concern of his ethical and social theory.

Dewey rejected the atomistic understanding of society of the Hobbesian social contract theory, according to which the social, cooperative aspect of human life was grounded in the logically prior and fully articulated rational interests of individuals. Dewey's claim in *Experience* and *Nature* that the collection of meanings that constitute the mind have a social origin expresses the basic contention, one that he maintained throughout his career, that the human individual is a social being from the start, and that individual satisfaction and achievement can be realized only within the context of social habits and institutions that promote it.[264]

Social problems, for Dewey, are concerned with the guidance of human action to the achievement of socially defined ends that are productive of a satisfying life for individuals within the social context. Regarding the nature of what constitutes a satisfying life; Dewey was intentionally vague, out of his conviction that specific ends or goods can be defined only in particular socio-historical contexts. *In* the *Ethics* (1932) he speaks of the ends simply as the cultivation of interests in goods that recommend themselves in the light of calm reflection. In other works, such as *Human Nature* and *Conduct* and *Art* as *Experience,* he speaks of (1) the harmonizing of experience (the resolution of conflicts of habit and interest both within the individual and within society), (2) the release from tedium in favor of the enjoyment of variety and creative action, and (3) the expansion of meaning (the enrichment of the individual's appreciation of his or her circumstances within human culture and the world at large). The attunement of individual efforts to the promotion of these social ends constitutes, for Dewey, the central issue of ethical concern of the individual; the collective means for their realization is the paramount question of political policy.

In large part, then, Dewey's ideas in ethics and social theory were programmatic rather than substantive, defining the direction that he believed human thought and action must take in order to identify the conditions that promote the human good in its fullest sense, rather than specifying particular formulae or principles for individual and social action. He studiously avoided participating in what he regarded as the unfortunate practice of previous moral philosophers of offering general rules that legislate universal standards of conduct. But there are strong suggestions in a number of his works of basic ethical and social positions. In *Human Nature* and *Conduct* Dewey approaches ethical inquiry through an analysis of human character informed by the principles of scientific psychology. The analysis is reminiscent of Aristotelian ethics, concentrating on the central role of habit in formulating the dispositions of action that comprise character, and the importance of reflective intelligence as a means of modifying habits and controlling disruptive desires and impulses in the pursuit of worthwhile ends.

The social condition for the flexible adaptation that Dewey believed was crucial for human advancement is a democratic form of life, not instituted merely by democratic forms of governance, but by the inculcation of democratic habits of cooperation and public spiritedness, productive of an organized, self-conscious community of individuals responding to society's needs by experimental and inventive, rather than dogmatic, means. The development of these democratic habits, Dewey argues in *Society* and *Democracy,* must begin in the earliest years of a child's educational experience. Dewey rejected the notion that a child's education should be viewed as merely a preparation for civil life, during which disjoint facts and ideas are conveyed by the teacher and memorized by the student only to be utilized later on. The school should rather be viewed as an extension of civil society and continuous with it, and the student encouraged to operate as a member of a community, actively pursuing interests in cooperation with others. It is by a process of self-directed learning, guided by the cultural resources provided by teachers that Dewey believed a child is best prepared for the demands of responsible membership within the democratic community.[266]

For Ambedkar, Drafting a Constitution is by no means an easy task. It requires the highest statecraft, statesmanship, scholarship, intellectual acumen endowed with a flood of knowledge of the nation's and world history, the working of Constitutions in the democratic, totalitarian and dictatorship governments. To Ambedkar, the Constitution was not just the basic law for the governance of the country. It was a vehicle of the nation's progress, reflecting the best in the past traditions of the country, to cope with the needs of the present and possessing enough resilience to meet the needs of the future. At the same time he was of the view that it must be a living organ, not for one or two generations, but for generations to come. In that perspective, the provisions of the Constitution are couched in the language of generalities with pregnant contents of significance which vary from age to age and have at the same time transcendental continuity without any hiatus.

The heart of the Constitution is the Fundamental Rights given to every citizen and the Directive Principles to the executive and legislature for governance of the country. The idea behind them is to ensure certain basic rights to the citizens, so that they are not at the mercy of the shifting opinions of the legislators. The chapter on Fundamental Rights ensures the dignity of man as a human being and emphasises the creation of a casteless, classless and homogeneous society. Pandit Jawaharlal Nehru remarked: " Ambedkar had played a most important part in the framing of India's Constitution. No one took greater trouble and care over Constitution-making than Dr. Ambedkar."[267] He carved a unique and impregnable pride of place and honour in the history of the free Indian nation. So long as the Indian Constitution survives, the name of Babasaheb Ambedkar will remain immortal. He lives forever in the hearts of every downtrodden.

Ambedkar's believed in a democratic system of government and power to the people had been a major concern for him. He was very clear that unless citizens have power in their own hands, there could be no democracy. That is why he says that democracy rests on four premises, where the citizen remains at the centre:

- The individual is an end in itself.
- The individual has certain inalienable rights, which must be guaranteed to him by the Constitution.
- The individual shall not be required to relinquish any of his constitutional rights as a price of any privilege.

The state shall not delegate power to private persons to govern others. The core of Dr Ambedkar's political thinking is contained in two of his statements: (1) rights are protected not by law but by the social and moral conscience of society; and (2) a democratic form of government presupposes a democratic form of society. Social conscience is the only safeguard of all rights, fundamental or non-fundamental. The prevalent view, that once rights are enacted in a law they are safeguarded, is unwarranted. The formal framework of democracy is of no value. Democracy is essentially a form of society, a mode of associated living. The roots of democracy are to be searched in the social relationship, in the terms of associated life between the people who form a society.

Ambedkar's expertise as a constitutional expert went a long way in enshrining the concepts of political democracy in the Indian Constitution. To him, political democracy cannot last unless there lies at the base of it social democracy. Social democracy is a way of life which recognizes liberty, equality and fraternity as the principles of life. These principles are not to be treated as separate items but in a trinity. They form a union of trinity in the sense that to divorce one from the other is to defeat the very purpose of democracy. Unless there is social democracy, power to the people would remain a distant dream.

Ambedkar knew that mere adoption of a democratic system of government in the Constitution would not be sufficient. Equality in society, equality before law and administration, constitutional morality, lack of tyranny of the majority and developing public conscience are conditions for the success of democracy in India. The foremost condition for democracy, in Ambedkar's opinion, is equality in society as equality is the foundation stone where the notions of liberty and fraternity develop. He remarked that equality is the original notion and respect for human personality is a reflection of it. If equality is denied, everything else may be taken to be denied.[268] Ambedkar also recognized the fact that the lofty ideals expressed in the Constitution would remain as they were, given the nature of contradictions inherent in society. Absence of equality on the social and economic plane is a cause of contradictions. This has resulted in a society based on the principle of graded inequality on the social plane which means elevation for some and degradation for others. On the economic plane there are some in society who have immense wealth as against many who live in abject poverty. To deny equality in social and political life would be putting political democracy in peril. If the contradictions are not removed, those who suffer from inequality will blow up the structure of political democracy which Constituent Assembly has laboriously built up.

The observations made by Ambedkar on November, 25, 1949 are prophetic and relevant considering the present political situation in our country. However the good a Constitution may be, it is sure to turn out bad because those who are called to work it, happen to be a bad lot. However bad a Constitution may be, it may turn out to be good if those who are called to work it, happen to be a good lot.[269] The working of the Constitution does not depend wholly upon the nature of the Constitution. The Constitution can provide only the organs of state such as legislature, the executive and the judiciary. The factors on which the workings of these organs of state depend are the people and the political parties they will set up as their instruments to carry out their wishes and policies. It is, therefore, futile to pass any judgment upon the Constitution without reference to the part which the people and their parties are likely to play.

Moreover, Dewey, the character and value of freedom was as the Idealists and New Liberals that he drew on, part of a debate about the proper scope of political action. The classical identification of liberty with negative liberty bolsters the identification of freedom with the sphere of life outside the scope of political action. By contrast, for Dewey the scope of legitimate social and political action had to be determined experimentally. The replacement of liberal policies with what Dewey called intelligent social control or social action is presented as a requirement of positive liberty or individuality, in modern industrial conditions. The identification of freedom with individuality in Dewey's sense allows the necessary means for achieving individuality to be understood as necessary conditions of freedom. So, for example, throughout his life he argued that education to produce undocile, unservile citizens was essential, in the name of individuality. More pointedly, Dewey argued, particularly in the 1930s, that a socialized economy was necessary for individuality. Dewey drew on a wide range of sources to bolster his conception of social action or social control (including the utopian Edward Bellamy and British guild socialist G. D. H. Cole), but much of his writing is unstructured and occasional and spread across many different contexts over a long period rather than systematic or prescriptive in a very specific way.

Dewey was anti-authoritarian, in the sense that he did not believe that the liberal rights protected in the name of individual liberty (such as freedoms of speech, thought, movement, and so on) should be dispensed with. Individuality as an ethical ideal requires that individuals find their own way, and not have particular doctrines or social roles imposed on them. Furthermore, viewing liberty through the prism of individuality only opens up the possibility of political action in the name of liberty, but it does not itself require it. Finally, and in contrast to technocratic critics of *laissez-faire* such as Walter Lippmann, Dewey argues that an extensive form of democracy is essential for social action.

Dewey's social philosophy was the importance of preparing people for democratic citizenship. He stressed that consciously guided social aimed at developing the "mental equipment" and moral character of people was essential to the development of civic character. He formulated a program for developing what he called "scientific thinking" the mental habit of free inquiry, tolerance of alternative viewpoints, and free communication. He also believed in cultivating people's capacity for the exercise of deliberative, practical reason in moral situations. He urged teachers to teach not "ready-made knowledge," as he called it, but a method that would enhance moral reasoning. The best way to do this, he said, was to introduce people at the outset to "a mode of associated living" characteristic of democracy. A school should be a community of full participation and "conjoint communicated experience" in which social sympathy and deliberative moral reason would develop.[270]

Dewey's social is the role of the public in a democracy. Dewey formulated what remains one of the most wide-ranging and persuasive arguments for a strong public sphere. His theory was initially developed in response to the widespread effort following World War I to reconstruct democratic theory according to the norms of objective science. Largely a product of the new alliance between psychology (especially behaviorism) and political analysis, this movement emphasized the irrational motivation underlying human social life and raised serious questions about the capacity of ordinary citizens for the sort of rational deliberation and judgment.

In the same line Ambedkar was, par excellence, a spokesman of the ignored humanity the workers, small peasants and landless labourers. He expressed the sorrows of the untouchables and tried sincerely to channel the activities of the depressed classes. In mobilising them, he created a sense of self-respect and pride in them. He dedicated his life to the cause of removal of untouchability and completely identified himself with the socially segregated section of the Indian society.

He launched a life-long crusade for liberating them from their centuries-old enslavement and ostracism. It is this crusade which "lifted him up high from a mere ghetto boy to a legend in his own lifetime". He was born an untouchable and therefore he had an intense yearning to see that the untouchables are better placed in social, political and economic fields. He rejected social reforms received as charity and accommodation. He wanted social reforms as of right. He was not so much for peripheral social reforms in Hindu society like widow remarriage and abolition of child marriage. He was for a total reorganization and reconstruction of the Hindu society on two main principles equality and absence of casteism.

The socially progressive values that Ambedkar's cherished were the basis of his social and political life. Though he was born in the dalit community, he never represented his own community but represented all those communities which were socially and economically downtrodden. He has been variously described as a crusader for the rights of the depressed classes of India, a literary genius, an eminent educationist, a political philosopher and an able parliamentarian. He was an indefatigable activist who by virtue of his formidable intellectual attributes started a movement for attainment of self-respect for the untouchables as well as depressed classes. He carried on a relentless struggle against the social, political and economic segregation of these classes.

Ambedkar's thinking arose out of his acute dissatisfaction with the anomalous treatment meted out to the people of his community. His mind was preoccupied with the social amelioration, political enlightenment, economic well-being and spiritual awakening of the downtrodden. He had a deep faith in fundamental human rights, in the equal rights of man and woman, in the dignity of the individual, in the promotion of better standards of life and, above all, in peace and security in all spheres of human life. He was a champion of a revolution to be brought about by the dynamics of public opinion through a change in the laws of the land. He was not a *Utopian,* but a realist. He saw a vast difference between a revolution and real social change. A revolution transfers political power from one party to another or one nation to another. The transfer of power must be accompanied by such distribution of power that the result would be a real social change in the relative strength of forces operating in society.[271]

Ambedkar was totally committed to the annihilation of the caste system. According to him, caste system is not merely a division of labour but a division of labourers. It is a hierarchy in which the division of labourers is graded one above other. This division of labour is based on neither natural aptitude nor choice of the individual concerned. It is, therefore, harmful inasmuch as it involves the subordination of man's natural powers and inclinations to the exigencies of social rules. Ambedkar reiterated: The caste system prevents common activity and by preventing it, it has prevented the Hindus from becoming a society with unified life and a consciousness of its own being.

Ambedkar's great vision enjoined the abolition of casteism in every shape and form, since he was opposed to all divisive forces and aimed at strengthening the impulse of national integration. The greatly cherished ideals of "fraternity and equality were the cement with which he wanted to bind together a totally cohesive nation". Ambedkar's philosophy was that self-respect and human dignity were of paramount importance in a free republic. He espoused the noble cause of equality of status and opportunity to every Indian, assuring the dignity of the individual and unity of the nation. He was not merely a learned man, but also an intellectual who sacrificed his life for the dignity and uplift of the poorest of the poor of the world. His aim was not communal and not limited to personal benefit, but it was essentially social and human, related to all whom suffered from slavery, injustice, tyranny and exploitation. Ambedkar's principle was not to fight against the particular persons who created a frustrating situation for him and his fellow sufferers, because the cause of the situation was not these persons but the social philosophy which supported a social system of inequalities. His long-range response was a direct attack against the root cause.

It is pertinent to raise some questions to reflect on Ambedkar's legacy. Have his projects shaped out as he would have wished? Has India moved in the direction that he thought optimal? Have his inheritors embalmed his ideas in dogma, or extended them while confronting new predicaments? Ambedkar's vision did not end at the horizon of Dalit power; rather, he envisaged an India liberated from caste consciousness, a futuristic society no longer trapped in the feudal binaries of master and slave, privilege and privation. Ironically, again, this vision has been negated by the perpetuation of caste attitudes in an electoral democracy whose political dynamics are fuelled by group antagonisms. With group identitities and interests raised to a cornerstone of political struggle, India now faces the long-running scenario of a caste war fought out on various social and economic fronts, at varying intensities.[272]

Ambedkar's dream of a society based on socio- economic justice, human dignity and equality is yet to be realised. So we cannot stop with Ambedkar and his programmed of social reform. We have to go beyond Ambedkar in our struggle to establish an egalitarian society. Ambedkar's legacy will have to be retrieved and extended by activists committed to the social and cultural renaissance he had envisioned; and not by the political purveyors of an exhausted rhetoric who claim to speak in his name.

Moreover Dewey's social justice is very philosophical and understandable. Postmodernists long for a time when all of society's ills and abuses will be eliminated and social justice will prevail. Richard Rorty elaborates his vision for America: "(Walt) Whitman and (John) Dewey tried to substitute hope for knowledge. They wanted to put shared utopian dreams of an ideally decent and civilized society in the place of knowledge of God's Will, Moral Law, the Laws of History, or the Facts of Science. As long as we have a functioning political left, we still have a chance to achieve our country, to make it the country of Whitman's and Dewey's dreams."[273]

Rorty's language is idealistic the goal is nothing less than "an ideally decent and civilized society."[274] Rorty further develops this idea: "(Whitman and Dewey) wanted utopian America to replace God as the unconditional object of desire. They wanted the struggle for social justice to be the country's animating principle, the nation's soul."[275] Elsewhere Rorty reiterates the desire to substitute "social justice for individual freedom as our country's principal goal."[276]

The Postmodern understanding of social justice revolves around the "other." Derrida's phrase "the singularity of the other" and Rorty's term "otherness" refer to those who are marginalized by society the poor, unemployed, migrants, Hispanics, blacks, women, gays and lesbians.[277] This is equivalent to the Marxist idea that virtue resides only among the oppressed and forms the foundation for identity politics.

Social justice in the Post modern sense means giving oppressed groups their due in society. Oppressed groups have traditionally been identified according to their race, sex, or gender as well as their economic level. To achieve economic equality requires governmental redistribution of wealth take from the rich and give to the poor a common theme among leftists. Rorty refers to Dewey's utopian dream, and while Dewey was not a Postmodernist, Rorty draws from Dewey's pragmatism to express his own political hopes. In that light, it is noteworthy that Dewey was himself the head of the League for Industrial Democracy, the American counterpart to the British Fabian Society a socialistic organization founded in 1883.[278] Both of these organizations attempted to influence their governments toward socialism.

In the same manner Ambedkar's theory of social justice has been defined in the paper as a principle that lays down the foundation of a society based on equality, liberty and fraternity. Although Plato and

Rawls have not defined social justice in these specific terms, yet these aforesaid principles can be inferred from their writings on social justice. Once this proposition about social justice is accepted it was easy to infer from Ambedkar's writings and speeches published posthumously, that equality, liberty, and fraternity are the basic principles of his theory as well. To begin with Ambedkar argues that for establishment of a society where individual is an end in himself and the aim and objective of society is the growth of the individual and development of his personality. He expected that there should be multiple channels and conjoint communicated experience. Further for Ambedkar Equality, liberty and fraternity cannot be divorced from each other. He had argued that, without equality liberty would produce the supremacy of the few over many. Equality without liberty would kill individual initiative. Without fraternity, liberty and equality could not become a natural course of things. Moreover, Ambedkar had envisaged that social justice could be brought when political democracy is extended in social and economic field as well. This has to be done through constitutional means and by breaking the monopoly of the erstwhile political and social elites. That is why he wanted that the Dalits and other marginalized sections of the society should join the administration. Ambedkar was aware of the existing corruption and biases in the Indian administration and judiciary. For him incorporation of aspiration of the marginalized categories in the rules and policy is not enough for dispensing social justice but incorporation of the individuals is also a must condition for dispensing justice.[279]

Hence Ambedkar's theory of social justice becomes akin to Plato and John Rawls's theory of social justice. Further, with the help of Beteille's analysis of distributive justice which includes distribution of benefits equally to every member of society, equality before law, equal protection of laws and equality of opportunity reflect upon the other elements of Ambedkar's theory of social justice. In this context we can observe that Ambedkar had already enshrined these values in the Constitution of India. The value of equality in the preamble of the Indian Constitution is not only a slogan. Rather it has been substantiated with equality of opportunity (Article 16) and equality of condition that is reservation (Articles 330, 332, 335 and 46). This was done specifically because he might have thought that in a hierarchical society, like India, equality of opportunity may in turn produce inequality and subordination.

Dewey's and Ambedkar's Thoughts on Political Philosophy

Dewey's political philosophy is liberal and ideal manner. The first is an important formative condition of his ethical and political thinking, the Idealist and New Liberal assault on the misguided individualism of the classical liberal tradition. From a very early point of his intellectual development, Dewey, like the British Idealist T. H. Green (on whom he wrote several essays) and the New Liberal L. T. Hobhouse, accepted that traditional liberalism in part rested on a false conception of the individual, which was ethically pernicious in its effect on liberal thought. Accordingly, many of the themes that characterised Dewey's thinking about social and political theory after his turn to 'experimentalism' were present in his earlier, overtly Idealist political philosophy. In texts such as 'The Ethics of Democracy' *(EW1)* and 'Christianity and Democracy' *(EW4)*, Dewey elaborates a version of the Idealist criticisms of classical liberal individualism. For this line of criticism, classical liberalism envisages the individual as an independent entity in competition with other individuals, and takes social and political life as a sphere in which this competitive pursuit of self-interest is coordinated. By contrast, the Idealists and New Liberals rejected this view of social and political life as the aggregation of inherently conflicting private interests. Instead, they sought to view individuals relationally: individuality could be sustained only where social life was understood as an organism in which the well-being of each part was tied to the well-being of the whole. Freedom in a 'positive' sense consisted not merely in the absence of external constraints but the positive fact of participation in such an ethically desirable social order. As Dewey puts it, 'men are not isolated non-social atoms, but are men only when in intrinsic relations' to one another, and the state in turn only represents them 'so far as they have become organically related to one another, or are possessed of unity of purpose and interest.'[280]

Dewey is anti-elitist, and argues that the capacity of the wise few to discern the public interest tends to be distorted by their position.

Democratic participation is not only viewed as a bulwark against government by elites, but also as an aspect of individual freedom - humanity cannot rest content with a good 'procured from without.' Furthermore, democracy is not 'simply and solely a form of government', but a social and personal ideal; in other words, it is not only a property of political institutions but of a wide range of social relationships. This ideal is common to a range of social spheres, and should take 'industrial, as well as civil and political' forms.[281] For this ideal to be effective requires a democratically educated citizenry. A distinctive emphasis of these early works is that it is through democracy in this extended and ideal sense that, Dewey believes, 'the incarnation of God in man ... becomes a living, present thing ... The truth is brought down to life, its segregation removed; it is made a common trust enacted in all departments of action, not in one isolated sphere called religious'[282] While the Christian conception of democracy recedes (but does not entirely disappear) in Dewey's later work, the idea that democracy should be viewed as a form of relationship that cuts across different spheres of social life and unifies them remains important. These crucial features of his early political philosophy survived, then, the jettisoning of Idealism: holism about the individual; anti-elitism; democratic participation as an aspect of individual freedom; and the unconventional view of democracy as a form of relationship inherent not merely in political institutions but in a wide range of social spheres.

While the Idealist and New Liberal assault on individualism is one important element of the intellectual background to Dewey's political philosophy, this should also be located against the background of his own mature conception of inquiry. A distinctive and central theme in Dewey's epistemology was the rejection of a 'spectator theory' of knowledge, which he thought dominated western philosophy. For this kind of theory, knowledge was understood on the model of the observation of a fixed and independent object on the part of a subject. The spectator account of knowledge was accompanied by a 'quest for certainty' in epistemology; that is, a search for a fixed and certain foundation for knowledge claims, for example in a *priori* truths or in the incorrigible data of our senses. Dewey aimed to displace this conception of knowledge with a notion of inquiry, understood as the struggle of human intelligence to solve problems. The goal of such inquiry was not to arrive at a certain picture of the nature of things, but at an inevitably provisional solution to the practical and intellectual problem that sparked inquiry.

Three features of this conception can be usefully underlined here: inquiry as problem-solving, as historical and progressive, and as communal. We engage in inquiry, Dewey thought, as part of a struggle with an objectively precarious but improvable environment. Inquiry is demanded by what he calls an 'incomplete' or 'problematic' situation, that is, one in which something must be done. The goal of inquiry is not simply a change in the beliefs of the inquirers but the resolution of the problematic situation, in what he calls a 'consummatory' course of action or state of affairs. The modern natural sciences, he argues, have been progressive and cumulative, giving us greater and greater control of the natural world. This has above all been the result of their *experimental* character, in which no intellectual element is taken to be beyond rational scrutiny. Theories and hypotheses are invented, used, tested, and revised, and so on. At the same time, new methods for the invention, use, testing and revision of theories and hypotheses are developed and refined, and so are new standards for evaluating theories and hypotheses. What counts as success in inquiry is some practice's meeting these standards, but these standards themselves may be judged in the light of how they square with ongoing practices of inquiry. In this way, the methods used by science are not fixed but themselves have a history and develop progressively and sometimes in unexpected ways. What counts as knowledge is defined as 'the product of competent inquiries'; beyond this, the meaning of the term 'is so empty that any content or filling may be arbitrarily poured in.'[283] Third, inquiry is social or communal, in the sense that its findings must be subject to scrutiny and testing by other inquirers: 'an inquirer in a given special field appeals to the experiences of the community of his fellow workers for confirmation and correction of results.'[284]

Dewey's conception of inquiry is intended as a general model of reflective intelligence, and he argues against drawing an a *priori* distinction between, for example, inquiry in ethics and politics and in the natural sciences. Indeed, he argues that *values* are constructed in order to resolve problematic situations, and valuation is conceived as reflective thought that responds to such situations, with the aim of providing means for what Dewey calls the 'directed resolution' of the situation. Strikingly, for example, in *Art* as *Experience,* he analyses the work of the French painters Paul Cézanne and Henri Matisse in terms of problem-solving, with the goal of 'consummatory' experience.

Dewey's political philosophy as the marriage of the Idealist and New Liberal view of liberalism with his pragmatist or experimentalist conception of inquiry. Many other influences were significant over a long working life. But to view matters in this way does capture a great deal of what is distinctive about Dewey's political thinking. Dewey suggested that Values can be viewed as constructs to solve practical problems. Like an outmoded piece of technology, a past value which was once constructed to address a problem in one set of circumstances can outlive its usefulness, and become a hindrance to the capacity of those in the present to deal with their practical needs and worries.

This, Dewey believes, is the case with values of classical liberalism. These have come to block the capacity to resolve social problems in a way compatible with what he takes to be liberalism's core commitment to individual liberty. It is in this way that 'the slogans of liberalism in one period can become the bulwarks of reaction' in the next.[285] He develops this thought in discussing the relation of individual and society, the character and value of freedom, and the scope of legitimate social and political action.

Whereas Ambedkar is influenced by all the major political traditions of his times. His political thought has emerged from the three grand traditions of political thought, i.e. liberal, conservative and radical. The unique feature about him is that he has transcended all these traditions. He was influenced by the ideas of John Dewey, the pragmatic American and the teacher of him. The Fabian Edwin R. A. Seligman had considerable impact on his thought. He often quoted Edmund Burke, the conservative thinker of British, though we can't brand Ambedkar as conservative. Ambedkar's notion of liberty comes close to T.H. Green.

Ambedkar's political philosophy is primarily ethical and religious. He thoroughly explored the Indian traditions and its philosophical systems in a unique way. He developed political concepts like democracy, justice, state and rights from his understanding of Indian society and the functioning of its institutions on the moral grounds. He is very critical of the institution of caste, which influences all the spheres of individual's life and the Indian society as a whole.

He further discusses how individual is related to society and how individual's freedom is limited by other social forces. He is critical of authoritarian Hindu social order and argued in favor of democratic society. He probed into the moral and social foundations of India and gave new meaning to the lives of disadvantaged people. His was a rationale approach. Reason plays a role in his writings and speeches. The methodology he used is very scientific rather speculative. He was influenced by the assumptions of modernity. He is well informed in many areas of Indian history, polity, culture, anthropology and philosophy. He quotes many thinkers in his writings those who are influenced him.

Ambedkar's political philosophy and its impact on Indian society and polity with reference to man and society, state and government, nation and nationalism, democracy, socialism, security, social justice, education and emancipation of the downtrodden. The notion of community is central to his thinking. To say that individuals make up society is trivial; society is always composed of caste system.

It may be exaggeration to assert the theory of class conflict, but the existence of definite castes in society is a fact... an individual in a society is always a member of a class. A caste is an enclosed class. Brahmins created caste and it is extended to other servile classes. Caste is endogamous unit and also a communal unit. His political theory was premised on moral community. It was as an ideal to be realised. He was very much critical about the Hindu social order. He argues that Hinduism is not qualified to be a community. Buddhism was projected as the ideal having the value of community grounding on morality. He considers that Buddhism attempted to found society on the basis of 'reason' and 'morality.'[287]

His conception of community is very novel. He does not confirm to either Hindu ideal community or Marxist conception of community based on participation in production process. His conception of community is moral and ethical. It is not automatically available for participation in common affairs. His idea of community has to be created through hard and torturous process of moral transformation.

Moreover Ambedkar has emerged as a major political philosopher with the rise of dalit movement in contemporary times. There are several attempts to understand Ambedkar and his philosophy. Confusion prevails among scholars due to the existence of diverse, and sometimes, contradictory theoretical assessment of Ambedkar. The social context of the scholars and their subjective positions play major role in the assessment of the thinker and very often the opinions of scholars evoke extreme reactions which either elevate or demean Ambedkar. Though he had a great influence on Indian politics from the nationalist movement onwards, till eighties, there has been not much academic debate on Ambedkar. The communities of knowledge and centre of power either ignored or deliberately marginalized him as a thinker and social scientist. Ambedkar is nowhere mentioned in the contemporary Indian philosophy and the philosophical discourses of India.

This exclusion of Ambedkar has to be understood with the implicit politics of the writers on Indian philosophy. Very interestingly, the masses /communities of under privileged of Indian society bring him into the forefront. It is not exaggeration to say that there is no major village in the country without the statue of Ambedkar.[288] He is the most celebrated symbol of the contemporary times. Due to the masses/Dalit communities symbolic association with Ambedkar, political parties and academics ranging from conservatives to radicals, are forced to look at Ambedkar. The celebration of Ambedkar has the undercurrent of failure of Indian democratic State to reach the majority of this nation and the assertion of these ignored communities in other words, Ambedkar's philosophy is a search towards the theories of social reconstruction of Indian society. Ambedkar was not merely an exploratory and idealistic political philosopher, in the conventional sense, like Plato and Aristotle. Nevertheless, he developed affairs. His political philosophy attempted to erode the dichotomies between theory and practice, materialism and spiritualism, more importantly between human beings stratified into contending castes and communities. Ambedkar's political ideology evolved from his total engagement with this predicament of Indian society.

Dewey criticizes classical liberalism for conceiving of the individual as 'something given, something already there', prior to society and for viewing social institutions for coordinating the interests of pre-social individuals. Instead, he argues, social institutions are not 'means for obtaining something for individuals. They are means for creating individuals.'[289] In this way, classical liberalism exemplifies 'the most pervasive fallacy of philosophical thinking.' This is the tendency to divide up experienced phenomena, and to take the distinct analyzed elements to be separate existences, independent both of the analysis and of each other. That this abstraction is in particular circumstances essential for inquiry is an important theme in Dewey's philosophy. But this abstraction goes wrong 'whenever the distinctions or elements that are discriminated are treated as if they were final and self-sufficient'[291] as when classical liberalism treats the individual as 'something given.' Instead, Dewey argues, 'liberalism knows that an individual is nothing fixed, given ready-made. It is something achieved, and achieved not in isolation but with the aid and support of conditions, cultural and physical: including in "cultural", economic, legal and political institutions as well as science and art.'[292]

The abstraction of the individual from social context in classical liberalism shapes its ethics. If the individual is thought of as existing prior to social institutions, then it is easier to envisage securing freedom for the individual in terms solely of the removal of external impediments on individual action, such as legal restrictions on freedom of speech. By contrast, Dewey argues that mere absence of external constraint is not a sufficient condition for freedom in the sense in which the latter is a value for liberals. For classical liberalism or 'old individualism', the individual is viewed as surrounded by a protective cordon of rights, which define his or her freedom.

Freedom is taken to consist in the absence of some intentional constraint on the individual's ability to pursue his or her chosen goals. For Dewey, this negative view of freedom is at the root of the wider social, ethical and political defects of this form of individualism.[293] What is valuable about freedom is not the negative absence of interference but the positive 'power to be an individualized self.'[294]

Dewey's view of individuality is complex, but three elements seem most prominent: individuality is reflective, it is social, and it must be exercised in order to be enjoyed. The first point is that freedom is held to consist in the capacity and willingness on the part of a person to reflect on her or his own goals, aims and projects, and to revise them as a result of this reflection. Individuality in what we may call a weak sense is universally possessed and consists in the distinctive patterns of response to the environment that each person displays, 'a distinctive way of feeling the impacts of the world and of showing a preferential bias in response to these impacts.'[295] In the strong sense in which it is a value for liberals, individuality consists in the personal capacity for *choice,* 'the most characteristic activity of a self.'[296] This is not a matter of arbitrarily or whimsically plumping for one option rather than another, for Dewey. Rather, choice that is expressive of individuality in the strong sense involves intelligent criticism of options. Accordingly, we can understand why Dewey claims that 'to foresee future objective alternatives and to be able by deliberation to choose one of them and thereby weigh its chances in the struggle for future existence, measures our freedom.'[297]

Second, freedom as individuality is social: it is thought to involve participation in shaping the social conditions that bear on individuality. As Dewey puts it in *The Public and Its Problems,* liberty 'is that secure release and fulfillment of personal potentialities which take place only in rich and manifold association with others: the power to be an individualized self making a distinctive contribution and enjoying in its own way the fruits of association.'[298] Freedom in its fullest sense, then, is only possible in a canonical form of social order, in which all take part in shaping the conditions of common life. Third, Dewey possesses what has been called an *exercise* rather than an *opportunity* concept of freedom. For some positive theories of *liberty,* including Dewey's, it is a necessary condition of an agent's being free that he or she should actually pursue those ends outlined by that theory as constitutive of the good that is, he or she should exercise the opportunity. He is in possession of my liberty in the valuable sense for Dewey only if he actually act in these ways. The value of individual liberty requires the reconstruction of the social order along the participatory and democratic lines that Dewey sees as intrinsic to this value.

In the same way Ambedkar was also shaped his ideas from western political liberalism into Indian democratic socio-political manner. Let us have a brief look at major philosophical traditions of politics before we proceed into the political philosophy of Ambedkar. Political philosophers sought to explore social phenomena and political behavior, (often in a historical context) as well as to clarify problematic concepts, evaluate existing institutions, and argue for social ideal. Political philosophy is about the critical reflection of politics and its practices. It is about the understanding of the governing principles of a society in a much more critical fashion. It tries to philosophize the values, principles, practices and institutions, which govern the society. Philosophers gave different interpretations about the meaning of public life and governing principles of good society. Morality of the society and the ways of functioning of institutions serve as source in deriving political theory. Socio-political developments and the ensuing conflicts in society provide conditions for the emergence of new social and political theories. Political thought seems to spring from the political experience of both the thinker and his society. Political theory is nothing but the systematization of moral and political judgments of our activities.

Historically, Greek thought followed the Christian natural law. In the west, Christian natural law was undermined by the individualism of seventeenth century. Relationship between individual and god was replaced by the relationship between individual and individual as the foundation of social enquiry. This individualism becomes the basic characteristic of the subsequent liberal tradition. The idea of social initiative and social control surrendered to the idea of individual initiative and individual control. In simple terms, new material conditions gave birth to new social relationships and new philosophy was evolved to afford a rational justification for the new world which had come into being. This new philosophy became known as liberalism. Liberalism acquired different flavors in different national cultures. The difficulties in liberal theory lie in its basic foundations of seventeenth century individualism and its quality of possessiveness. The possessive quality lies in the conception of the individual as essentially the proprietor of his own person or capacities owing nothing to society. The individual was seen neither as a moral whole, nor as a part of a larger social whole, but as a proprietor of himself. The basic assumption of possessive individualism that man is free and human by virtue of his sole proprietorship of his own person, and that human society is essentially a series of market relations, were deeply embedded in seventeenth century foundations.[300] The inconsistency lies inherently in the market society itself. Market society automatically brings the class differentiations. The propertied class would like to hold power over the subordinate classes. Men no longer saw themselves fundamentally equal in an inevitable subjection to the determination of market. Alternatives emerged for the market system. Articulation of proletarian politics gave a serious blow to the liberal politics. There are altogether different assumptions about man and society. The community has replaced individual. Marxist theory aims at the radical change in society and its human relations.

Human society has seen from the perspective of the class considers human being as primarily a producer. His relations are determined by his involvement in social production. Other than the Marxist notion there is a conservative political theory would like to see society from the point of view of community. Conservatism has reverence for tradition, religion and age old custom. Edmund Burke is the one of the examples for conservative tradition. Burke more than any thinker of eighteenth century approached the political tradition with a sense of religious reverence. The conservative view of politics is known as politics of tradition. The state in particular and society in general must operate with respect to traditions and customs. The rights of the groups are acknowledged in that particular society. Conservative perspective works within the limits of the given order accepting forms of political action within the structural framework of existing institutions. Conservative theory of politics is known as politics of imperfection. It finds limitations with human beings and believes that human beings will be unable to create a social order through their own spontaneous efforts. People are inherently greedy and selfish. To restrain them there is a need for a state. The power is state. State plays a central role in conservative thought. It is the backbone of social order and authority, the guarantor of social hierarchy. As per the conservative views, the inherent imperfections of human nature make a strong state necessary. It is needed to control the anti-social impulses of the individual. As per the traditional conservative perspective, social order is not and can never be achieved spontaneously by the free play of individual activities as claimed by liberals and anarchists. Social order has to be maintained through the strong leadership of those who hold positions of political responsibility. It does not mean that state is the only agency which maintains social order. Conservatives stress the importance of tradition, custom and of network of longstanding groups and associations, all pre- requisites of social order.

In the late1970s political scientist Fred R. Dallmayr reiterated the statement of Peter Laslett, "the great tradition of theoretical literature stretching from Hobbes to Bosanquet had been broken and that for the moment, anyway, political philosophy is dead."[301] The crisis in political philosophy may be understood with the changed socio-economic developments and the un-relatedness of intellectual to the politics. In twentieth century, western political philosophy is marked with its defense of liberal democracy and legacy of civil rights against totalitarian or repressive forces. The economic practices and scientific rationality of west got different meaning in the developing nations. In recent times, the culmination of western science and economics leading towards dominance over other parts of the world invites competition and confrontation at global level. This situation has compelled the west to rethink and reformulate its central premises of its philosophy, and its conception of 'reason'. And at the same time, there is a need to critically understand what constitutes 'subjectivity' and its cognitive activity.

This dilemma seems to be aptly captured by Fred Dallmayr, 'In the domain of political thought, the contemporary dilemma can be phrased broadly in terms of the relationship between 'contract' and 'community.''[302] Society is of collectives and generates political community. Far from involving only the aspect of inter subjective or inter individual contracts, a revision or modification of individualism in the light of communal bonds necessitates a general reconsideration of man's relation to the world and nature-a reconsideration that inevitably conjures up the peril of objectivism and naturalism. Contemporary political theory appears precariously lodged at the cross roads of liberal individualism and post individualist communalism. Christian Bay elaborates this in his article 'From Contract to Community', he links up the major predicaments of post-industrial society with the basic assumptions and preferences of 'individualistic contract liberalism' as inaugurated by Hobbes and Locke and it manifested in different forms.

He notes that, liberals have 'persistently tended to cut the citizen off from the person', putting on their pedestal 'a cripple of a man' without a 'moral or political nature' and without 'moorings in any real community.' However, the debates of political philosophy in later days tried to articulate from the point of community or individual in relation to community.

Ambedkar's thoughts, as reflected in his writings and speeches has great importance in tracing the history and growth of western social thought in India. It is necessary to understand the philosophy of Ambedkar which is the theoretical foundation for the Dalit movement. The core of political thinking of Ambedkar is contained in two of his statements- the rights are protected not by law but by social and moral conscience of society, and a democratic form of government presupposes a democratic form of society. He considers democracy essentially as a form of society of a more associated living and a social conscience is the only safe guard of all rights. The roots of democracy are to be searched in social relationships, in terms of associated life among the people who form a society. For him, social relationships are the key to democracy. Ambedkar is a social democrat in spirit and practice. His special contribution to political thought lies in his linking up liberty, equality and fraternity to the concept of social democracy, which in turn, he relates to democracy as a form of government. He further reminds the limitations of social democracy in everyday functioning. As he categorically stated while addressing the constituent assembly.[304] 'Political democracy cannot last unless there lies at the base of it social democracy' which means, a way of life which recognize liberty, equality and fraternity as the principles of life.' In this sense he defined democracy as a form and method of government whereby revolutionary changes in the economic and social life of people are brought about without bloodshed.

In most of the speeches and writings of Ambedkar, the central theme is social reformism. He often debated and confronted on the issue of precedence of social over political issues. Politics have to be necessarily connected to the social issues. The very foundations of democracy lie in associated living in society. On the issue of giving primacy to social over political, he differs with congress and socialists. This is well reflected in all his writings in general and his writings 'Annihilation of caste' and 'what congress and Gandhi have done to untouchables' in particular.[305]

In contemporary times, once 'caste' got theoretically recognized and established as the Indian social reality, the established political and social theories got new meanings. Ambedkar as a thinker got prominence because of his scholarly conceptualization of the institution of caste and its functioning in Indian society. He interpreted the Indian social world in order to change the lives of the Dalit masses who are the victims of caste system. The situation demands proper assessment of Ambedkar's political philosophy in relation to other prominent political streams of the time. Ambedkar is a real philosopher in the Marxian sense. He has interpreted the Indian social reality in order to change it.

Gail Omvedt, well known scholar in social movements assesses Ambedkar's political thought in search of new vision for India. Her interpretations of Ambedkar's ideas as enunciated in a memorial lecture, "Liberty, Equality, Community, Ambedkar's Vision of a New Social Order"[306] will be discussed here. Ambedkar, like Marx, is against exploitation, but not against development and accumulation. At a social level, he believes in progress in history, and at an individual level he gives legitimating to honest and energetic efforts of 'householders' to work and earn. While he doesn't fit clearly into a historical materialist position, his writings show an evolutionary and 'strategist' view of history. This social evolutionary model differed from the more economically based versions offered by Marx or more conventional sociologists. History then does show progress. What plays the basic role in determining social structure and conditioning human actions? This is the great question of sociological and historical materialism versus idealism (pluralism). Was Ambedkar an idealist because he gave so much importance to the role of religion and ideas in action?

Gail Omvedt finds difficulty in fixing him to a particular political and philosophical position. At the same time she makes an attempt to develop Ambedkar's political thought. She notes that Ambedkar doesn't spend any time developing or explicitly stating his methodology. She identifies different phases in Ambedkar and also tries to provide a comprehensive and coherent thought of Ambedkar as a whole in the concrete situations of India. She observes that in his early essay on Russell, he projects the economic interpretation of history and at the other end of his life he seems to have moved towards idealism. He argued against the basic theses of Marx that the economic interpretation of history is the only explanation of history. In Buddha and his *Dhamma,* he gives clear priority to 'mind' as a determinant. He recognizes mind as the centre of everything. Mind precedes things, dominates them, creates them.... Mind is the chief of all faculties. The first thing to attend to is the culture of the mind. His study of Indian past in religious terms can be seen in his 'Revolution and Counter Revolution'. He reads the stages in history as Brahmanism, Buddhism and Hinduism. Gail Omvedt characterizes Ambedkar's views pluralistic.'[307]

Omvedt considers that Ambedkar has a significant sociological theory though he was not a trained sociologist or historian. Ambedkar does show a concern for a logical and a scientific method. Though he stresses 'mind' as primary in his final work, the orientation is very much towards the material world. Ambedkar's philosophy of history is consistent with the pluralistic explanation of history, though not of a purely materialistic one. This would be a Weberian position. Even in his rejection of Marx, Ambedkar, who was never one to use words sloppily, rejects the 'economic interpretation' as the 'only explanation.' He never denies the role of material factors and economic impulses as a necessary part of any overall historical and social explanation.'[308] In spite of these shifting phases, there is no doubt that Ambedkar's political-economic philosophy was a form of liberalism. He was an individualist and rationalist, returning always to the basic enlightenment values linked to Indian tradition.'[309]

Further, Gail Omvedt elaborates the liberal position of Ambedkar in the light of many shades of liberalism. She considers Ambedkar as representing the 'social liberalism'. According to this, the State will intervene in resolving the contradiction between inherited inequality and human rights. In this sense, it is different from classical and neo-liberalisms.

Further, Ambedkar realized the necessity of political power for the attack on caste system. Even to bring about residual change in the belief system either through the cultural or religious route, he stressed the necessity of political power. At the same time, in the given time, he was not prepared to confront the State. As an alternative he proposed, feudal relations in the village could be destroyed only if the private ownership of the land is abolished and co operativisation of farming is introduced. He thought this structural change Could be effected through the constitution.

Dewey's and Ambedkar's Philosophy of Democracy

Dewey's Meaning of Democracy

The key to understanding Dewey on democracy is that it is not just as a form of government. It is surely that, but it is simultaneously a way of life, an ethical ideal, and a personal commitment.[310] Specifically, it is a way of life in which individuals are presumed to be self directing and able to pursue their own goals and projects. No society which maintains order through constant supervision and/or coercion can be rightly called democratic. Further, individual benefit and the common good are mutually enhancing in a democracy. He also reminds us, though this is hardly original with Dewey, that citizenship in a democratic state is not just a condition; it is an office. We, therefore, not only have rights, but also responsibilities. These latter appear to be in conflict with the pursuit of our individual interests only if we misapprehend the true nature of our interests. An article of faith for Dewey is that we are each best served by a democracy that is so constituted as to maximize the common good..[311] The key to this compatibility between public and private goods is their democratic reciprocity: social membership entails certain responsibilities; in return, the society has the responsibility to take those actions and pursue those policies that remove obstacles to the realization of any individuals' full membership and participation. This is the nature of "rights." That there is this public responsibility commits the individuals who constitute the public to its pursuit.

Further, there is no form of social life that can allow for greater human development than democracy. An entailment of this view is that true human good is maximized for every individual in a democracy just to the extent that the society maximizes the common good.

This aspect of Dewey's argument is teleological; it trades on the notion that there is a best and most human life made possible by a best and most human social form. It is also, in keeping with Dewey's pragmatism, offered as a hypothesis to be tested, not a dogma to be followed.

John Dewey has been described as "a philosopher who combined the stubborn perseverance of a New England farmer with the zeal of a reckless liberal."[312] He was a progressive and far-sighted thinker with a distinctly American sensibility, one who espoused the virtues of pragmatism and experience over absolute and metaphysical truths and who advanced a social and political philosophy perhaps more thoroughly democratic than any that has been formulated before or since. Today, some fifty years after his death, John Dewey remains if not America's premier political philosopher, then at least its greatest spokesman for civil society, community values, grass-roots liberalism, and some would argue even democracy itself.

The philosophy of John Dewey is often identified with Charles Sanders Pierce, William James, and other thinkers loosely identified as 'pragmatic.' As a school of thought, pragmatism made its entrance into history under the banner of modernism, with its emphasis on scientific progress and its disdain of historical and metaphysical truths.

The pragmatists rejected Hegel's notion that "philosophy aims at knowing what is imperishable, eternal, and absolute. "Since objective truth is not something that can be discovered through the faculty of reason, they argued, epistemology and its preoccupation with the "foundations" of knowledge must be abandoned altogether. They believed that ideas and propositions cannot be judged by objective criteria since it is impossible to establish such criteria; instead, they should be judged by the results they produce when put into practice. In Santayana's memorable phrase, the pragmatists insisted that "it's better to pursue truth than to possess it."[313]

In *John Dewey and American Democracy,* Robert Westbrook chronicles the development of Dewey's thinking from his initial disenchantment with idealist metaphysics in the late 1880s to his formulation of pragmatic naturalism which culminated in a volume, written in collaboration with some of his colleagues, entitled *Studies in Logical Theory.* The book was rescued from likely obscurity by noted Harvard philosopher William James who praised it as an example of the kind of thinking he had begun to call "pragmatism." As James saw it, Dewey had abandoned the belief in an "absolute behind or around the finite world" in favor of an empiricism in which "'life' or 'experience' is the fundamental conception"[314]

Dewey welcomed the association with James enthusiastically. *Studies in Logical Theory* was dedicated to James, in fact, and he regarded James's *Principles of Psychology* (1890) as one of his greatest inspirations. Robert Westbrook observes that? James's influence on Dewey has recently been called into question, but if one carefully specifies its character, this influence was as undeniable and important as Dewey claimed it to be. Dewey's greatest debt to James was his pragmatic critique of epistemology. While epistemology sought to objectify knowledge as something separate from experience,

Dewey clearly subordinated knowledge to action,? According to Westbrook, the link between Dewey and James is significant because pragmatism has often been criticized as overly identified with individualism, capitalism, and material success, when, in fact, Dewey often spoke out *against* these values. If anything, Dewey saw the necessity of going beyond James's version of pragmatism to develop a philosophy that would bind Americans to a moral community, as he put it, and provide criteria for decisions that were socially important and politically useful.

It was this social dimension that informed most of Dewey's philosophy during the second half of his life. Following his arrival at Columbia University in 1905, Dewey's primary mission was to reconstruct philosophy and shift its attention from "the problems of philosophers" to "the problems of men."

This demand for relevance grew out of his sense that social progress is the true end of philosophy, and that philosophy, if it is to have any meaning, must be firmly rooted in human experience not in epistemological notions of an independent cogito, City of God, a *priori* category, or Transcendental Mind. According to Dewey, philosophers have mistakenly insisted on making a problem of the relation between the mind and the world when, in fact, "mind" and "reality" are meaningless epistemological abstractions drawn from a single indivisible process.

According to Westbrook, Dewey believed that philosophy had reached a "fatal turning point" and that the role of the philosopher needed to be radically transformed to meet the needs of a progressive society. "American philosophy," Dewey stated in 1904, "must be born out of and must respond to the demands of democracy." So long as knowledge is conceived as something external to experience, he said, human beings are deprived of the capacity to direct their societies and control the institutions that affect their lives. "Pragmatism was the logic of this new conception of intelligence," Westbrook writes, "deployed to close down an epistemology industry at odds with both science and democracy in order to erect a philosophy responsive to both. Democracy was the immanent, oppositional value that Dewey's philosophy idealized."[315]

While Dewey's early career was deeply influenced by Hegel and other speculative philosophers, he began to turn away from the idealism of his youth in the late 1880s to explore the practical dimensions of consciousness and action. Having already defined an ethic of self-realization the notion that each individual has a unique and normative purpose or "function" his thinking now shifted to a systematic examination of the practical and environmental requirements of this idea. Out of this search grew a highly original and carefully worked out social philosophy that continues to influence American political thought to this day.

The ideal of self-realization, as Dewey conceived it, held that freedom was the opportunity to actualize oneself as a social being. Freedom was defined in the positive, in contrast with many of Dewey's contemporaries who maintained that freedom could only be properly understood in the negative as "freedom from" this or that constraint. The key to Dewey's ideal was the notion of "function" which described the relationship between an individual and his or her environment. A person's function was a normative concept that prescribed how a person might best fit into society in order to actualize his or her highest capacities. Dewey insisted that the relationship between the individual and his or her environment must be based on mutual adjustment. In fact, he said, fitting into society might well involve radically changing it. (He later used this argument as a justification for extensive social reforms.)

Formulated in this way, democracy could be seen as "organic," as synergistic and evolving, rather than "atomistic" composed of individual parts held together by a social contract. A society was not an entity unto itself, Dewey said, but rather an aggregate of individuals who grow and evolve. By extension, only a society that could grow and evolve as its citizens did would be truly free. Dewey maintained that the ends of democratic politics were to secure the conditions for the self-realization of all the individuals in a society.

Democracy was not so much a political matter for Dewey as it was a quality inherent in each individual. While this idea did not go over well with Dewey's contemporaries, he stood fast in his conviction that "humanity cannot be content with a good that is procured from without, however high and otherwise complete that good."[316] The way for individuals to realize the democracy "in their own hearts" was through community. As Dewey wrote, "it is through association that man has acquired his individuality and it is through association that he exercises it. The theory which sets the individual over against society, of necessity contradicts itself."[317]

Already, Dewey had firmly established himself as a political thinker in the tradition of Plato, Rousseau, and Marx as one who believes in the inherent virtues of human beings and whose outlook is oriented toward what Glenn Tinder has called "the politics of redemption." For Dewey, the ends and means of democratic life were the fulfillment of human virtue and nobility, not the preservation of the political status quo or the securing of individual liberties.

The democratic ideal represents "a demand to be realized," Dewey said. It holds that "each individual shall have the opportunity for release, expression, fulfillment, of his distinctive capacities, and that the outcome shall further the establishment of a fund of shared values. Like every true ideal, it signifies something to be done rather than something already given, something ready-made."[318]

"Everything about Dewey's analysis pointed to the need for a politics of knowledge that would end the bewilderment of the public."[319] Westbrook observes, "But this politics remained, at best, an implicit, wholly undeveloped element of his argument. In laying out the 'infinitely difficult' conditions for the emergence of the Great Community and offering little guidance for overcoming them, he inadvertently and ironically made almost as good a case as Lippmann had that the phantom public would not materialize."[320]

John Dewey embraced a wide range of public roles over the course of his long career philosopher, educator, pragmatist, political activist, intellectual but Westbrook interprets him first and foremost as a political thinker whose philosophy was always driven by a commitment to the values of community, public life, and shared experience. For Dewey, metaphysics, epistemology, psychology, and ethical theory were all means toward the same end: securing the conditions of a viable participatory democracy.

Peter Gay has observed that there are two ways of being un-political "to think that politics can do everything, and to think that politics can do nothing."[321] The former leads to "utopianism and fanaticism," in his view, the latter to "Epicureanism and apathy." "Yet despite their opposite effects, both are symptoms of the same disease, a failure of realistic vision."[322] Dewey may be justifiably described as unrealistic. Indeed, his faith in ordinary citizens, in "the public," was roundly criticized by the democratic realists for what they saw as its excessive idealism. Yet Dewey was not un-political. As he wrote in *Ethics,* democracy, rightly conceived, is not so much a goal as it is a process and a highly political one at that. It involves constant meeting and solving of problems that is to say, the desired harmony is never brought about in a way which meets and forestalls all future developments. There is no shortcut to it, no single predestined road which can be found once for all and which, if human beings continue to walk in it without deviation, will surely conduct them to the goal.

Ambedkar's Meaning of Democracy

Abraham Lincoln said, "As I would not be a slave, so I would not be a master. This expresses my idea of democracy." Various philosophers, political scientists and writers have given numerous definitions of democracy. A relentless champion of human rights and staunch believer in democracy, Ambedkar said, "Democracy is not a form of government, but a form of Social Organization."[323]

Ambedkar believed that in democracy revolutionary changes in the economic and social life of the people are brought about without bloodshed. The conditions for that are as follows: (1) there should not be glaring inequalities in society i.e. privilege for one class; (2) the existence of an opposition; (3) equality in law and administration: (4) observance of constitutional morality: (5) no tyranny of the majority: (6) moral order of society: (7) public conscience" (Jatava.1991. 126).

Addressing the Constituent Assembly, he suggested certain devices essential to maintain democracy: "(i) Constitutional methods (ii) not to lay liberties at the feet of a great man (iii) Make political democracy a social democracy."[324]

Ambedkar firmly believed that political democracy cannot succeed without social and economic democracy. In his talk given on the Voice of America he argued that "democracy could not be equated either with republic or parliamentary form of government. The roots of democracy lay not in the form of government, parliamentary or otherwise. A democracy is a mode of associated living. The roots of democracy are to be searched in social relationship, in terms of the associated life between the people who form the society."[325]

Ambedkar had a lengthy discussion on democratic form of government in his writings. His conception of democracy is different from the parliamentary democracy of Western Europe. Democracy came with the principles of liberalism. His conception of democracy makes different with parliamentary forms of in a significant way. Parliamentary democracy has all the marks of a popular government, a government of people, by the people and for the people. Ambedkar considered the problems and expressed discontent against the parliamentary democracy in the nations like Italy, Germany, Russia, Spain and some other European nations in proposing the parliamentary democracy in India. Ambedkar finds reasons for the failure of parliamentary democracy that 'parliamentary democracy gives no free hand to dictatorship and that is why it became a discredited institution in the countries like Italy, Spain and Germany which readily welcomed dictatorships.'[326] The nations that are opposing dictatorship and pledged to democracy to find their discontent with democracy. First, the parliamentary democracy began with equality of political rights in the form of equal suffrage. There are very few countries having parliamentary democracy that have not adopted adult suffrage. It has progressed by expanding the notion of equality of political rights to equality of social and economic opportunity. It has recognized that corporations, which are anti-social in purpose, cannot hold state at bay. With all this, 'the reason for discontent is due to the realization that it has failed to assure to the masses the right to liberty, property or the pursuit of happiness. The causes for this failure may be found either in wrong ideology or wrong organization or in both.'[327] He elaborated this point by pointing out the fault with both wrong ideologies and the bad organization in carrying the ideals of democracy.

The idea of freedom of contract is one of the responsible factors for parliamentary democracy in terms of ideology. Parliamentary democracy took no notice of economic inequalities and didn't care to examine the result of freedom of contract on the parties to the contract, in spite of the fact that they were unequal in bargaining power. It didn't mind if the freedom of contract gave the strong opportunity to defraud the weak. The result is that parliamentary democracy in standing out as a protagonist of liberty has continuously added to economic wrongs of the poor, downtrodden and disinherited class.'[328] The second wrong ideology which has vitiated parliamentary democracy is the failure to realize that political democracy cannot succeed where there is no social and economic democracy.' He illustrated this point by comparing the collapse of parliamentary democracy in the countries of Italy, Germany and Russia with England and USA. He felt that there was a greater degree of economic and social democracy in the latter countries than existed in the former. 'Social and economic democracy are the tissues and fiber of a political democracy. The tougher the tissue and the fiber, the greater the strength of the body.'[329] Democracy is another name for equality. Parliamentary democracy developed a passion for liberty. It never made even nodding acquaintance with equality. It failed to realize the significance of equality and didn't even strike a balance between liberty and equality, with the result the liberty swallowed equality and has made democracy a name and farce.

More than the bad ideology, bad organization is responsible for failure of democracy. All political societies get divided into two classes-the rulers and the ruled. This is almost stratified that rulers are always drawn from ruling class and the class that is ruled never become the ruling class. This happens because generally people do not see that they govern themselves. They are content to establish a government and leave it to govern them.

This explains why parliamentary democracy has never been a government of the people or by the people and why it has been in reality a government of hereditary subject class by a hereditary ruling class. It is this vicious organization of political life which had made parliamentary democracy such a dismal failure.'[330] It is wrong to believe that democracy and self government is automatically became realities of life. In fact, the existing governing class is inconsistent with democracy and self- government and made all its efforts to retain its power to govern. Ambedkar felt that self government and democracy become real not when the constitution based on adult suffrage comes into existence but when the governing class loses its power to capture the power to govern. In some of the countries the servile classes may succeed in ousting the governing class from the seat of authority with just by adult suffrage. In some other countries the governing class may be so deeply entrenched that the servile classes will need other safeguards besides adult suffrage to achieve the same end.[331]

Ambedkar accused the western writers that they are superficial and not provided the realistic view of democracy. They superficially touched the constitutional morality, adult suffrage and frequent elections as the be-all and end-all of democracy. Ambedkar proposed a written constitution for the effective democracy. The habits of constitutional morality may be essential for the maintenance of a constitutional form of government. He puts more emphasis on moral society and its custom than the written legal law in governing its people. He heavily invested on social morality for effective functioning of the democratic form of government. He reminds us very often, in devising the constitution one has to keep in mind that the principle aim of constitution must be to dislodge the governing class from its position and to prevent it from remaining as a governing class forever.[332]

Dewey's and Ambedkar's Model of Political Democracy

Dewey remarks, "It is often thought to be the very beginning of wisdom, of moral discrimination, to make this distinction [between the intrinsic and the instrumental good]. . . arrived into practice it has an import that is tragic. Historically it has been the source and origin of a hard and fast difference between ideal goods on the one side and material goods on the other."[333] Whether educated people consider the intrinsic good to be intellectual contemplation, as in ancient Greece, or religious observation, as in the Middle Ages, or aesthetic enjoyment, as occasionally in our time, the effect is similar.

Dewey claims that, from the beginning of Western political thought, this conception has reinforced the class structure of society. The case of Aristotle is illuminating. In his sketch of an ideal state, Aristotle proposed that the laboring masses be excluded from participation in civic activity. Their manual labor was needed by the state, so they had to be kept around, but their exercise of this labor, because it was a burden and good only for its consequences, distorted their lives and by implication their morals. The assumption was that manual labor is inherently burdensome and thus merely instrumental. Aristotle reasoned that only persons freed from menial tasks to engage in governing and contemplation could live truly worthwhile lives and thus only a non-laboring class could identify with the state which made these lives possible.

Since manual labor was still required by the system of production, Aristotle looked for a subspecies of the human race, individuals whose limited mental powers made them fit for this kind of service. He located some of them not enough, by the way in a human subgroup he called natural slaves, and he judged that it would not violate their potential to assign them to such a subordinate and politically powerless role.

The harmful effect of these ideas goes beyond injury to the group which Aristotle regarded as natural slaves. This theory helps persuade people devoted to the perfection of the mind and soul that they should withdraw as much as possible from activity involving material things. Business and even politics are then left to persons least concerned with intelligence and decency. The result, says Dewey, is the brutalization of ordinary life.[334]

Dewey urges us to reinsert intrinsic value into the material life, into economics. Not, of course, that we should make profit a god. Rather we should see production of goods as a moral service to people who will use them. A vocation can be a sacred duty or trust. If life is to be worthwhile (economic ends) must acquire ideal and intrinsic value. Esthetic, religious and other ideal' ends are not thin and meager or else idle and luxurious because of the separation from instrumental or economic ends. Only in connection with the latter can they be woven into the texture of daily life and made substantial and pervasive.[335]

The next distinction which Dewey attacks is the distinction between moral goods and natural goods. This is also an ancient distinction, going back to Plato and Aristotle. Something like it was important for the Stoics, whose ethical ideas we present elsewhere on this site. Moral goods are conditions of the soul such as courage, wisdom, justice of character, and other virtues. Unlike moral goods, natural goods do not entirely depend on us. Such values include health, wealth, honor, economic security, art, and technical know how. In classical times, the Aristotelians and the Stoics agreed on the lowly status of these values. But so insistent was Stoicism on the secondary position of these values that it said that happiness does not depend upon them at all. Stoicism even refused to call them goods, labeling them instead merely 'preferred' things.

Dewey wants to undermine this distinction, to dethrone the virtues from their position at the summit of values. He doesn't take the position of regarding the virtues merely as a means to something else. Early Utilitarian such as Jeremy Bentham went to this extreme when they said that virtues were valuable only because they promoted pleasure and diminished pain. But for Dewey virtuous action is not the only thing intrinsically worthwhile. And he thinks that all so-called virtues should be evaluated in terms of their actual and predictable consequences. If middle-level bureaucrats would evaluate in this way the so-called virtue of loyalty to superiors, perhaps some of history's greater crimes would have been prevented.

The radical and unconventional character of Dewey's conception of democracy and his political philosophy generally derives from its boldness, which some readers find hard to stomach. The abstract character of conception of democracy is as far from a common and 'realist' view of democracy as the name of a set of specific political procedures and institutions as it is possible to find. Participation may not be a good, or appreciated as one, by every individual, such as those who are too shy or busy.

Dewey too contributed much on the construction of a democratic society which is based on liberty equality and fraternity. he foundation of democracy is faith in the capacities of human nature; faith in human intelligence and in the power of pooled and cooperative experience. It is not belief that these things are complete but that if given a show they will grow and be able to generate progressively the knowledge and wisdom needed to guide collective action. Every autocratic and authoritarian scheme of social action rests on a belief that the needed intelligence is confined to a superior few, who because of inherent natural gifts are endowed with the ability and the right to control the conduct of others; laying down principles and rules and directing the ways in which they are carried out. It would be foolish to deny that much can be said for this point of view. It is that which controlled human relations in social groups for much the greater part of human history.

The democratic faith has emerged very, very recently in the history of mankind. Even where democracies now exist, men's minds and feelings are still permeated with ideas about leadership imposed from above, ideas that developed in the long early history of mankind. Belief in equality is an element of the democratic credo. It is not, however, belief in equality of natural endowments. Those who proclaimed the idea of equality did not suppose they were enunciating a psychological doctrine, but a legal and political one. All individuals are entitled to equality of treatment by law and in its administration. Each one is affected equally in quality if not in quantity by the institutions under which he lives and has an equal right to express his judgment, although the weight of his judgment may not be equal in amount when it enters into the pooled result to that of others. In short, each one is equally an individual and entitled to equal opportunity of development of his own capacities, be they large or small in range. Moreover, each has needs of his own, as significant to him as those of others are to them. The very fact of natural and psychological inequality is all the more reason for establishment by law of equality of opportunity, since otherwise the former becomes a means of oppression of the less gifted.

While what we call intelligence is distributed in unequal amounts, it is the democratic faith that it is sufficiently general so that each individual has something to contribute, whose value can be assessed only as enters into the final pooled intelligence constituted by the contributions of all. Every authoritarian scheme, on the contrary, assumes that its value may be assessed by some prior principle, if not of family and birth or race and colour or possession of material wealth, then by the position and rank a person occupies in the existing social scheme. The democratic faith in equality is the faith that each individual shall have the chance and opportunity to contribute whatever he is capable of contributing and that the value of his contribution be decided by its place and function in the organized total of similar contributions, not on the basis of prior status of any kind whatever.

Whereas Ambedkar political democracy was too expressed his views, and strongly advocated for a democratic form of governance for India. In fact, there was almost unanimity in favour of a democratic form of governance. For Ambedkar, was the way democracy was being defined by the privileged social groups? The privileged social groups were insistent on continuing with varna/ caste institutions - which would continue to regulate social life of the people, but at same time asked for a modern State-system, to regulate the political life of society. Ambedkar could foresee the consequences of such a theoretical design, wherein the institutions of *varna*/caste, would decisively undermine the authority of the modern State, and thus retain the status-quo.

Ambedkar in 1943, argued that, "A democratic form of Government presupposes a democratic form of society. The formal framework of democracy is of no value and would indeed be a misfit if there was no social democracy."[336] He further emphasized, "The politicals never realized that democracy was not a form of Government: it was essentially a form of society."[337] He was extremely apprehensive of the Dalits` fate in the independent India. For, he could clearly see that most political outfits of his time were preparing for a democratic form of government, without even questioning the *varna*/caste organization of the Indian society. That is why, he was insistent on a thoroughgoing social reform movements along radical lines, of which, most political conflicts were averse to. He could also see that, no political organization was prepared to intervene in the internal affairs of the society. While referring to the experiences of other societies, he had cautioned, "As experience proves, rights are protected not by law but by the social and moral conscience of society. If social conscience is such that it is prepared to recognize the rights which law chooses to enact, rights will be safe and secure. But if the fundamental rights are opposed by the community, no law, no Parliament, no Judiciary can guarantee them in the real sense of the word."[338]

The Constituent Assembly, while drafting the Constitution for an independent India, could not ignore the vital questions of civil society and citizenship, and therefore, assigned A twine role to the Indian Republic, i.e., the State to accomplish the task of democratising Indian social order, and also to regulate the socio-political affaires of the society. The Constitution, in its preamble itself, directs the State, to secure to all its citizens: Justice, social, economic and political; Liberty, of thought, expression, belief, faith and worship; Equality of status and opportunity; and to promote among them all; Fraternity assuring the dignity of the individual.

The Indian Constitution sounds like manifesto of some radical political organization, seeking revolutionary transformation in a particular society. The caste society had then, when the Constitution was being framed, very reluctantly agreed to opt for a civil society, and the task was to be accomplished by the modern State.

Unlike the democratic realists, Dewey believed that direct participation in a democracy would foster an unexpected talent for thoughtful deliberation in ordinary citizens. "We lie in the lap of an immense intelligence,"[339] he said. The difficulty was to unleash this intelligence, which remained "dormant" until "it possesses the local community as its medium." In *The Public and its Problems* Dewey's only work of formal political philosophy, he outlined an elaborate program of truly participatory democracy, one built around face-to-face interactions in "neighborly communities."[340] Dewey insisted that most of his contemporaries had failed to properly distinguish between democracy as a way of life and democracy as a system of government. Though the two were closely related, the idea of democracy in the former sense was, in Dewey's words, "a wider and fuller idea than can be exemplified in the state even at its best. To be realized it must affect all modes of human association, the family, social life and religion. And even as far as political arrangements are concerned; governmental institutions are but a mechanism for securing to an ideal channel of effective operation."[341] As such, democracy was an inherently participatory ideal and the "realist" proposal for democracy with a limited degree of self-government was for Dewey a contradiction in terms. "Whatever his weaknesses as a political theorist and strategist, Westbrook notes, "Dewey was never guilty of shortchanging democracy as a moral ideal."[342]

Moreover Ambedkar's views of democracy as an instrument of bringing about change peacefully. Democracy does not merely mean rule by the majority or government by the representatives of the people. This is a formalistic and limited notion of democracy. We would understand the meaning of democracy in a better fashion if we view it as a way of realizing drastic changes in the social and economic spheres of society. Ambedkar's idea of democracy is much more than just a scheme of government. He emphasises the need for bringing about an all-round democracy. A scheme of government does not exist in vacuum; it operates within the society. Its usefulness depends upon its relationship with the other spheres of society. Elections, parties and parliaments are, after all, formal institutions of democracy. They cannot be effective in an undemocratic atmosphere. Political democracy means the principle of 'one man one vote' which indicates political equality. But if oppression and injustice exist, the spirit of political democracy would' be missing. Democratic government, therefore, should be an extension of a democratic society.[343]

In the Indian society, for instance, so long as caste barriers and caste-based inequalities exist, real democracy cannot operate. In this sense, democracy means a spirit of fraternity and equality and not merely a political arrangement. Success bf democracy in India can be ensured only by establishing a truly democratic society. Along with the social foundations of democracy, Ambedkar takes into consideration the economic aspects also. It is true that he was greatly influenced by liberal thought. Still, he appreciated the limitations of liberalism. Parliamentary democracy, in which he had great faith, was also critically examined by him. He argued that parliamentary democracy was based on liberalism. It ignored economic inequalities and never concentrated upon the problems of the downtrodden. Besides, the general tendency of the western type of parliamentary democracies has been to ignore the issues of social and economic equality. In other words, parliamentary democracy emphasized only liberty whereas true democracy implies both liberty and equality. This analysis becomes very important in the Indian context. Indian society was demanding freedom from the British. But Ambedkar was afraid that freedom of the nation would not ensure real freedom for all the people. Social and economic inequalities have dehumanized the Indian society. Establishing democracy in such a society would be nothing short of a revolution. This would be a revolution in the social structure and attitudes of the people. In the place of hereditary inequality, the principles of brotherhood and equality must be established. Therefore, Ambedkar supported the idea of all-round democracy.[344]

Ambedkar favored the parliamentary form of government. For the successful functioning of this form of government, it is necessary that certain other conditions must be fulfilled. To begin with, political parties are necessary for the effective working of parliamentary democracy. This will ensure existence of the opposition which is very important. Parliamentary government is known as responsible government mainly because the executive is constantly watched and controlled by the opposition. Respect and official status for the opposition means absence of absolute power for the executive. The other condition is a neutral and non-political civil service. A neutral civil service means that administrators would be permanent not dependent on the fortunes of the political parties and that they would not take sides with political parties.

This will be possible only when appointments of civil servants are not made on the basis of political consideration. Success of democracy depends on many ethical and moral factors also. A country may have a constitution. But it is only a set of rules. These rules become meaningful only when people in the country develop conventions and traditions consistent with the constitution. People and politicians must follow certain norms in public life.[345]

Similarly, there must also exist a sense of morality and conscientiousness in the society. Law and legal remedies can never replace a voluntary sense of responsibility. No amount of law can enforce morality. Norms of honest and responsible behavior must develop in the society. Democracy can be successful only when every citizen feels duty bound to fight injustice even if that injustice does not put him into any difficulty.

This will happen when equality and brotherhood exist in the society. To make democracy successful in India, Ambedkar suggested a few other precautions also. Democracy means rule of the majority. But this should not result into tyranny of the majority. Majority must always respect the views of the minority. In India there is a possibility that the minority community will always be a political minority also. Therefore, it is very essential that the minority must feel free, safe and secure.

Otherwise, it will be very easy to convert democracy into a permanent rule against the minority. Caste system could thus become the most difficult obstacle in the successful functioning of democracy. The castes which are supposed to be of low status will never get their proper share in power. Caste will create barriers in the development of healthy democratic traditions. This means that unless we achieve the task of establishing democracy in the social field, mere political democracy cannot survive.

Dewey's and Ambedkar's Concept of Social Democracy

For Dewey understands of democracy is basically social, in a sense that every day good congregation- and family life reveals. The priority of the social becomes in a similar way visible in his organic understanding of society, which understands the social connection of all with all in the community as given by nature and through a pragmatic venture which can be achieved.

The vision of democracy as a large community can finally be understood as a social-liberal inner-worldly theology of society. Here one need to emphasize the concept of social-liberal, for with the options of the classical liberal thinking, which laces only the individual into the focus of attention, Dewey's social philosophy cannot be combined. Dewey is as a liberal in many ways an opponent to liberalism, which he criticizes as laissez faire-liberalism. What he understands under liberal democracy is a liberal form of socialism, which of course is to be seen as separate from illiberal, dictatorial forms of socialism. Finally the connection of Dewey to liberal thought needs quite a restriction: Dewey's battle for a just society becomes only through a new definition of liberalism possible. The consequences of this new definition remain ambivalent.

One needs to realize that the democratic and the liberal idea come politically from two opposing historical sources. To opt for both ideas at the same time leads to a paradox. The democratic idea wants the social, economic and political equality of all citizens. She fights against the inequality of certain social classes and groups. Its political voice is ideally the gathering of the people, in which all confer everything and if possible decide unanimously. The democratic state needs strength in order to establish the idea of justice. It leans thus already in the "politics" of Aristoteles either towards dictatorship or to chaos, today we would say: to instability.

The liberal idea fights for the rights and the free development of the individual (whereby the single person as well as a group can be meant); societal difference, competition and plurality, e.g. groups in society are seen as enlivening for the societal progress; next to the freedom of religion and conviction is property one of the most liberal basic rights. The state has according to liberal understanding essentially the task to assure security of justice: All infringes into the social and economic life through the state the convinced liberal attempts if possible to avoid.

How both ideas, the democratic and the liberal, enter complicated balances in the modern society, shows the democratic liberal constitutions of western countries. It is the task of the science of state or politics to closer describe the different forms of power, the political institutions, their power balances and their control and in a time of historical-international comparison of the systems to reflect.[347]

This as entirely outside of Dewey's consideration. His (hardly developed) theory of state is limited to pointing to the American

Constitution, the laws, the president. Again and again Dewey spoke to political questions and to the role of America in the world. Of a deciding role always played the basic sentences of his social philosophy societal equality of the unequal, justice, overcoming social barriers for social integration.

The social federalism as well as ethnic segmentation of the American society, the diversity of groups standing next to one another, in different subcultures living groups of people, generated the clear need of tools as Dewey would say, which would bring about the necessary social Dewey's achievement is that he created a general pragmatic philosophy of societal integration on the basis of the free individual development and that he as person represented it convincingly. Dewey's philosophy gives the people confidence for a life in a good society. What makes his philosophy trustworthy is the special power of radiation. But a social theory of a highly complex society cannot possibly do justice to all principles in the same way. The emphasis of certain aspects of societal life sees to it that some aspects are fewer foregrounds. Which aspects Dewey held as being less important we shall deal with now.

This distinction is helpful, because it clarifies that Dewey was not interested in a democracy as ruling form. He could only criticize forms of dominion, but could not give it a place in a theory of political institutions. The more strongly Dewey identified himself with democracy as a form of life. Dewey democracy as form of society, he recognized the plurality of societal life and its potential of conflict, but essentially under the concept of a theory of social integration.[348] It could give the different groups in the country on the basis of human values identity, for social integration of immigrants is helpful. One needs to ask if a theory of society, which connects the moment of freedom of the individual with the social goal of societal peace, is able to accept the interests of groups and respects ethnical wishes of autonomy.

Democracy is much broader than a special political form, a method of conducting government, of making laws and carrying on governmental administration by means of popular suffrage and elected officers. It is that, of course. But it is something broader and deeper than that The political and governmental phase of democracy is a means, the best means so far found, for realizing ends that lie in the wide domain of human relationships and the development of human personality. It is, as we often say, though perhaps without appreciating all that is involved in the saying, a way of life, social and individual. The key-note of democracy as a way of life may be expressed; it seems to me, as the necessity for the participation of every mature human being in formation of the values that regulate the living of men together: which is necessary from the standpoint of both the general social welfare and the full development of human beings as individuals.[349]

Universal suffrage, recurring elections, responsibility of those who are in political power to the voters, and the other factors of democratic government are means that have been found expedient for realizing democracy as the truly human way of living. They are not a final end and a final value. They are to be judged on the basis of their contribution to end. It is a form of idolatry to erect means into the end which they serve. Democratic political forms are simply the best means that human wit has devised up to a special time in history. But they rest back upon the idea that no man or limited set of men is wise enough or good enough to rule others without their consent; the positive meaning of this statement is that all those who are affected by social institutions must have a share in producing and managing them. The two facts that each one is influenced in what he does and enjoys and in what he becomes by the institutions under which he lives, and that therefore he shall have, in a democracy, a voice in shaping them, are the passive and active sides of the same fact.

The development of political democracy came about through substitution of the method of mutual consultation and voluntary agreement for the method of subordination of the many to the few enforced from above. Social arrangements which involve fixed subordination are maintained by coercion. The coercion need not be physical. There have existed, for short periods, benevolent despotisms. But coercion of some sort there has been; perhaps economic, certainly psychological and moral. The very fact of exclusion from participation is a subtle form of suppression. It gives individuals no opportunity to reflect and decide upon what is good for them. Others who are supposed to be wiser and who in any case have more power decide the question for them and also decide the methods and means by which subjects may arrive at the enjoyment of what is good for them. This form of coercion and suppression is more subtle and more effective than is overt intimidation and restraint. When it is habitual and embodied in social institutions, it seems the normal and natural state of affairs. The masses usually become unaware that they have a claim to a development of their own powers. Their experience is so restricted that they are not conscious of restriction. It is part of the democratic conception that they as individuals are not the only sufferers, but that the whole social body is deprived of the potential resources that should be at its service.[350] The individuals of the submerged mass may not be very wise. But there is one thing they are wiser about than anybody else can be, and that is where the shoe pinches, the troubles they suffer from.

The foundation of democracy is faith in the capacities of human nature; faith in human intelligence and in the power of pooled and cooperative experience. It is not belief that these things are complete but that if given a show they will grow and be able to generate progressively the knowledge and wisdom needed to guide collective action. Every autocratic and authoritarian scheme of social action rests on a belief that the needed intelligence is confined to a superior few, who because of inherent natural gifts are endowed with the ability and the right to control the conduct of others; laying down principles and rules and directing the ways in which they are carried out. It would be foolish to deny that much can be said for this point of view. It is that which controlled human relations in social groups for much the greater part of human history. The democratic faith has emerged very, very recently in the history of mankind. Even where democracies now exist, men's minds and feelings are still permeated with ideas about leadership imposed from above, ideas that developed in the long early history of mankind. After democratic political institutions were nominally established, beliefs and ways of looking at life and of acting that originated when men and women were externally controlled and subjected to arbitrary power persisted in the family, the church, business and the school, and experience shows that as long as they persist there, political democracy is not secure.

Belief in equality is an element of the democratic credo. It is not, however, belief in equality of natural endowments. Those who proclaimed the idea of equality did not suppose they were enunciating a psychological doctrine, but a legal and political one. All individuals are entitled to equality of treatment by law and in its administration. Each one is affected equally in quality if not in quantity by the institutions under which he lives and has an equal right to express his judgment, although the weight of his judgment may not be equal in amount when it enters into the pooled result to that of others. In short, each one is equally an individual and entitled to equal opportunity of development of his own capacities, be they large or small in range. Moreover, each has needs of his own, as significant to him as those of others are to them. The very fact of natural and psychological inequality is all the more reason for establishment by law of equality of opportunity, since otherwise the former becomes a means of oppression of the less gifted.

While what we call intelligence is distributed in unequal amounts, it is the democratic faith that it is sufficiently general so that each individual has something to contribute, whose value can be assessed only as enters into the final pooled intelligence constituted by the contributions of all. Every authoritarian scheme, on the contrary, assumes that its value may be assessed by some prior principle, if not of family and birth or race and color or possession of material wealth, then by the position and rank a person occupies in the existing social scheme. The democratic faith in equality is the faith that each individual shall have the chance and opportunity to contribute whatever he is capable of contributing and that the value of his contribution be decided by its place and function in the organized total of similar contributions, not on the basis of prior status of any kind whatever.

We have emphasized in what precedes the importance of the effective release of intelligence in connection with personal experience in the democratic way of living. we have done so purposely because democracy is so often and so naturally associated in our minds with freedom of action, forgetting the importance of freed intelligence which is necessary to direct and to warrant freedom of action.

Unless freedom of individual action has intelligence and informed conviction back of it, its manifestation is almost sure to result in confusion and disorder. The democratic idea of freedom is not the right of each individual to do as he pleases/ even if it be qualified by adding "provided he does not interfere with the same freedom on the part of others."[351] While the idea is not always, not often enough, expressed in words, the basic freedom is that of freedom of mind and of whatever degree of freedom of action and experience is necessary to produce freedom of intelligence. The modes of freedom guaranteed in the Bill of Rights are all of this nature: Freedom of belief and conscience, of expression of opinion, of assembly for discussion and conference, of the press as an organ of communication. They are guaranteed because without them individuals are not free to develop and society is deprived of what they might contribute.

It is a disputed question of theory and practice just how far a democratic political government should go in control of the conditions of action within special groups. At the present time, for example, there are those who think the federal and state governments leave too much freedom of independent action to industrial and financial groups, and there are others who think the government is going altogether too far at the present time. Dewey does not need to discuss this phase of the problem, much less to try to settle it. But it must be pointed out that if the methods of regulation and administration in vogue in the conduct of secondary social groups are non- democratic, whether directly or indirectly or both, there is bound to be unfavorable reaction back into the habits of feeling, thought and action of citizenship in the broadest sense of that word. The way in which any organized social interest is controlled necessarily plays an important part in forming the dispositions and tastes, the attitudes, interests, purposes and desires, of those engaged in carrying on the activities of the group. For illustration, we do not need to do more than point to the moral, emotional and intellectual effect upon both employers and laborers of the existing industrial system.[352] Just what the effects specifically are is a matter about which we know very little. But we suppose that everyone who reflects upon the subject admits that it is impossible that the ways in which activities are carried on for the greater part of the waking hours of the day; and the way in which the share of individuals are involved in the management of affairs in such a matter as gaining a livelihood and attaining material and social security, cannot but be a highly important factor in shaping personal dispositions; in short/ forming character and intelligence.

There are certain corollaries which clarify the meaning of the issue. Absence of participation tends to produce lack of interest and concern on the part of those shut out. The result is a corresponding lack of effective responsibility. Automatically and unconsciously, if not consciously, the feeling develops, "This is none of our affair; it is the business of those at the top; let that particular set of Georges do what needs to be done." The countries in which autocratic government prevails are just those in which there is least public spirit and the greatest indifference to matters of general as distinct from personal concern.

Where there is little power, there is correspondingly little sense of positive responsibility. It is enough to do what one is told to do sufficiently well to escape flagrant unfavorable notice. About larger matters, a spirit of passivity is engendered. In some cases, indifference passes into evasion of duties when not directly under the eye of a supervisor; in other cases, a carping, rebellious spirit is engendered. Habitual exclusion has the effect of reducing a sense of responsibility for what is done and its consequences. What the argument for democracy implies is that the best way to produce initiative and constructive power is to exercise it. Power, as well as interest, comes by use and practice. It is also true that incapacity to assume the responsibilities involved in having a voice in shaping policies is bred and increased by conditions in which that responsibility is denied. We suppose there has never been an autocrat, big or little, who did not justify his conduct on the ground of the unfitness of his subjects to take part in government.[354]

Dewey concludes by saying that the present subject is one of peculiar importance at the present time. The fundamental beliefs and practices of democracy are now challenged as they never have been before. In some nations they are more than challenged. They are ruthlessly and systematically destroyed. Everywhere there are waves of criticism and doubt as to whether democracy can meet pressing problems of order and security. The causes for the destruction of political democracy in countries where it was nominally established are complex. But of one thing Dewey think we may be sure. Wherever it has fallen it was too exclusively political in nature. It had not become part of the bone and blood of the people in daily conduct of its life. Democratic forms were limited to Parliament, elections and combats between parties. What is happening proves conclusively, Dewey think that unless democratic habits of thought and action are part of the fiber of a people, political democracy is insecure? It cannot stand in isolation. It must be buttressed by the presence of democratic methods in all social relationships. The relations that exist in educational institutions are second only in importance in this respect to those which exist in industry and business, perhaps not even to them. There are three main lines of argument for democracy in Dewey's mature political philosophy: democracy as the protection of popular interests; democracy as social inquiry; and democracy as the expression of individuality.[355]

At the minimum, for Dewey, democracy involves the expression of interests on the part of voters; the vote helps to protect individuals from putative experts about where the interests of people lie. A class of experts will inevitably slide into a class whose interests diverge from those of the rest and becomes a committee of oligarchs. So 'the strongest point to be made in behalf of even such rudimentary political forms as democracy has attained, popular voting, majority rule and so on, is that to some extent they involve a consultation and discussion which concerns social needs and troubles.' [356] Dewey stresses the importance of discussion, consultation, persuasion and debate in democratic decision-making. These processes extend and deepen the public awareness of the problems under discussion, and help to inform the 'administrative specialist' of social needs.

This way of viewing the desirability of democracy is instrumental and minimal; instrumental, in that the desirability of democracy derives from its protecting the interests of each individual against the depredations of an elite class, and minimal, in that the rationale for popular participation is limited to the need for the elite to be informed where the shoe pinches, if its policies are not to be misguided. Dewey deepens this minimal and instrumental justification by taking democracy to be a form of social inquiry: Democracy as public discussion is viewed as the best way of dealing with the conflict of interests in a society: 'The method of democracy in as far as it is that of organized intelligence is to bring these conflicts out into the open where their special claims can be discussed and judged in the light of more inclusive interests than are represented by either of them separately.' Democratic societies are thought of as both seeking to attain desirable goals, and arguing over how to do so, and also as arguing over what a desirable goal is. In other words, democratic politics is not simply a channel through which we can assert our interests (as it is for the first argument), but a forum or mode of activity in which we can arrive at a conception of what our interests are. As the experimentalist conception of inquiry insists, this does not imply that we need a *priori* criteria in order to establish if this process has been successful. Rather, criteria for what counts as a satisfactory solution may be hammered out in the process of searching for one. Democracy is experimental for Dewey in that it allows, or should allow, a profound questioning of the idéas fixes of the established order, even if, of course, much democratic politics will not take the form of such questioning.

The third line of argument is that democracy is a requirement of freedom in Dewey's sense of individuality. The collective exercise of the experimental ethos is an ethical demand of this conception of freedom. Exercised properly, this experimental ethos allows individuals to arrive at a common good. From the standpoint of the individual, it consists in having a responsible share according to capacity in forming and directing the activities of the groups in which one belongs and in participating according to need in the values which the groups sustain. From the standpoint of the groups, it demands liberation of the potentialities of members of a group in harmony with the interests and goods which are common.[358] Full liberation of an individual's potentialities can only be achieved in a democratic social order, one in which social conflicts are treated as the subject of social inquiry. Dewey's argument that the experimental character of democracy renders it desirable should not merely be interpreted instrumentally, then. He is not only saying that democracy allows a clearer view of social problems and how to address them. His suggestion is also that individuality can only be properly expressed if the individual participates in democratic practices, since social inquiry is a constitutive part of the individual good. And this is a claim about individuality in the specific ethical sense in which he develops the notion in his critique of classical liberalism.

The radical and unconventional character of Dewey's conception of democracy and his political philosophy generally derives from its boldness, which some readers find hard to stomach. The abstract character of conception of democracy is as far from a common and 'realist' view of democracy as the name of a set of specific political procedures and institutions as it is possible to find. Participation may not be a good, or appreciated as one, by every individual, such as those who are too shy or busy. Furthermore, it is a bold assumption to hope, as Dewey does, that complex industrial societies can be characterized by a high level of harmony among the interests of their members, to be secured through public discussion and communication. Of course, this very boldness is appealing to others, for whom the connection Dewey makes between an ethos of flexible openness and democratic self-government stands as an enduring critical challenge to a circumscribed democratic pessimism.

In Ambedkar's social vision of democracy was closely related to his ideal of a "good society". He did not leave room for any ambiguity regarding the nature of this ideal. On many occasions, he stated that he envisaged a good society as one based on 'liberty, equality and fraternity'. Democracy, as he saw it, was both the end and the means of this ideal. It was the end because he ultimately considered democracy as coterminous with the realisation of liberty, equality and fraternity. At the same time, democracy was also the means through which this ideal was to be attained.

Ambedkar's notion of 'democratic government' went back to the fundamental idea of 'government of the people, by the people and for the people'. But "democracy" meant much more to him than democratic government. It was a way of life: "Democracy is not merely a form of government. It is primarily a mode of associated living, of conjoint communicated experience. It is essentially an attitude of respect and reverence towards fellowmen."[359]

Another crucial feature of Ambedkar's conception of democracy is that it was geared to social transformation and human progress. Conservative notions of democracy, such as the idea that it is mainly a device to prevent bad people from seizing power, did not satisfy him. In one of the most inspiring definitions of the term, he defined democracy as "a form and a method of government whereby revolutionary changes in the economic and social life of the people are brought about without bloodshed."[360]

Ambedkar's passion for democracy was closely related to his commitment to rationality and the scientific outlook. At an obvious level, rationality is necessary for democratic government since public debate (an essential aspect of democratic practice) is impossible in the absence of a shared adherence to common sense, logical argument and critical enquiry. Rational thinking is even more relevant if we adopt Ambedkar's broad view of democracy as a state of 'liberty, equality and fraternity.' Indeed, rationality is conducive if not indispensable to the realisation of these ideals. ...

There is also a close affinity between rationality and equality. For one thing, propaganda and manipulation are common tools of subjugation. The caste system, for instance, has been propped over the centuries by an elaborate edifice of unscientific dogmas. The scientific outlook is essential to liberate and protect oneself from ideological manipulation. For another, the scientific spirit has a strong anti-authoritarian dimension. Authority rests on the notion that one person's view or wish counts more than another's. In scientific argument, this is not the case. What counts is the coherence of the argument and the quality of the evidence. In that sense, the scientific outlook is a protection against the arbitrary exercise of power.

There is a view that reason and science are 'western' notions, alien to the people of India, who have their own 'modes of knowledge'. This view is bound to astonish anyone who has cared to read the Buddha's teachings. Many centuries before Descartes,

Buddha urged his followers to use their reason and not to believe anything without proof. In '*Buddha or Karl Marx*', one of his last speeches, Ambedkar includes the following in his summary of the essential teachings of the Buddha: "Everyone has a right to learn. Learning is as necessary for man to live as food is ... Nothing is infallible. Nothing is binding forever. Everything is subject to inquiry and examination."[361]

In a multi-denominational society like India, the common denominator is secularism which is one of the pillars on which the superstructure of our democracy rests. It is a unifying force of our associated life. He says: "The conception of a secular state is derived from the liberal democratic tradition of the West. No institution which is maintained wholly out of state funds shall be used for the purpose of religious instruction irrespective of the question whether the religious instruction is given by the state or by any other body."[362] Participating in a debate in Parliament, he further emphasized: "It (secular state) does not mean that we shall not take into consideration the religious sentiments of the people. All that a secular state means that this Parliament shall not be competent to impose any particular religion upon the rest of the people. That is the only limitation that the Constitution recognizes."[363]

Social unity can be achieved by coercive methods. For true democracy to flower and flourish, social union is must. For that he suggested safeguards for the minority. In democracy, minority does not become the victim of the tyranny of the majority. He suggested certain safeguards for the protection of the minority. "The State should guarantee to its citizens the liberty of conscience and the free exercise of his religion including the right to profess, to preach and to convert within limits compatible with public order and morality."[364]

A crusader against social and economic injustice and a great champion of human rights with a firm belief in democracy, he exhorted his audience at the All India Depressed Classes Conference: "It seems to me that there lies on us a very important duty to see that democracy does not vanish from the earth as the governing principle of human relationship. If we believe in it, we must both be true and loyal to it. We must not only be staunch in our faith in democracy, but we must resolve to see that whatever we do not help the enemies of democracy to uproot the principles of liberty, equality and fraternity." For that he exhorted the Dalits to defend and support democracy and secularism to safeguard their rights, life and liberty.

Ambedkar laid much emphasis on the term moral and said: "The Declaration of Independence does not assert that all men are equal; it proclaims that they are created equal."[366] He further argued: "For the successful working of democracy there must not be glaring inequalities in the society. There must not be an oppressed class. There must not be a suppressed class." In case of inequalities "State intervention is a must". Right to treatment as an equal must precede the right to equal treatment as a state policy. Equality of opportunity is a misleading term. There should be opportunity for equality.

Ambedkar emphasized on the need for liberty of movement, liberty of speech and liberty of action and political liberty to choose his government for securing "unalienable rights such as life, liberty and pursuit of happiness. Political liberty is really a deduction from the principle of human personality and equality."[367] Liberty and equality exist together.

One without the other is absurd. Commenting on failure of democracy in some countries, he said: "Parliamentary democracy developed a passion for liberty. It failed to realise the significance of equality and did not even Endeavour to strike a balance between liberty and equality, with the result that liberty swallowed equality and has made democracy a name and a farce."[368] He was against violence. A firm believer in the Buddhist doctrine of non-violence he asked his followers to 'agitate' for their rights in a peaceful manner. Violence undermines the spirit of democracy.

At the time of adoption of the Constitution, Ambedkar warned: "On 26th of January 1950, we are going to enter into a life of contradictions. In politics we will have equality and in social and economic life we will have inequalities. In politics we will be recognizing the principles of one man one vote and one vote one value. In our social and economic life, we shall, by reason of our social and economic structure, continue to deny the principle of one man one vote. How long shall we continue to live this life of contradictions? How long shall we continue to deny equality in our social and economic life? If we continue to deny it for long, we will do so only by putting our political democracy in peril. We must remove this contradiction at the earliest possible moment or else those who suffer from inequality will blow up the structure of our political.

Reference

264. John Dewey.1985. *'Experience and Nature').* Southern Illinois University Press, Carbondale, IL.p.104

265. John Dewey. (1922/1983). *Human Nature and Conduct.* Southern Illinois University Press, Carbondale, ILp.4

266. John Dewey.1973. *"Society and Democracy."* Southern Illinois University. Carbondale.p.22

267. Jatava, D. R. 1965.*The Political Philosophy of B.R.Ambedkar,* Phoenix publishing Agency, Agra. P.76

268. Jatava, D. R. 1965.*The Political Philosophy of B.R.Ambedkar,* Phoenix publishing Agency, Agra. p.77

269. Jatava, D. R. 1965.*The Political Philosophy of B.R.Ambedkar,* Phoenix publishing Agency, Agra. p.78

270. John Dewey. 1952. *"Philosophy and Society."* Southern Illinois University. Carbondale.p.55

271. Jatava, D. R. 1965. *The Political Philosophy of B.R.Ambedkar, Phoenix* publishing Agency, Agra. P.54

272. Jatava, D. R. 1965.*The Political Philosophy of B.R.Ambedkar,* Phoenix publishing Agency, Agra. P.78

273. Rorty, Richard.1999.' *Achieving Our Country: Leftist Thought in Twentieth-Century* America, Harvard University Press, Cambridge.p.106-107

274. Rorty, Richard.1999.' *Achieving Our Country: Leftist Thought in Twentieth-Centur America,* Harvard University Press, Cambridge p.107

275. Ibid, p.108

276. Ibid

277. Carolyn Graglia.1998. *"Domestic Tranquility: A Brief Against Feminism"* Spence Publishing Co.Dallas.TX.p.222
278. Patricia McCarran.1954. *"Political Boss of Nevada,"* Jerome E. Edwards Books Publisher. Nevada.p.134
279. David Miller,1989. *"Ambedkar's Political and Social Thought"* Clarendon Press, Oxford.p.214
280. Beerbohm, E. 2006. *'The Ethics of Democracy' EW1*, Princeton University Press,.Princeton.p.231-232
281. Beerbohm, E. 2006. *'The Ethics of Democracy' EW1*, Princeton University Press,.Princeton.p.246
282. John Dewey, 1892. *Christianity and democracy. EW4,* Southern Illinois University Press. Carbondale, IL.p.9
283. John Dewey. (1938a/1986). *"Philosophy and Democracy"*, EW12, Southern Illinois University Press. Carbondale, IL.p.16
284. Ibid, p.484
285. John Dewey. (1923/1983). *"Logial Method and Law"*, EW15, Southern Illinois University Press. Carbondale, IL.p.76
286. Jatava, D. R. 1965.*The Political Philosophy of B.R.Ambedkar.* Phoenix publishing Agency, Agra.p.34
287. Ibid, p.35
288. Jatava, D. R. 1965.*The Political Philosophy of B.R.Ambedkar*, Phoenix publishing Agency, Agra.p.36
289. John Dewey. *Reconstruction in Philosophy, MW12,* Southern Illinois University Press. Carbondale, IL p.190-192
290. John Dewey, 'Context and Thought', LW5, Southern Illinois University Press. Carbondale, IL p. 5
291. Ibid, p.7
292. John Dewey, *'The Future of Liberalism', LW*11., Southern Illinois University Press. Carbondale, IL p.291
293. John Dewey, *'Religion and Morality in a Free Society'* LW15, Southern Illinois University Press. Carbondale, IL p.181
294. John Dewey,1927/1984). *"The Public and Its Problems"* LW2, Southern Illinois University Press. Carbondale.p.329
295. John Dewey,1897/1972). "Individualism Old and New,"LW5, Southern Illinois University Press. Carbondale.p.121
296. John Dewey,1899/1976). "Ethics, 2ndedition" LW1, Southern Illinois University Press. Carbondale.p.285

297. John Dewey, (1922/1983). *Human Nature and Conduct.* MW14, Southern Illinois University Press. Carbondale, IL.p.210
298. John Dewey,1927/1984). *"The Public and Its Problems" LW2*, Southern Illinois University Press,Carbondale. p.329
299. Jatava, D. R. 1965. *The Political Philosophy of B.R.Ambedkar,* Phoenix publishing Agency, Agra.p.p.37
300. Jatava, D. R. 1965. *The Political Philosophy of B.R.Ambedkar,* Phoenix publishing Agency, Agra.p.p.38
301. Dallmayr, Fred R. 1978. *'Political Theory at Cross Roads' in From Contract to Community,* Marcel Dekkar, Inc, New York. p.1
302. Dallmayr, Fred R. 1978. *'Political Theory at Cross Roads' in From Contract to Community,* Marcel Dekkar, Inc, New York. p.9
303. Dallmayr, Fred R. 1978. *'Political Theory at Cross Roads' in From Contract to Community,* Marcel Dekkar, Inc, New York. p.9
304. Ambedkar B.R, 1987. *"Social and Political Democracy'* Dalit Sahitya Academy, Bangalore.p.25
305. Ambedkar B.R, 1987. *"Social and Political Democracy'* Dalit Sahitya Academy, Bangalore.p.26
306. Gail Omvedt, 2000. *"Dalits and the Democratic Revolution,"* Sage Publications, London, p.33
307. Gail Omvedt, 2000. *"Dalits and the Democratic Revolution,"* Sage Publications, London. p.34
308. Gail Omvedt, 2000. *"Dalits and the Democratic Revolution,"* Sage Publications, London. p.34
309. Ibid, p.35
310. John Dewey, 1961. *"Democracy and Politics"* Southern Illinois University Press. Carbondale, IL.p.127
311. John Dewey, 1961. *"Democracy and Politics"* Southern Illinois University Press. Carbondale, IL.p.127
312. Scott London, 1977. *"The Emergence of American Political Issues."* West Pub. Co. University of Michigan, p.258
313. Scott London, 1977. *"The Emergence of American Political Issues,"* West Pub. Co. University of Michigan, p.259
314. Scott London, 1977. *"The Emergence of American Political Issues,"* West Pub. Co. University of Michigan, Michigan. p.260
315. Scott London, 1977. *"The Emergence of American Political Issues,"* West Pub. Co. University of Michigan, p.272

316. Scott London, 1977. *"The Emergence of American Political Issues."* West Pub. Co. University of Michigan, p.274
317. Ibid, p.275
318. Scott London, 1977. *"The Emergence of American Political Issues,"* West Pub. Co. University of Michigan, Michigan. p.283
319. Ibid, p.284
320. Scott London, 1977. "The Emergence of American Political Issues," West Pub. Co. University of Michigan, Michigan. p.283
320. Ibid, p.284 -285
321. Ibid, p.287
322. Ibid, p.289
323. Jatava, D. R.1991. *The Political Philosophy of B.R.Ambedkar,* Phoenix publishing Agency, Agra. p.125
324. Ibid, p. 127
325. Ibid, p.128-129
326. Valerian Roudrigs, (Ed.) 2002. *"The Essential Writings of B.R.Ambedkar,"* Oxford University Press, New Delhi. p.61
327. Ibid, p.62
328. Ibid
329. Valerian Roudrigs (Ed.) 2002. *"The Essential Writings of B.R.Ambedkar,"* Oxford University Press, New Delhi p.62
330. Valerian Roudrigs (Ed.) 2002. *"The Essential Writings of B.R.Ambedkar,"* Oxford University Press, New Delhi . p.63
331. Ibid
332. Valerian Roudrigs (Ed.) 2002. *"The Essential Writings* of B.R.Ambedkar," Oxford University Press, New Delhi p.64
333. John Dewey,1916.*"Political Philosophy and Democracy,* "MW11,Southern Illinois University Press, Carbondale. p.177
334. John Dewey, 1916. *"Political Philosophyand Democracy,* "MW11,Southern Illinois University Press,Carbondale. p.178
335. Ibid
336. Jatava, D. R.1991. *The Political Philosophy of B.R.Ambedkar,* Phoenix publishing Agency, Agra. p.130

337. Ibid,p.131

338. Ibid, p.132-133

339. John Dewey, (1927;1984). *"The Public and Its Problems"LW3,* Southern Illinois University Press. Carbondale.p.20

340. Ibid, p.21

341. John Dewey.1952. *"Democracy and Society"* Southern Illinois University Press. Carbondale.p.57

342. Ibid

343. Jatava, D. R.1991. *The Political Philosophy of B.R.Ambedkar,* Phoenix publishing Agency, Agra. p.134

344. Ibid

345. Jatava, D. R.1991. *The Political Philosophy of B.R.Ambedkar,* Phoenix publishing Agency, Agra. p.136

346. John Dewey, 1939. *"The Meaning of Democracy: its politico-economic structure and ideals"* Liveright Publishing Corporation, New York.p.27

347. John Dewey, 1939. *"The Meaning of Democracy: its politico-economic structure and ideals"* Liveright Publishing Corporation, New York.p.36

348. John Dewey, 1939. *"The Meaning of Democracy: its politico-economic structure and ideals"* Liveright Publishing Corporation, New York. p.43

349. John Dewey, 1939. *"The Meaning of Democracy: its politico-economic structure and ideals"* Liveright Publishing Corporation, New York.p.47

350. John Dewey, 1939. "The Meaning of Democracy: its politico-economic structure and ideals" Liveright Publishing Corporation, New York.p.51

351. John Dewey, 1939. "The Meaning of Democracy: its politico-economic structure and ideals" Liveright Publishing Corporation, New York.p.53

352. John Dewey. (1922/1983). Human Nature and Conduct. MW14 Southern Illinois University Press. Carbondale, IL.p.335

353. Ibid, p. 336

354. John Dewey. (1922/1983). Human Nature and Conduct. MW14 Southern Illinois University Press. Carbondale, IL.p.337

355. Ibid, 338

356. John Dewey, 1984. "Individuality and experience." LW2, Southern Illinois University Press. Carbondale, IL.p.364

357. John Dewey, 1984 "The crucial role of intelligence". LW11, Southern Illinois University Press. Carbondale, IL.p.56

358. John Dewey, 1984. "Individuality and experience." LW2, Southern Illinois University Press. Carbondale, IL.p.327-328

359. Ambedkar, B.R. (1979-98),"States and Minorities", Vol. I&II, printed in Government of Maharashtra, Bombay. p.406

360. Ibid, p.407

361. Ambedkar, B.R. (1979-98). "States and Minorities", Vol.I&II, printed in Government of Maharashtra, Bombay. p.408

362. Syam Chand.2007. "Ambedkar ond Democracy," Blue Moon Books, New Delhi.p.184

363. Syam Chand.2007. "Ambedkar ond Democracy," Blue Moon Books, New Delhi.p.185

364. Ibid, p.186

365. Ibid, p.187

366. Ibid

367. Syam Chand.2007. "Ambedkar ond Democracy," Blue Moon Books, New Delhi.p.188

368. Ibid,p.189

Conclusion

The present study tries to examine John Dewey and Ambedkar's views on religious morality and socio- political philosophy in which both Ambedkar and John Dewey share same ideas. Dewey discusses that Religion should be rational and secular and it should be based on proper reason and facts but not by fiction. But there are two facts where first was a question of choice and personnel resolution on behalf of individuals but not of nature. Secondly as an individual, one carries one's personal attitude into secular activities, which is beyond the range of religion, and constitutes an enormous change, in terms of the belief that secular subjects should be impregnated by the spirit of religion. This is where a religion can be distinguished from the religious function.

Dewey observed that the future of the religious function should be related all religions by integrating the truth in them and emancipating the false illusions. According to Dewey, history illustrates three stages of religious growth. In the first stage man considered all the natural calamities are result of the wrath of the super natural elements and they should seek redemption by offering rituals as a solace to them. The following stage, connected with distinctive religious values, where liberal theologists take up position. In the third stage that values in the religion should be associated with the normal life of human beings produced by them but not by the divine projection of supernatural kingdom in which salvation and punishment plays a vital role.

Dewey said that many religions generally consider themselves to be great and their religious morality is important but he says the religion which gives more impertinence to human values and practice of present social life is greatest religion than other religions.

In the same way, Ambedkar's model of theory on religion is a good model available for us in India to emulate. We need to follow Ambedkar's methodology not only to learn from the great master and achieve what he did, also to carry forward his struggle, and the liberation of all. It is quite clear that Ambedkar's intervention in the philosophical realm is clearly guided by the socio-political reason. Ambedkar holds a perception that the religion is a vital force, a scheme of moral governance and foundation for human society. In Ambedkar's sense, religion is necessary as a system of values and as a science of social reconstruction. He looked at the religion not as an instrument for the individual salvation but as the basis for social interaction. And Ambedkar focuses on the notion of Liberative religion. Through this notion what he emphasizes that notion of religion is quite essential to social transformation. But for him, all the factors in the social transformation are self-subsistent in itself (i.e. social structure, individuals, religion etc). Ambedkar redefines the notion of religion also in the basis of reason and scientific method. He redefines the purpose of the religion.

In Dewey's view religions are human inventions; they were born and disappeared, evolved and decayed and blended and split apart throughout human history. He argues that religious systems do more harm than good and will continue to do so unless they are completely removed of their supernatural elements. They would cease to be religious as the term is generally understood. If we look at any religion in terms of supernatural elements, we may not see good sense in any of the religions. So one should encourage the abandonment of ethical systems based on supernatural religion. In response to this proposal, some would argue that we must first find a replacement. Personally, he finds this line unconvincing.

In the same manner Ambedkar stressed that religion is for humans and not humans for religion. For him, man and morality must be the centre of religion. Humanist to the core, Ambedkar was ready to throw away any religion or religious practice however ancient and sanctified if that does not promote human welfare. According to Ambedkar, Buddhism demands living experience and it was realism and never idealism. It upheld liberty, equality, truth and justice; it emphasized humanity, love and peace. It was dynamic, scientific and all embracing. Its explanation of life and its meaning and purpose of birth and death and its aftermath were very clear, intelligible and logical. Above all, man was the center of his study and examination and not anything outside of him.

Ambedkar says that Religion emphasizes, universalizes social values and brings them to the mind of the individual who is required to be familiar with them in all his acts in an order that he may function as an approved member of the society. He observed, man cannot live by bread alone.

He has a mind, which needs food for thought. Religion instills hope in man and drives him to activity. Religion is not an end in itself. It meant for the preservation of life and human welfare. Hence, religion is not the one that has the final say; it is not infallible, absolute, inflexible nor permanent. Ambedkar stressed that religion is for humans and not humans for religion. For him, man and morality must be the centre of religion. Religion instills hope in man and drives him to activity. Hindu religion has watered down the enthusiasm of the downtrodden. He says that Religion emphasizes, universalizes social values and brings them to the mind of the individual who is required to be familiar with them in all his acts in an order that he may function as an approved member of the society. The concern for the universal well-being is the main consideration of his scheme of religion.

Ambedkar reveals that his address towards religion is not a mere crave towards addressing a religion as a social institution but it was very deep that concentrated on the structure of social system in its wholeness. The religion is a vital force, a scheme of moral governance and foundation for human society. It is necessary as a system of values and as a science of social reconstruction. He looked at the religion not as an instrument for the individual salvation but as the basis for social interaction. He redefines the purpose of the religion.

Finally Dewey comes to conclusions through his books "common faith" he defines three points regarding the religion. First one is to point out the differences in meaning among religions, in its historic-religious experience perspective. Second is to present a new basis of faith which is product of religious experience and it should be divorced from historic religions with their supernatural connotations. Third is to demonstrate the superiority of the proposed new basis of faith over the old. Then Dewey concerns himself first with the task of differentiating between the meaning of religious and the religion. The actual of the religion is "Recognition on the part of man of some unseen higher power as having control of his destiny and as being entitled to obedience, reverence and worship. There is no great similarity in the ways in which reverence and obedience have been expressed by different groups and at different times in history. Historic religions have been relative to the conditions of social culture in which people live. He asserts that historical fact supports the need for a restructuring of religions in the light of current cultural developments. After explain the religion from the historic perspective he also describes about religious experience and harmony which is essentially religious in nature. This quality of experience can result from participation with an institutionalized religion. Religious experiences such as the aesthetic, scientific, moral and friendship should be charged with "religious" potentiality.

Lastly, Dewey's criticism can be made concerning the fact that he qualifies historical religions as superstitions and God as 'supernatural being with powers' is somehow quite simplistic and many believers certainly will not recognize themselves in such a description of their God or religion. Moreover, the 'religious' which he highlighted because of its 'power in action' can also be found in the religions he criticizes, as they sometimes also lead to social change and action. And finally, the ideal ends and experience he requires and add up to a new religion in which he himself seems to believe, and his concept of the 'religious' can't really be empirically verified.

According to Ambedkar, God and faith is a human creation. In the primitive period the primitive man regarded anything as divine power, which he was not able to understand. This power was originally malevolent, but later on, it was felt that it could also be benevolent. Later the power has become God or it was called the creator. So man developed the theory of God to explain natural phenomena. Ambedkar raised a question that if God was benevolent then why his own creations are considered untouchables. In his perception, God was an embodiment of hatred and injustice because it was said that the unjust social structure, which gave birth to untouchability, is a God given one hence it cannot be changed. Hence, Ambedkar rejected the idea of God created by religion which is exactly what he reproaches to traditional belief and faith.

Ambedkar's Religion is praiseworthy on many counts. It has emphasized the social function of religion without neglecting to emphasize its necessity for personal growth. It laid more stress on orthopraxis, the right moral conduct based on love, than doctrines, cults, rituals and devotional practices. Many magical trappings of religion and doctrinal binding chains have been broken down by his theology. He has emphasized the liberative, prophetic, critical dimension of religion.

Ambedkar's Religion is humanistic and anthropological; his thought is social humanism. His main concern was to regain the full humanity deprived of caste oppression and sex discrimination, which are not only economic alienations but also primarily anthropological alienations. In his theology, Ambedkar gave importance to the common good, and the establishment of a humane social order, a society based on liberty, equality and fraternity of all the people. As a part of it, Holistic human development was much insisted upon. He would never take rest only with the fulfilment material well-being, and often reminded his people of the spiritual salvation, mental enlightenment, cultural transformation, social status, unity, love and peace, which are essential for happy and holy life.

Ambedkar's religion is essentially stereological and eschatological. Its aim and dream was to build up the Kingdom of Righteousness and *Dhamma Raj* by perfecting the social order gradually. To begin with, socio-religious reform for equality, national independence, democratic constitutional forms of government and state socialism are to be realized. The transformation of the social relationships and attitudes, based on the new value-system of liberty, equality and fraternity, is the foundation of the new just egalitarian society. Justice, social, economic and political, is to be secured for every member of the national and the human family. Only then can humane divine state of love and peace can reign in the universe, with blessedness and happiness for all creatures, the humans and the nature. At the same time, we also find his theological approach universalistic in nature. It wishes the welfare of all people. Ambedkar's Theology emphasized the common good, the just social order that will secure justice and equality for all the citizens. It strives for the universal peace of the Kingdom.

In next step Dewey speaks about morality. In his view it represents no universal 'good' and 'bad', as it is not connected to 'truth'. No morality is needed to make human beings 'social', because they always act in associations with the meaning of 'social realm. He states that there is an artificial division between morality and life-activity with the consequence of morality as a separate entity which is imposed upon human actions. But he emphasizes that even 'no action' is action in reference to the social process because there are always lead to consequences. The morality provides for only 'right' and 'wrong' action in reference to something stable outside of the perceivable reality. Dewey explains in accordance to his concept, how one can perceive that morality as something imposed upon us. As Dewey have argued, that religious morality does more harm than good, then we can only gain by forsaking it. If it is replaced it should not be based on supernaturalism but on equality and justice. Religious morality is thought to be authoritarian in spirit and antagonistic to the freedom of an individual? However, the possibility that morality might be need of religious foundations but its authoritarian character is not considered. It is the opposition to religious authority in the matter of motives and norms which alienates the fellow human beings rejected by Dewey.

In the same line how Ambedkar justify morality without reference to transcendental religious beliefs is a first step to make the realm of morality as an autonomous one. The concern for the universal well-being is the main consideration of Ambedkar's scheme of morality.

Thus, external considerations are no longer being above moral principles. Ambedkar makes such a morality the basis of religion, which he construes as *Dhamma.* In this construal, he redefines the centre of religion as morality rather than God. According to Ambedkar, Natural law is the basis of moral order of universe. *Dhamma* for Ambedkar is all-inclusive. The underlying meaning of the *Dhamma* is a message of equality.

Ambedkar's morality of love arises from the direct necessity for man to love man. He makes it comprehensible that it is not to please the God that man has to be moral but for his own good qualities, man has to love man. In the struggle for existence the individual's rights may not' be catered for, and at times his or her interests can be, rare by the group. Similarly, a weak group may also be discriminated by a stronger group, hence the indispensability ability of the *law of love,* fraternity and goodwill, which is another name for morality. The most important in, *Saddhamma,* more than *Prajna* and *Sila, Sila* is *Karuna,* love of human beings and *Maitri* that is all living beings.

It must be remembered that Ambedkar categorically defends the autonomy of morality. Like Spinoza, Ambedkar says that the good life is not a means to something else but is itself a supreme end. Hence according to Ambedkar morality must be autonomous in the sense that, no alien considerations, like the fear of tyrannical God or deity from an absolute Hindu religious *Dharma* should be admitted as valid determining the conduct of human persons. Again he says that any consideration of earthly gain or worldly reward and success should not determine the truly moral conduct. The good is to chosen for its own sake, just as the good life is to be lived for its own sake. Thus in any respect according to Ambedkar the morality is truly autonomous. However, Ambedkar persistent question is still remains that which morality is dependent for its content on the norms and concepts derived from which religion. Here, Ambedkar makes clear difference between Buddhism and Hinduism and takes the position that the Hindu social order is immoral and it is against the human freedom and fraternity. For Ambedkar, religion must be essentially moral; religion cannot live unless it interacts with other forms of spiritual life as morality, beauty, and truth. Religion is thus when compared with morality it turns out to be at once *infra* and *supra* ethical. The fact that the religion takes as its point of departure human life, for this it provides a goal. Without such a destiny in sight religion cannot exist, provided with it faith passes on far beyond the realm of morality.

Ambedkar's position is that morality in religion would not be an effective one. In religion, morality is only a wagon which is attached to it. It is attached and detached as the occasion requires. Ambedkar notes that the morality comes in only wherein man comes in relation to man. Morality comes into religion as a side wind to maintain peace and order….Be good to your neighbour because you are both are human beings….The action of morality in the functioning of religion is therefore casual and occasional. Ambedkar affirms that morality is *Dhamma* and *Dhamma* is morality.

After discussion of morality, Dewey concludes that Political Ideology is dynamic and political culture is static. Political ideologies and political cultures are related in certain aspects. Political cultures are the basic rights and they should be protected by the people, whereas political ideologies are just more in depth and specific. These are very important aspects of ideals in explaining political ideologies and cultures.

Dewey says Political ideology will seem quite apparent when the definitions and related examples are explained in postdating sections. Political ideology is a certain set of ideals or principles dealing with a nation, or even a group, that explains how society should work. A political ideology largely concerns itself with how to allocate power and to what ends it should be used. It is often seen as the background of a political party and their policy. Political culture, in simple terms, is what most citizens expect from their government. Most of these are basic rights, such as those outlined in the Constitution. Political culture is usually determined by the government ,which is considered as a static however, political ideology is dynamic because it is usually determined by the people and even a certain period in time, not by the government.

The Dewey basic principles of political philosophy are liberty, equality and fraternity. Liberty is the condition of being free from restriction. It also relates with free will the right to act or believe in a manner of your choosing. Equality would be defined, obviously, as the state of being equal. Whether it is socially, religiously, and economically, equality is a goal that the government has striven for its adopted. Fraternity is defined as the right to maintain relation with others. However, authority seems to corrupt the equality of our nation. Yet, so many people in the name of power they ignore the social needs of the people.

Dewey Liberalism of political ideology is People who are liberal are in favor of a more active federal government. These people believe that the poor should be helped by the government and that thing such as minority rights are preserved and protected. A basic definition of a liberal person is openness to progress and change. Most liberals are also, open-minded and willing to give rather than receive. What distinguishes liberals from conservative is that liberals apply a greater degree of government support, defense and promotion of the free market. Those who are conservative seek to limit governmental activities. They are usually the ones who don't like helping others at their own expenses. Conservatives have a strong orientation to value and they believe all others should think the same. They tend to reject other political ideologies.

In the same ideology, we have concluded that Ambedkar political philosophy was nurtured in the liberal tradition; he makes a difference from it. On many issues, he differs from liberal thinkers like Nehru. While embracing Buddhist religion, he seems to be conservative, but it is clearly evidenced that he is not conservative by his attack of Gandhi and the Hindu social order. At certain points, he seems to be radical (Marxist). But, he throughout his life, he maintains his differences with Marxist thought, particularly in understanding Indian society. However, the primary concern for Ambedkar is liberation of Downtrodden, the people of the lower strata of Indian society. He approached any political tradition from this point only. This has implications in providing the principles of reconstruction of Indian society. In other words, one feels that his political thought demanda whole new language and the existing political language fails short in assessing or understanding his philosophy. Ambedkar's political philosophy has a great potential in mediating both liberal and communitarian traditions of the west. He connects the individual and community based on morality. He proposes the democratic, humanistic and rationalistic religion such as Buddhism is the source for morality and associate living. When Ambedkar criticizes the Hindu community for its oppressive nature, he does it with a standard of individual liberty and freedom. When he is talking about suffering of individual members of Dalit community he is projecting an ideal moral community based on equality, liberty and fraternity. So it is not correct to call Ambedkar as either a fierce individualist or as a strong communitarian.

Moreover Ambedkar Liberalism, as a political theory developed in the west has a theoretical basis and reflection of modern industrial capitalist society. It implies individual rights as natural and absolute. Ambedkar seems to reject the liberal notion of society as an aggregation of individuals related to each other as individuals in terms of the goal of promoting individual interest. He has given importance to justice than utility. According to him utility is only a secondary criterion for judging right or wrong. That is, primacy of justice over utility is axiomatic for him. By subordinating utility to justice in his philosophical analytical scheme, he departs from the very first tenet of utilitarianism in particular and liberal philosophy in general.

It is very difficult to fit him into dominant political traditions like liberalism, Marxism and conservatism. He himself finds difficulty in explaining his political position. It doesn't mean that there is no consistency in his political thinking. The problem lies only in explaining his thought in existing political vocabulary. He critically engaged with liberalism, Marxism and Gandhism. He describes himself as a progressive radical and occasionally as a 'progressive conservative'. One thing is clear that he would like to be a progressive, and distinguish himself from liberals and communists depending on the case.

The social philosophy of Ambedkar, who faced the terrible discrimination ,terrible suffering, pain and pathos of cultural deprivation, cultural exploitation, social ostracism, and political domination caused by the ruthless monstrous caste-system, made Ambedkar whole-heartedly hate the caste system and anything or anyone related with its continuation he has choosed the Buddism where equality prevails from king to common man.. As he admits, such hatred for injustice is necessary for the activists who wish to fight for a justice and self-governing order. The core of Ambedkar's social philosophy of life happened to be the basics tenets of liberty, equality and fraternity. To him, A great man must be motivated by the dynamics of a social purpose and must act as the curse and the scavenger of society. These are the elements which distinguish an eminent individual from a great man and constitute his title-deeds to respect and reverence.

Indeed, he himself fulfilled all the conditions of being a great man. His title to this dignity rests upon the social purposes he served and in the way he served to them. His life is a history of great struggles and achievements. His message to the people was we must have firm belief in sacredness of our mission. Noble is our aim and inspiring and glorious is our mission. Blessed are those who are awakened to their duty to those among whom they are born. Towards the end of his life, Ambedkar had to stand lone most of his life, with no support from other ideologists, parties, and religions, because of his non-compromising attitude. His strong critique of them all and avoidance, made them also shun him.

Bibliography

- Alfred North Whitehead. 1926. *'Religion in the Making,'* Macmillan, New York.
- Ambedkar, B.R. 1998. *'Ambedkar's Philosophy of Religion,'* INA Shree Publishers, Jaipur.
- Ambedkar, B. R. (1957),1991, *'The Buddha and His Dhamma,'* Siddharth Publications, Bombay.
- Ambedkar, B. R. 1950. *"The Buddha and the Future of His Religion,"* The Mahabodhi Publications, Bangalore.
- Ambedkar, B.R.1989. *'Slavery and Untouchability: Which is worse?,'* Dalit Dayal, New Delhi.
- Ambedkar, B.R. (1979-98), *"States and Minorities",* Vol.I&II, printed in Government of Maharashtra, Bombay.
- Ambedkar, B. R.1968. *The Buddha and the Future of His Religion,* The Mahabodhi, Bombay.
- Anand Teltumbde. 1997. *'Ambedkar' In and for the Post-Ambedkar Dalit Movement,* Sugawa Prakashan, Pune.
- Aristotle, 1998. *'Politics,' Book* 1, Hackett *Publishing Co.* Indianapolis.
- Asghar Ali Engeneer, ed., 1984. *'Islam and Revolution,' Ajanta Published,* New Delhi.
- Bakshi, P.M. 1990. *'B.R.Ambedkar: Statesman and Constitutionalist,'* Anmol Publications, New Delhi.

- Beerbohm, E.,2006. *'The Ethics of Democracy' EW*1, Princeton University Press.Princeton
- Benedict.1927, *'Divine Truth,'* Ignatius Press and the Vatican's *Publishing* House,San Francisco
- Bergson, Henri (1932; 1956) *The Two Sources of Religion and Morality.* Doubleday Anchor Books. Garden City, NewJersy.
- Bernabé. 2006. *"Diversity as Fraternity Lite"* El Diario La Prensa, New York .
- Bernard Murchland.1967. *"The Meaning of the Death of God"* Random House, New York.
- Billy Graham, 1983. *"The Bible is a Book",* American Bible Society, New york, Verse.27
- Bloom, Allan. 1987. *'Closing of the American mind.,'* Simon & Schuster, New York.
- Bohman, James, 2005. *'Democracy as Inquiry, Inquiry as Democratic: Pragmatism, Social Science and the Cognitive Division of Labor."* Blackwell Publishing Ltd Garsington Road, Oxford UK
- Campbell, James, 1993. *'Democracy as Cooperative Inquiry.'* In John J. Stuhr (ed.), Philosophy and the Reconstruction of Culture, SUNY, Albany.
- Carolyn Graglia.1998. *"Domestic Tranquility: Arief against Feminism"* SpencepublishingCo.Dallas.Texas.
- Caspary, William R. 2000. *'Dewey on Democracy.'* Cornell University Press, Ithaca, New York.
- Christopher. 1997. *"Reconstructing Dewey",* Cornell University Press, Berlin.
- Cohn and Dirks. 1996. 2001. *'Castes of Mind: Colonialism and the Making of Modern India ,'* published by Princeton University Press. New Jersey.
- *Coomaraswarmy,* Ananda K.1979& 2007. *'Hinduism And Buddhism,'* Kessinger Publishing, Newyork.
- Coomaraswarmy, Ananda K.2004. *'World Wisdom,'* Inc, Newyork.
- Coomaraswarmy, Ananda K. 1979. *'Comparative Religion: The Democracy, Freedom, and Equality,'* Ministry of Information and Broadcasting, Government of India, New Delhi.

- Craig & Raymond.1987 *"Morality and Religion"* Simon & Schuster Publishers, New York.
- Dallmayr, Fred R. 1978. *'Political Theory at Cross Roads' in From Contract to Community,* Marcel Dekkar, Inc, New York.
- Damico, Alfonso, 1978. *'Individuality* and *Community: The Social* and *Political Thought of John Dewey,'* University Presses of Florida, Gainesville.
- David W. Noble.1965. *"The American Political Tradition",* University of Minnesota Press, Minneapolis.
- David Miller,1989. *"Ambedkar's Political and Social Thought"* Clarendon Press. Oxford.
- Debra Morris and Ian Shapiro, eds., *'John Dewey: The Political Writings,'* Indianapolis: Hackett, 1993
- Dhananjay Keer, 1991. *'Dr. Ambedkar Life and Mission,'* Popular Prakashan, Bombay..
- Diggins, John Patrick. 1994. 'The Promise of Pragmatism,' University of Chicago Press, Chicago.
- Dutt, Naraendra Kumar. 1984., *'Origin and growth of caste in India,'* Vol.I Firma K.L Mukhopadhya press,Calcutta.
- Eakman, B.K. 1998. *'Cloning of The American Mind: Eradicating Morality Through* Education' Huntington House Publishers, Lafayette, LosseAnjels.
- Farr, James, 1968. *'John Dewey and American Political Science', American Journal of Political Science,'* Markham Publishers, Chicago.
- Festenstein, Matthew, 1997. *'Pragmatism and Political Theory: From Dewey to Rorty,'* Chicago University Press, Chicago.
- Festenstein, Matthew,1997. *'The Ties of Communication: Dewey on Ideal and Political Democracy', History of Political Thought,'* Chicago University Press, Chicago.
- Festenstein, Matthew,2001. *'Inquiry as Critique: On the Legacy of Deweyan Pragmatism for Political Theory', Political Studies,'* Festenstein, M.Publishers, New York.

- Fott, David, 1998. *'John Dewey: America's Philosopher of Democracy,'* Rowman and Littlefield, Lanham, Maryland.
- Franklin & David Hartley, 1789. *"The Love of Liberty"* Poor Richard's Almanack and The Pennsylvania Gazette.United States.
- Gail Omvedt, 2000. *"Dalits and the Democratic Revolution"* , Sage Publications, London.
- George, Lawrence, 1966. (Trans) *'A common Faith,' Harper & Row,* Part II, chap. 2. New York.
- Ghurye, G.S. 1979. *'Caste and Race in India,'* Popular Prakashan, Bombay.
- Gokhale, Jayasree, 1993. *"The Politics of an Indian Untouchable Community,"* Popular Prakashan, Mumbai.
- Gore, M.S,1993. *'Social Context of an ideology: Ambedkar's Political and Social Thought,'* Sage publications, New Delhi.
- *Guenter Lewy,* 1974. *'Religion and Revolution,'* Oxford University Press, New York.
- Herbert Wallace Schneider, 1946. *"International Journal of Ethics* and *'A History of American Philosophy,'* Columbia University Press, New York.
- Hickman, Larry (ed.), 1998. *'John Dewey: Interpretations for a Postmodern Generation,'* Indiana University Press, Indianapolis.
- Honneth, Axel, 1998 . *'Democracy as Reflexive Cooperation: John Dewey and the Theory of Democracy Today'*, Honneth, Axel, Burlington.
- Honneth, Axel,200.1 *'Staunchly Modern, Non-Bourgeois Liberalism.'* In Avital Simhony and David Weinstein (eds.), The *New Liberalism: Reconciling Liberty and Community.* Cambridge University Press, Cambridge.
- Hunumanthan, K.R.1991. *'Evolution of Untouchability in Tamil Nadu up to AD 1600',* in Aloka Parasher-Sen,(ed)., *'Subordinate and Marginal Groups in Early India,'* New Delhi.
- Hutton, J.H.1946. *'Caste in India: its Nature Function and origins,'* University Press, Cambridge.
- Jatava, D.R. 1991. *'The Political Philosophy of B. R. Ambedkar,' Popular* Prakashan, New Delhi.

- Jatava, D.R.1965. *'The Social Philosophy of B. R. Ambedkar,'* Phoenix Publishing Agency, Agra.
- James Campbell, 1995. *'Understanding John Dewey: Nature and Cooperative Intelligence,'* Open Court, Chicago.
- Janine Marie Idziak, 1978. *'Divine Commands are the foundation of Morality,'* Clarendon Press, Oxford.
- John Dewey, 1925. *'Science and the Modern World'.* Lowell Lectures: Macmillan, New York.
- John Dewey, 1961. *"Democracy and Politics"* Southern Illinois University Press. Carbondale.
- John Dewey, (1927/1984). *'The Public and Its Problems,' LW*3 Southern Illinois University Press, Carbondale.
- John Dewey, 1982. *'Reconstruction in Philosophy and Essays 1920',* Southern Illinois University Press, Carbondale.
- John Dewey,1922/1983. *'Human Nature and Conduct',* Southern Illinois University Press. Carbondale.
- John Dewey. (1933/1986). *"How We Think"* Southern Illinois University Press. Carbondale, IL.p.33
- John. Dewey,1892/1997. *Christianity and democracy.* EW3, Southern Illinois University Press, Carbondale.
- John Dewey, (1952). *'The Impact of Science on Society'.* George Allen &Unwin. London
- John Dewey. (1923/1983). *"Logial Method and Law",* EW15, Southern Illinois University Press, Carbondale
- John Dewey, (1919; 1988).' *Philosophy and Democracy.' MW*11.Southern Illinois University Press, Carbondale.
- John Dewey.1973. *"Society and Democracy."* Southern Illinois University. Carbondale
- John Dewey. 1952. "Philosophy and Society." Southern Illinois University. Carbondale.
- John Dewey. *Reconstruction in Philosophy, MW*12, Southern Illinois University Press. Carbondale.

- John Dewey, *'Context and Thought', LW5*, Southern Illinois University Press. Carbondale.
- John Dewey, *'The Future of Liberalism', LW*11., Southern Illinois University Press. Carbondale.
- John Dewey, *'Religion and Morality in a Free Society'* LW15, Southern Illinois University Press. Carbondale.
- John Dewey,1927/1984). *"The Public and Its Problems" LW2*, Southern Illinois University Press. Carbondale.
- John Dewey,1897/1972). *"Individualism Old and New,"LW5*, Southern Illinois University Press. Carbondale.
- John Dewey,1899/1976). *"Ethics, 2ndedition "LW1, Southern Illinois University Press.* Carbondale.
- John Dewey, 1939. *'The Meaning of Democracy: its politico-economic structure and ideals,'* Liveright Publishing Corporation, New York.
- John Dewey, 1984. *"Individuality and experience." LW2*, Southern Illinois University Press. Carbondale.
- John Dewey, 1984 *"The crucial role of intelligence". LW*11, Southern Illinois University Press. Carbondale.
- John Dewey, 1983/2008. *"Religion and Morality,"* Southern Illinois University Press. Carbondale.
- John Herman Randall Sr and Jr .1929. *"Religion and Modern World"*, Stokes Co., New York.
- John Neville Figgis 1965. *"Religion and Society"* Rand McNally & Co., Chicago.
- Joshi Lal Mani, 1977. *'Studies in the Buddhistic Culture of India,'* Motilal Banarasidass, NewDelhi.
- John Dewey. (1910a/1978). *'How We Think,' MW*16, Southern Illinois University Press. Carbondale.
- John Dewey, 1925. *"Experience and Nature," LW*1 Southern Illinois University Press, Carbondale.
- John Dewey, and James H. Tufts. 1963. *Ethics.* John Somerville and Ronald E. Santoni, *Social and Political Philosophy. Anchor Books, New York.*

- John Dewey, 1951. *Biography of John Dewey:The philosophy of John Dewey.* Ed. Paul A. Schilp. New York, Tudor.
- John Dewey, 1894. John Dewey to Alice Dewey, *"Dewey papers,"* Morris Library, Southern Illinois University, Carbondale.
- John Dewey, 1960, *'The New American Liberty,'* Cambridge University Press, New York.
- John Dewey, 1934. *'A Common Faith,'* New Haven, Yale University Press, New York.
- John Dewey, 1925. *'Science and the Modern World.'* Lowell Lectures: Macmillan, New York.
- John Dewey,1934. *'Art as Experience.' LW*2 Southern Illinois University Press, Carbondale.
- John Dewey,1984. *'The Quest for Certainty 1929,'LW*4 Southern Illinois University Press, Carbondale.
- John Dewey, 1985. *Ethics* 1932, LW7 Southern Illinois University Press, Carbondale.
- John Dewey,(1916;1985). *Democracy and Education MW*9 Southern Illinois University Press, Carbondale.
- John Dewey,(1939;1988). *'Freedom and Culture,' LW*13 Southern Illinois University Press. Carbondale.
- John Dewey, (1993). Eds. Debra Morris and Ian Shapiro. *'The Political Writings.'* Hackett Publishing Company, Indianapolis.
- John Dewey, (1934), *'The Future of Liberalism,'* Yale University Press, New Haven.
- John Dewey, 1925. *'Science and the Modern World. Lowell Lectures,'* Macmillan, New York.
- Joseph Haroutunian, 1964. *'Theology and American Experience,'* Criterion WinterPublishers, New York.
- Kadam K.N, 1993. *'Ambedkar: The Emancipator of the Oppressed,'* Sangam Books, London.
- Keer, Dhananjay, 1982. *'Ambedkar: A Memorial Album',* Sangan Books, London

- Kelley's, M.study, 1972. *'Why Conservative Churches are Growing; A Study in Sociology of Religion,'* Harper & Row, New York.
- Kevin Reilly, Stephen Kaufman, Angela Bodino,2003. *'Racism: A Global Reader'* M.E .Sharpe Inc, New Delhi.
- Klass, Morton.1993. *'Caste: The Emergence of the South Asian Social System',* Monhar Publishers, New Delhi,
- Klass 1980; Yurlova 1989. *'Caste hierarchies in India ,'* Indian Institute of Dalit Studies.New Delhi.
- Koch, Adrienne. 1965. *'Pragmatic Wisdom and the American Enlightenment,'* Vol. 18, No. 3 in JSTOR, New York.
- Kosambi, D.D. 1977. *'The Culture and Civilisation of Ancient India,'* Vikas Publishers, New Delhi.
- Krishnasagar, R.K.1989. *'Untouchability In India,'* Deep & Deep Publications, New Delhi.
- Kuber, W. N. 1990. *'B.R. Ambedkar,'* Publication Division, Ministry of Information and Broadcasting, Govt. of India, New Delhi.
- Lakshmana, Chintamani.1973.' *Caste Dynamics in Village India,'* Nachiketa Publications, Bombay.
- Lederle M, 1976. *The Untouchables' Claim to Human Dignity,* Journal of University of Poona, Humanities Section, Poona.
- Margaret Patricia McCarran, 1954. *'Fabianism In The Political Life Of Britain, 1919-1931'* The Heritage Foundation, Chicago.
- Martin B. Marty, 1961. *'The Infidel; Free Thought and American Religion,'* World Pub. Co.'s Meridian Books, Cleveland.
- Mary Kelley. 1975. *"Religion and American Revolution,"* Seabury Press, New York .
- Massey,James. 1991. *Roots: A Concise History of Dalits,* CISRS, Bengalore.
- Mendelsohn, Oliver & Vicziany, Maria,1998. *"The Untouchables",* Cambridge Publisher,.New Delhi.
- Moon, Vasant. Vol.I, 1989. (ed.), *'Babasaheb Ambedkar's: Writings and Speeches',* Dept. of Education, Govt. of Maharastra, Bombay.
- Moon, Vasant. Vol.III, 1987. (ed.), *Babasaheb Ambedkar's: Writings and Speeches,* Dept. of Education, Govt. of Maharastra, Bombay.

- Moon, Vasant. Vol.V, 1989. (ed.), *'Babasaheb Ambedkar's: Writings and Speeches,'* Dept. of Education, Govt. of Maharastra, Bombay.
- Moon, Vasant. Vol.IX, 1989. (ed.), *'Babasaheb Ambedkar's: Writings and Speeches,'* Dept. of Education, Govt. of Maharastra, Bombay.
- Moon Vasanth, 1989. *'B.R.Ambedkar, Writings and Speeches.'* Vol.III, Govt of Maharastra, Bombay.
- Moon Vasant, 1987. *Why Go for Conversion?* Dalit Sahitya Akademy, Bangalore.
- Gore M.S. 1993. *'The Social Context of an Ideology - Ambedkar's Political and Social Thought,'* Sage Publications, New Delhi.
- Nathaniel William Taylor, 1942. *"A Connecticut Liberal,"* Chap IV&VI,University of Chicago Press, Chicago.
- Niles. 1818. *"The American Revolution"* Samuel and John AdamsPublisher, Baltimore.
- Omvedt, Gail. 2000. *'Liberty, Equality, Community. Dr.Babasaheb Ambedkar's vision of a New Social Order'* New Age International Publishers, New Delhi.
- Orrill, Robert E., ed. 1997. *'Education and Democracy: Re-Imagining Liberal Learning in America,'* College Entrance Examination Board, New York.
- Otto Maduro, 1982. *Religion and Social Conflicts,* Orbis Books, New York.
- Panikkar and A. Koothothil, 1981. *"Man and Religion,"* Jeevadhara Publications, New Delhi.
- Patricia McCarran.1954. *"Political Boss of Nevada,"* Jerome E. Edwards Books Publisher. Nevada.
- Paul Kurtz, 2002 *"Are Science and Religion Compatible?Skeptical Inquirer,'* Vol. 26, no. 2, Amherst Publisher, New. York.
- Paulos Gregorios, 1989, *"East and West : pointers in the quest for India's secular identity"* B. R. Publishing House, New Delhi
- Panikar R and Koothothil A, 1981. *"Man and Religion,"* Jeevadhara Publishers, New Delhi.
- Paradkar B.A.M,1972. *'The Religious Quest of Ambedkar,'* in T.S.Wilkinson and M.M.Thomas, eds., *'Ambedkar and the Neo-Buddhist Movement,' Bangalore. CISRS.*

- Paul Arthur Schilpp. (ed)., 1951. *'The Philosophy of John Dewey,'* Tudor Publishing Company, New York.
- Paul Kurtz, 2002. *"Are Science and Religion Compatible? Skeptical Inquirer,'* Vol. 26, no. 2, Newark Publisher, New Jersey.
- Paul Rasor, 1997. *'Written for Unitarian Universalist Theologies',* Andover-Newton Theological School. Seminar Press, New York.
- Paulos Mar Gregorios, 1989. *'Enlightenment East and West: Pointers in the Quest for India's Secular Identity,'* Simla. I. I. S. A.
- Philip Mathew and Ajit Murican, eds.,1987. *"Religion, Ideology and Counter - Culture, his "Non - Brahmin and Dalit Movements and their implications for Anti - Caste Struggle,"* Horizon book, Bangalore.
- Pieris A, 1988. *'Love Meets Wisdom: A Christian Experience of Buddhism,'* Orbis Books, New York.
- Putnam, Hilary, 1991. *'A Reconsideration of Deweyan Democracy.'* Melvin L. Rogers Publishers, California.
- Rabb, Peter (ed.), 1993. *"Dalit Movements and the Meaning of Labour in India"* Oxford University Press, Oxford.
- Robert Cummings Nuville, 2002. *"Functions: New Essays in The Philosophy of Psychology"* Oxford University Press, Oxford.
- Robert E. Enger (ed.), *'Bertrand Russell's Best,'* The New American Library Press, New York.
- Robert M. Brown, 1967 *"In Conscience I Must Break the Law"* M. Ryan, editor New york.
- Rockefeller, Steven C., 1991 *'John Dewey: Religious Faith and Democratic Humanism,'* Columbia University Press, New York.
- Roger. Mead, 1967. *"social and cultural continuity"* International Publishers, New York.
- Roger, Williams.1967. *"Separation of Church and State."* John Milton's publisher,United States (US)
- Rorty, Richard.1999. *'Achieving Our Country: Leftist Thought in Twentieth-Centuy America'.* Harvard University Press, Cambridge.
- Rorty, Richard. 1999. *'Achieving Our Country: Leftist Thought in Twentieth-Century America,'* Harvard University Press, Cambridge, MA.

- *Rorty,* Richard. 1998. *'Achieving Our Country'* Harvard University Press, Cambridge, MA.
- Shourie, Arun. 2000. *'Worshipping False Gods: Ambedkar and the Facts which have been Erased.'* Harper Collins, New Delhi.
- Roudrigues, Valerian (Ed.) 2002. *'The Essential Writings of B.R.Ambedkar,'* Oxford University Press, New Delhi.
- Ryan, Alan, 1985. *'John Dewey and the High Tide of American Liberalism,'* New York:
- Ryan, Alan, 1985. *'Pragmatism, Policy Science, and the State',* American Journal of Political Science, 29. New York.
- Ryan, Alan ,1991. *'Politics/Sense/Experience,'* Cornell University Press, Ithaca, New York.
- Saul K. Padover. 1943. *'Religious freedom,'* Duell, Sloan and Pearch, Inc., New York.
- Savage, Daniel M., 2002. *'John Dewey's Liberalism: Individuality, Community, and Self-Development,'* Southern Illinois University Press, Carbondale and Edwardsville.
- Scott London, 1977. *"The Emergence of American Political Issues,"* West Pub. Co. University of Michigan, New Delhi.
- Segundo J. L , 1977. *'Faith and Ideologies.'* Orbis Books, New York.
- Srinivas M.N, 1988. *'Social Change in Modern India,'* Orient Longman, Hyderabad.
- Steven Rockefeller,1995. *'John Deey:Religious Faith and Democratic Humanism',* Columbia University Press, Columbia.
- Syam Chand.2007. *"Ambedkar ond Democracy,"* Blue Moon Books, New Delhi.
- Teltumbde, Anand. 1997. *'Ambedkar': in and for Post-Ambedkar Dalit Movement.* Sugawa Prakashan, Pune.
- Thomas Paine, 1794. *'The Age of Reason,'* preface to Part II, Dell *Publishing* Co., New York.
- Thumma Anthony Raj, 2000 *"Wisdom of the Weak: Foundations of People's Theology,* " ISPCK, New Delhi.

- Tinder, Glenn. 1995. *'Political Thinking: The Perennial Questions,'* HarperCollins, New York.
- Untermeyer, Louis. 1955. *'Makers of the Modern World,'* Simon & Schuster, New York.
- Tiles, J. E., 1992. *'John Dewey: Critical Assessments,'* vols 4 Routledge, , London.
- Valerian Roudrigs, (Ed.) 2002. *"The Essential Writings of B.R.Ambedkar,"* Oxford University Press, New Delhi.
- Walton, Christopher L.1997. *'The Religious Availability of John Dewey's God.'* Philocrites Publisher, New York.
- Weaver (eds.), 2004. *'Pragmatism in Law and Society'* Westview, , Boulder.
- Weaver (eds.), 1994. *'Words and Life,':* Harvard University Press, Cambridge Mass.
- Welchman, Jennifer, 1995. *'Dewey's Ethical Thought,'* Cornell University Press, Ithaca, New York.
- Westbrook, Robert B.1991. *'John Dewey and American Democracy,'* Cornell University Press, Ithaca, New York.
- William James. 1994. *'The Varieties of Religious Experience.'* Longmans, Green, 1902; Modern Library, New York.
- Winthrop, John (1630) *'A Model of Christian Charity,'* in Pery Miller, 1956. ed. *The American Puritans: Their Prose and Poetry.* Anchor Books, NewYork.
- Zelliot E, 1969. *"Religion and Legitimation"*, Princeton University Press, Princeton city.

Secondary Sources

- Alexander, Thomas M. 1987. *'The Horizons of Feeling: John Dewey's Theory of Art, Experience,* and Nature.' State University of New York Press, Albany.
- Boisvert, Raymond D. 1988. *'Dewey's Metaphysics.'* Fordham University Press, New York.
- Boisvert, Raymond D. 1998. *'John Dewey: Rethinking Our Time.'* State University of New York Press, Albany.

- Bullert, Gary. 1983. *'The Politics of John Dewey.'*: Prometheus Books, Buffalo. NewYork.
- Campbell, James. 1995. *'Understanding John Dewey: Nature and Cooperative Intelligence.'* Open Court, Chicago and La Salle.
- Damico, Alfonso J. 1978. *'Individuality and Community: The Social and Political Thought of John Dewey.'* Gainesville, University Presses of Florida, Florida.
- Dykhuizen, George.1973. *'The Life and Mind of John Dewey.'* Southern Illinois University Press, Carbondale.
- Eames,S.Morris. 2003. *'Experience and Value: Essays on John Dewey and Pragmatic Naturalism,'* Elizabeth R. Eames and Richard W. Field, eds. Southern Illinois University Press, Carbondale.
- Eldridge, Michael. 1998. *'Transforming Experience: John Dewey's Cultural Instrumentalism'.* Vanderbilt University Press, Nashville.
- Gouinlock, James. 1972. *'John Dewey's Philosophy of Value.'* Humanities Press, New York.
- Hickman, Larry. 1990. *'John Dewey's Pragmatic Technology.'* Indiana University Press, Bloomington.
- Hickman, Larry A, (ed). 1998. *'Reading Dewey: Interpretations for a Postmodern Generation'* Indiana University Press, Bloomington and Indianapolis.
- Hook, Sidney. 1995. *'John Dewey: An Intellectual Portrait.'* John Day Co., Prometheus Books, New York.
- Jackson, Philip W. 1998. *'John Dewey and the Lessons of Art'* Yale University Press, New Haven.
- Haskins, Casey and David I. Seiple, (eds). 1999..*'Dewey Reconfigured: Essays on Deweyan Pragmatism.'* State University of New York Press, Albany.
- Levine, Barbara. 1996. *'Works about John Dewey: 1886-1995.'* Southern Illinois University Press, Carbondale and Edwardsville.
- Rockefeller, Steven C. 1991. *'John Dewey: Religious Faith and Democratic Humanism.'* Columbia University Press, New York.
- Schilpp, Paul Arthur and Lewis Edwin Hahn, (eds). 1989. *'The Philosophy of John Dewey, The Library of Living Philosophers',* vol. 1. La Salle, IL. Open Court. New York.

- Sleeper, Ralph. 1987. *'The Necessity of Pragmatism: John Dewey's Conception of Philosophy.'* Yale University Press, New York.
- Thayer, H. S. 1952. *'The Logic of Pragmatism: An Examination of John Dewey's Logic.'* Humanities Press, New York.
- Tiles, J. E. 1988, . *'Dewey.'* Routledge, London.
- Welchman. Jennifer, 1995. *'Dewey's Ethical Thought.'* Cornell University Press, Ithaca.